CHOCTAW BY BLOOD

ENROLLMENT CARDS

1898-1914

VOLUME XVII

TRANSCRIBED BY

JEFF BOWEN

NATIVE STUDY
Gallipolis, Ohio
USA

Originally published:
Baltimore, Maryland
2017

Reprinted by:

Native Study LLC
Gallipolis, OH
www.nativestudy.com

Library of Congress Control Number: 2020911767

ISBN: 978-1-64968-020-4

Made in the United States of America.

Other Books and Series by Jeff Bowen

1901-1907 Native American Census Seneca, Eastern Shawnee, Miami, Modoc, Ottawa, Peoria, Quapaw, and Wyandotte Indians (Under Seneca School, Indian Territory)

1932 Census of The Standing Rock Sioux Reservation with Births And Deaths 1924-1932

Census of The Blackfeet, Montana, 1897- 1901 Expanded Edition

Eastern Cherokee by Blood, 1906-1910, Volumes I thru XIII

Choctaw of Mississippi Indian Census 1929-1932 with Births and Deaths 1924-1931   Volume I

Choctaw of Mississippi Indian Census 1933, 1934 & 1937, Supplemental Rolls to 1934 & 1935 with Births and Deaths 1932-1938, and Marriages 1936-1938   Volume II

Eastern Cherokee Census Cherokee, North Carolina 1930-1939 Census 1930-1931 with Births And Deaths 1924-1931 Taken By Agent L. W. Page   Volume I

Eastern Cherokee Census Cherokee, North Carolina 1930-1939 Census 1932-1933 with Births And Deaths 1930-1932 Taken By Agent R. L. Spalsbury   Volume II

Eastern Cherokee Census Cherokee, North Carolina 1930-1939 Census 1934-1937 with Births and Deaths 1925-1938 and Marriages 1936 & 1938 Taken by Agents R. L. Spalsbury And Harold W. Foght Volume III

Seminole of Florida Indian Census, 1930-1940 with Birth and Death Records, 1930-1938

Texas Cherokees 1820-1839 A Document For Litigation 1921

Choctaw By Blood Enrollment Cards 1898-1914 Volumes I thru XVI

Visit our website at **www.nativestudy.com** to learn more about these and other books and series by Jeff Bowen

This series is dedicated to
Mike Marchi,
who keeps my spirits up.

CREEK CENSUS.

SECOND NOTICE.

Members of the Dawes Commission will be present at the following times and places for the purpose of enrolling Creek citizens, as required by Act of Congress of June 10, 1896:

At Muskogee, Nov. 8 to 30, 1897, inclusive.
At Wagoner, Nov. 8 to 13, " inclusive.
At Eufaula, Nov. 8 to 13, " inclusive.
At Sapulpa, Nov. 15 to 20, " inclusive.
At Wetumpka, Nov. 15 to 20, " inclusive.
At Okmulgee, Nov. 22 to 30, " inclusive.

All persons who have not heretofore enrolled before the Dawes Commission should appear and enroll. Parents and guardians can enroll their families and wards.

TAMS BIXBY,
FRANK C. ARMSTRONG,
A. S. McKENNON,
THOS. B. NEEDLES,
Commissioners.

The above illustration is similar in nature to what was found throughout Indian Territory for different tribes as far as postings on bulletin boards, public centers, or wherever they could be read so people would be notified of where and when they needed to be for enrollment with the Dawes Commission.

This is a picture of the Dawes Commission at Camp Jones in Stonewall, Indian Territory on September 8, 1898.

The images below are of two of the original cards given on the microfilm. The cards given in this book have been formatted to fit on one page and still give all the information found on the original cards.

Introduction

This series of Choctaw Enrollment Cards for the Five Civilized Tribes 1898-1914 has been transcribed from National Archive Film M-1186 Rolls 39-46.

The series contains more than 6100 Choctaw enrollment cards. All of the cards list age, sex and degree of blood, the parties' Dawes Roll Numbers, and date of enrollment by the Secretary of Interior for each person. The contents also give the enrollee's parents' names as well as miscellaneous notes pertaining to the enrollee's circumstances, when needed. Most entries indicate whether or not a spouse is an Intermarried White, with the initials I.W.

Enrollment wasn't as simple a process as most would think just by going through these pages. The relationships between the Five Tribes and the Dawes Commission were weak at best. There were political battles going on between the tribes and the U.S. Government as it was, but the struggles didn't stop there. Each tribe had its own political factions pulling it from every direction. On top of everything else, people from every corner of the United States were trying to figure how to get in on the spoils (Money and Land Allotment) by means of political favor. Kent Carter, author of *The Dawes Commission*, describes the continuous effort required to enroll the different tribes and the pressure the Commission incurred from people all over the country who tried to insinuate themselves into the equation:

"In May 1896 the Dawes Commission Returned To Indian Territory for its third visit, establishing its headquarters at Vinita in the Cherokee Nation. It now had to process applications for citizenship in addition to negotiating allotment agreements; these circumstances make the narrative of events more confusing because the commission attempted the two tasks concurrently. The commissioners resumed making their usual speeches to tribal officials and public gatherings to promote negotiations, but now they inevitably had to respond to questions about how the application process for citizenship would work. They also began receiving letters from people all over the United States asking how they could 'get on the rolls' so they could 'get Indian land'."[1]

For the actual process of Choctaw enrollment, "A commission was appointed in each county of the Choctaw Nation under an act of September 18 to make separate rolls of citizens by blood, by intermarriage, and freedmen; it was to deliver them to recently elected Chief Green McCurtain by October 20, but he rejected them even before they were completed because of charges that people were being left off for political reasons. On October 30, the National Council authorized establishment of a five-member

---

[1] *The Dawes Commission* by Kent Carter, page 15, para. 1

ix

commission to revise the rolls within ten days and then directed McCurtain to turn them over to the Dawes Commission on November 11, 1896. The Choctaws hired the law firm of Stuart, Gordon, and Hailey, of South McAlester to represent the tribe at all proceedings held by the Dawes Commission,"[2] another indication that throughout the Commission's efforts there was always controversy between the tribes and the negotiators.

When completed, this multi-volume series will contain thousands of names, all of them accounted for in the indexes carefully prepared by the author. Hopefully this work will help many researchers find their ancestors and satisfy the questions that so many have had about their Native American heritage.

Jeff Bowen
Gallipolis, Ohio
NativeStudy.com

---

[2] *The Dawes Commission* by Kent Carter, page 16, para. 5

Choctaw By Blood Enrollment Cards 1898-1914

RESIDENCE: Tobucksy	COUNTY.					CARD NO.		
POST OFFICE: Choate	**Choctaw Nation**			**Choctaw Roll** *(Not Including Freedmen)*		FIELD NO. **4801**		

Dawes' Roll No.	NAME	Relationship to Person	AGE	SEX	BLOOD	TRIBAL ENROLLMENT		
						Year	County	No.
13247	1 Choate Jefferson 23	First Named	20	M	1/4	1896	Tobucksy	2342
	2							
	3							
	4							
	5							
	6							
	7							
	8							
	9							
	10							
	11							
	12							
	13							
	14							
	15	ENROLLMENT OF NOS. ~~~1~~~ HEREON APPROVED BY THE SECRETARY OF INTERIOR Mar 19 1903						
	16							
	17							

TRIBAL ENROLLMENT OF PARENTS

Name of Father	Year	County	Name of Mother	Year	County
1 Ed. Choate	Dead	Tobucksy	Arabelle Choat[sic]	Dead	Tobucksy
2					
3					
4					
5					
6					
7					
8					
9					
10					
11					
12					
13					
14					
15				Date of Application for Enrollment.	
16				Sept 14th 1899	
17					

1

Choctaw By Blood Enrollment Cards 1898-1914

RESIDENCE: Tobucksy COUNTY.
POST OFFICE: So. McAlester

Choctaw Nation

Choctaw Roll *(Not Including Freedmen)*

CARD No.
FIELD No. **4802**

Dawes' Roll No.	NAME	Relationship to Person	AGE	SEX	BLOOD	TRIBAL ENROLLMENT		
						Year	County	No.
15961	1 James, Agnes 19	First Named	16	F	1/2	1896	Tobucksy	6678
	2							
	3							
	4							
	5							
	6							
	7							
	8							
	9							
	10							
	11							
	12							
	13	ENROLLMENT OF NOS. ~~1~~ HEREON						
	14	APPROVED BY THE SECRETARY						
	15	OF INTERIOR Nov 27, 1905						
	16	G.W. McMillard So McAlester I.T. Atty for appl.						
	17							

TRIBAL ENROLLMENT OF PARENTS

	Name of Father	Year	County	Name of Mother	Year	County
1	Wm James	Dead	Skullyville	Sina Tom	Dead	Skullyville
2						
3						
4						
5						
6	No1 also on 1896 Choctaw roll, Skullyville County, Page 159: #6482					
7	~~Enrollment of No1 cancelled by order of Department March 4, 1907~~					
8	No1 denied by Dawes Commission in 1896: Choctaw Case #1019. No appeal.					
9	No1 restored to roll by Departmental authority of January 19, 1909 (File 5-51)					
10	No1 is duplicate enrollment of No2 on Choctaw					
11	Card #D 249: Which is cancelled					
12						
13						
14	GRANTED					
15	Oct 4-1905			Date of Application for Enrollment.		
16				Sept 12th 1899		
17						

2

Choctaw By Blood Enrollment Cards 1898-1914

RESIDENCE: Tobucksy COUNTY.
POST OFFICE: Alderson, I.T.

Choctaw Nation

Choctaw Roll
(Not Including Freedmen)

CARD NO.
FIELD NO. 4803

Dawes' Roll No.	NAME	Relationship to Person First Named	AGE	SEX	BLOOD	TRIBAL ENROLLMENT		
						Year	County	No.
13248	1 Impson, William ³⁴	First Named	31	M	Full	1896	Tobucksy	6255
	2							
	3							
	4							
	5							
	6							
	7							
	8							
	9							
	10							
	11							
	12							
	13							
	14							
	15							
	16							
	17							

ENROLLMENT
OF NOS. ~~~ 1 ~~~ HEREON
APPROVED BY THE SECRETARY
OF INTERIOR MAR 19 1903

TRIBAL ENROLLMENT OF PARENTS

	Name of Father	Year	County	Name of Mother	Year	County
1	Kanashambe	Dd	Boktuklo[sic]	Elaiamma	Dd	Boktuklo
2						
3						
4						
5						
6						
7	No.1 "Died prior to September 25, 1902; not entitled to land or money."					
8	(See Indian Office letter of June 20, 1910, D.C. #840-1910)					
9						
10						
11				See wife on Chic card #643- Millie Worcester		
12						
13						
14						
15					Date of Application for Enrollment.	
16						
17						9/12/99

3

RESIDENCE:		COUNTY.					CARD NO.		
POST OFFICE:		**Choctaw Nation**				**Choctaw Roll** *(Not Including Freedmen)*	FIELD NO. **4804**		

Dawes' Roll No.	NAME	Relationship to Person First Named	AGE	SEX	BLOOD	TRIBAL ENROLLMENT		
						Year	County	No.
DEAD	1 ~~Gibson Susan~~ DEAD	~~Named~~	~~48~~	~~f~~	~~1/2~~	~~1896~~	~~Gaines~~	~~6636~~
	2							
	3							
	4							
	5							
	6							
	7							
	8							
	9							
	10							
	11							
	12							
	13							
	14							
	15 No. 1 HEREON DISMISSED UNDER							
	16 ORDER OF THE COMMISSION TO THE FIVE							
	17 CIVILIZED TRIBES OF MARCH 31, 1905.							

TRIBAL ENROLLMENT OF PARENTS

Name of Father	Year	County	Name of Mother	Year	County
1 ~~Jas Williams~~	~~dead~~		~~Charlotte Williams~~	~~Dead~~	San[sic] Bois
2					
3					
4					
5					
6					
7 On page 35, No 355-PR 1893 San[sic] Bois Co					
8					
9 On 1896 roll as Susan Jipson					
10 No.1 died June 12 1900. Proof of death filed Aug 5, 1901					
11					
12					
13					
14					
15					
16				Date of Application for Enrollment.	
17				Sept 15th 1899	

CANCELLED

Applicant died on ratification of Choctaw Chickasaw agreement, Sept. 25, 1902

Choctaw By Blood Enrollment Cards 1898-1914

Dawes' Roll No.	NAME	Relationship to Person First Named	AGE	SEX	BLOOD	TRIBAL ENROLLMENT		
						Year	County	No.
13249	1 Bruner, Rosa ²⁴	First Named	21	F	1/2	1893	Sans Bois	950
13250	2 Morrell, Lee T ⁵	Son	2	M	1/4			
15592	3 Walker, Willie ②	"	4	M	1/4			
	4							
	5							
	6							
	7							
	8							
	9							
	10							
	11	ENROLLMENT OF NOS. 3 HEREON APPROVED BY THE SECRETARY OF INTERIOR Sep 22, 1904						
	12							
	13							
	14							
	15	ENROLLMENT OF NOS. 1 & 2 HEREON APPROVED BY THE SECRETARY OF INTERIOR Mar. 19, 1903						
	16							
	17							

TRIBAL ENROLLMENT OF PARENTS

Name of Father	Year	County	Name of Mother	Year	County
1 Jack Rowe	Dead	Non Cit	Sina Rowe	Dead	San Bois
2 Lee F Morrell		Non Cit	No1		
3 Willie Walker		Creek	No1		
4					
5					
6 On P. 97 #950, 1893 P.R. San[sic] Bois Co as Rosa Roe					
7 No3 Born April 15, 1900. Application received Aug 14, 1901 and returned on					
8 account of being irregularly executed. Corrected affidavits received and No2 enrolled May 18, 1904					
9 For children of No1 see NB (Apr 26-06) Card #621					
10					
11					
12					
13					
14					
15				#1 & 2	
16				Date of Application for Enrollment.	
17				Sept 15ᵗʰ 1899	

5

Choctaw By Blood Enrollment Cards 1898-1914

RESIDENCE: San Bois COUNTY. **Choctaw Nation**   **Choctaw Roll** CARD NO.
POST OFFICE: Bower   *(Not Including Freedmen)* FIELD NO. 4806

Dawes' Roll No.	NAME		Relationship to Person First Named	AGE	SEX	BLOOD	TRIBAL ENROLLMENT Year	County	No.
I.W. 934	1 Beck, Elijah	(49)	First Named	45	M	IW	1896	San[sic] Bois	14279
13251	2 " Joanna	37	Wife	34	F	1/2	1896	" "	666
13252	3 " Milo	14	S	11	M	1/4	1896	" "	667
13253	4 " Delora	11	D	8	F	1/4	1896	" "	668
13254	5 " Grover	8	S	5	M	1/4	1896	" "	669
13255	6 " Joseph D	3	S	1 week	M	1/4			
13256	7 " Green Taylor	2	Son	2mo	M	1/4			
	8								
	9								
	10								
	11	ENROLLMENT							
	12	OF NOS. 1 HEREON APPROVED BY THE SECRETARY							
	13	OF INTERIOR Aug 3, 1904							
	14								
	15	ENROLLMENT							
	16	OF NOS. 2 3 4 5 6 & 7 HEREON APPROVED BY THE SECRETARY							
	17	OF INTERIOR Mar 19, 1903							

TRIBAL ENROLLMENT OF PARENTS

	Name of Father	Year	County	Name of Mother	Year	County
1	Thos Beck	Dead	Non Cit	Eliza Beck	Dead	Non Cit
2	Stephen Wood	"	Wade	Mary Wood	"	Wade
3	No1			No2		
4	No1			No2		
5	No1			No2		
6	No1			No2		
7	No1			No2		
8						
9						
10	No1 as to marriage see his testimony					
11			No7 Enrolled March 26, 1901			
12						
13						
14						
15				#1 to 6 inc		
16				Date of Application for Enrollment.		
17				Sept 15th 1899		

Choctaw By Blood Enrollment Cards 1898-1914

RESIDENCE: Atoka COUNTY:	Choctaw Nation	Choctaw Roll (Not Including Freedmen)	CARD NO.
POST OFFICE: Atoka			FIELD NO. 4807

Dawes' Roll No.	NAME	Relationship to Person First Named	AGE	SEX	BLOOD	TRIBAL ENROLLMENT Year	County	No.
	1 Stone Oscar L		24	M	IW			
13257	2 " Agnes 21	wife	18	f	Full	1896	Atoka	4974
	3							
	4							
No.1	5							
	ACTION APPROVED BY SECRETARY OF INTERIOR. MAR 2- 1907							
	8							
	9 NOTICE OF DEPARTMENTAL ACTION FORWARDED ATTORNEYS FOR CHOCTAW AND CHICKASAW NATIONS. APR 4- 1907							
	NOTICE OF DEPARTMENTAL ACTION MAILED APPLICANT. APR 4- 1907 13							
	14							
	15 ENROLLMENT OF NOS. ~~ 2 ~~ HEREON APPROVED BY THE SECRETARY 16 OF INTERIOR MAR 19 1903							
	17							

TRIBAL ENROLLMENT OF PARENTS					
Name of Father	Year	County	Name of Mother	Year	County
1 Z T Stone		Non Cit	Sarah Stone		Non cit
2 Ellis Gibson		Jacks Fork	Listie Gibson		Jacks Fork
3					
4					
5 As to marriage see his testimony					
6					
7 No2 transferred from Card 1737					
8					
9 No2 on 1896 roll as Agnes Gipson					
10 For child of No2 see NB (March 3, 1905) #1444					
11					

REFUSED FEB 14 1907

RECORD FORWARDED DEPARTMENT FEB 14 1907

Date of Application for Enrollment.
Sept 15th 1899

7

Choctaw By Blood Enrollment Cards 1898-1914

Choctaw Nation

Choctaw Roll
(Not Including Freedmen)

CARD No.
FIELD No. **4808**

Dawes' Roll No.	NAME		Relationship to Person First Named	AGE	SEX	BLOOD	TRIBAL ENROLLMENT		
							Year	County	No.
13258	1 Harlan, Aaron	32		29	M	1/4	1896	Tobucksy	5352
I.W. 1264	2 " Etta	26	Wife	23	F	I.W.			
13259	3 " Willie Louisa	2	Dau	1 wk	F	1/8			
	4								
	5								
	6								
	7								
	8								
	9								
	10								
	11								
	12								
	13								
	14								
	15								
	16								
	17								

ENROLLMENT
OF NOS. ~~~2~~~ HEREON
APPROVED BY THE SECRETARY
OF INTERIOR Dec 30, 1904

ENROLLMENT
OF NOS. 1&3 HEREON
APPROVED BY THE SECRETARY
OF INTERIOR Mar. 19, 1903

TRIBAL ENROLLMENT OF PARENTS

	Name of Father	Year	County	Name of Mother	Year	County
1	Buck Harlan	Dead	Tobucksy	Emily Harlan	Dead	Tobucksy
2	Joseph Kilpatrick	Dead	Non Citizen	Millie Fitzpatrick	Dead	Non Citizen
3	No.1			No.2		
4						
5						
6						
7						
8	No1 on 1896 roll Aaron Harlen					
9	License issued by U.S. Clerk					
10	at So. McAlester Married					
11	by E.R. Cheadle, Mayor of					
12	South Canadian Choctaw					
13	Nation, July 23-1899					
	For child of Nos 1 and 2 see NB (Apr 26,1906) No. 563					
14	No3 Enrolled July 13, 1900. Correct name "Willie Louisa"					
15	For child of Nos 1 and 2 see NB (Mar 3'05) #384					
	Affidavit of No2 as to her marriage to No1 and					
16	naming witnesses to the ceremony filed July 10, 1903.			Date of Application for Enrollment.		
17	P.O. Paola I.T.			Sept 15, 1899		

8

Choctaw By Blood Enrollment Cards 1898-1914

RESIDENCE: Tobucksy   COUNTY: **Choctaw Nation**   **Choctaw Roll** *(Not Including Freedmen)*   CARD No.
POST OFFICE: South Canadian   FIELD NO. **4809**

Dawes' Roll No.	NAME		Relationship to Person	AGE	SEX	BLOOD	TRIBAL ENROLLMENT		
							Year	County	No.
13260	1 Smith, Eliza A	58	First Named	55	F	1/16	1896	Tobucksy	11289
13261	2 Heskett, Henry	23	Son	20	M	1/32	1896	"	5345
13262	3 " , Wesley	21	"	18	M	1/32	1896	"	5346
13263	4 " , Inez O	16	Dau	13	F	1/32	1896	"	5348
I.W. 688	5 " , Nettie	24	Wife of No 2	24	F	I.W.			
I.W. 1140	6 Smith, Charles	42	Husband	42	M	I.W.			
	7								
	8								

ENROLLMENT
OF NOS. ~~~~6~~~~ HEREON
APPROVED BY THE SECRETARY
OF INTERIOR Nov 16-1904

ENROLLMENT
OF NOS. 5 HEREON
APPROVED BY THE SECRETARY
OF INTERIOR Mar 26, 1904

ENROLLMENT
OF NOS. 1 2 3 & 4 HEREON
APPROVED BY THE SECRETARY
OF INTERIOR Mar 19, 1903

TRIBAL ENROLLMENT OF PARENTS

	Name of Father	Year	County	Name of Mother	Year	County
1	Amos Gary	Dead	Non Cit	Lucy Gary	Dead	Atoka
2	Elijah Heskett		" "	No 1		
3	" "		" "	No 1		
4	" "		" "	No 1		
5	J. W. Watterson	Dead	Non Citizen	Mary E Watterson		Non Citizen
6	Jno Smith		" "	Mary Smith		" "

7 No 1 on 1896 roll Eliza Smith
8 No 4 " " " Orella "
9 No 2 Married to Nettie Heskett Choc D.785, on June 16, 1901
Evidence of marriage filed Sept. 8, 1902
10 No 6 transferred from Choctaw card #D-445 Oct 31, 1904. See decision of Oct 15, 1904
11 No 5 transferred from Choctaw card D-785 January 21, 1904. See decision
12 of January 4, 1904
No 6 Admitted by Dawes Com as an intermarried citizen in 1896, Choc Citizenship Case #812
13 Nos 1 and 6 are divorced and No 6 has since married again
14 For child of Nos 2&5 see NB (Mar 3-1905) Card No 30
15 " " " No 3 " " " " No 31
16 " " " No 4 " (Apr 26 '06) " 1232

Date of Application for Enrollment.

17 No 6. P. O. New Castle I. T.   Sept 15 1899

Choctaw By Blood Enrollment Cards 1898-1914

RESIDENCE: Sans Bois	COUNTY.	Choctaw Nation		Choctaw Roll	CARD NO.	
POST OFFICE:				*(Not Including Freedmen)*	FIELD NO. 4810	

Dawes' Roll No.	NAME	Relationship to Person First Named	AGE	SEX	BLOOD	TRIBAL ENROLLMENT		
						Year	County	No.
13264	1 Oquinn, Addie 24	First Named	21	F	1/4	1896	San[sic] Bois	5139
	2							
	3							
	4							
	5							
	6							
	7							
	8							
	9							
	10							
	11							
	12							
	13							
	14	ENROLLMENT						
	15	OF NOS. ~~~ 1 ~~~ HEREON						
	16	APPROVED BY THE SECRETARY						
	17	OF INTERIOR Mar 19 1903						

TRIBAL ENROLLMENT OF PARENTS

Name of Father	Year	County	Name of Mother	Year	County
1 Jno Herron		Non Cit	Susan Herron		San[sic] Bois
2					
3					
4					
5					
6		On roll Addie Herron			
7					
8					
9					
10	No.1 died March 20, 1902: Enrollment cancelled by Department Sept. 10, 1906.				
11					
12					
13					
14					
15				Date of Application for Enrollment.	
16					
17				Sept 15- 1899	

Choctaw By Blood Enrollment Cards 1898-1914

RESIDENCE: Tobucksy   COUNTY.

POST OFFICE: ~~South~~ Canadian

Choctaw Nation

Choctaw Roll
(Not Including Freedmen)

CARD NO.

FIELD NO. 4811

Dawes' Roll No.		NAME		Relationship to Person First Named	AGE	SEX	BLOOD	TRIBAL ENROLLMENT		
								Year	County	No.
IW 587	1	Connors John P	45	Named	42	M	IW	1896	Tobucksy	14394
13265	2	" Aran	21	wife	28	f	1/2	1896	"	2334
13266	3	" William J B	6	son	3	M	1/4	1896	"	2340
13267	4	" Annie	4	D	1	f	1/4			
13268	5	" Edward	20	S	17	M	1/4	1896	Tobucksy	2335
13269	6	" Daniel	18	S	15	"	1/4	1896	"	2336
DEAD	7	~~" John~~		~~S~~	~~12~~	~~"~~	~~1/4~~	~~1896~~	~~"~~	~~2337~~
13270	8	" Cora	12	D	9	f	1/4	1896	"	2338
13271	9	" Fannie	11	D	8	f	1/4	1896	"	2339
13272	10	Cook Lizzie	14	S.D.	11	f	1/4	1896	"	2341
13273	11	Connors Patrick	2	Son	5mo	M	1/4	ENROLLMENT		
13274	12	" Michael	1	Son	1/2	M	1/4	OF NOS 2 3 4 5 6 7 8 9 10 11 12 HEREON APPROVED BY THE SECRETARY OF INTERIOR Mar. 19. 1903		
	13	No1 admitted by Dawes Com Case 698 as Jno P Connors								
	14	No2 on 1896 roll Arian Connors								
	15	No1 " " " Jno P "						ENROLLMENT		
	16	No3 " " " Wm B "						OF NOS ~1~ HEREON APPROVED BY THE SECRETARY OF INTERIOR Feb. 8 - 1904		
	16	No7 " " " John Jr "								
	17	No12 born Jany 24,1902: Enrolled July 7,1902								

TRIBAL ENROLLMENT OF PARENTS

	Name of Father	Year	County	Name of Mother	Year	County
1	John Connors	Dead	Non Cit	Ann Connors		Non Cit
2	Ben Jones	"	Tobucksy	Jenny Jones	Cherokee	Tobucksy
3	No1		"	No2		
4	No1		"	No2		
5	No1		"	Fannie Connors	Dead	Tobucksy
6	No1		"	Do Do	"	"
7	~~No1~~		~~"~~	~~Do Do~~	~~"~~	~~"~~
8	No1		"	Do Do	"	"
9	No1		"	Do Do	"	"
10	Lewis Cook	Dead	"	No2		
11	No1	No. 7 hereon dismissed under order of the Commission to the Five Civilized Tribes of March 31, 1905.		No2		
12	No1			No2		
13			As to marriage of parents			
14			see enrollment Mary Arnult			
15			No.11 Enrolled February 4, 1901			
16			No 7 Died Sept 15.1901· Proof of death filed Dec. 23, 1902		DATE OF APPLICATION FOR ENROLLMENT.	
17			For child of No10 see NB(Apr 26-06) Card #511		Sept 15- 1899	

" " " No5 " " #1184
" " " Nos1&2 " " (Mar 3-05) " #1216

11

Choctaw By Blood Enrollment Cards 1898-1914

RESIDENCE:	Tobucksy	COUNTY.	**Choctaw Nation**		**Choctaw Roll**	CARD No.	
POST OFFICE:	South Canadian				*(Not Including Freedmen)*	FIELD No.	4812

Dawes' Roll No.	NAME	Relationship to Person	AGE	SEX	BLOOD	TRIBAL ENROLLMENT		
						Year	County	No.
13275	1 Hammons Lizzie ¹⁹	First Named	16	f	1/32	1896	Tobucksy	5347
DEAD.	2 " John Henry DEAD	Son	1mo	M	1/64			
13276	3 " Cecil Emery ¹	Dau	3wks	F.	1/64			
	4							
	5							
	6							
	7							
	8							
	9							
	10							
	11							
	12	No. 2 HEREON DISMISSED UNDER ORDER OF THE COMMISSION TO THE FIVE CIVILIZED TRIBES OF MARCH 31, 1905.						
	13							
	14							
	15	ENROLLMENT OF NOS. 1 and 3 HEREON APPROVED BY THE SECRETARY OF INTERIOR MAR 19 1903						
	16							
	17							

TRIBAL ENROLLMENT OF PARENTS

Name of Father	Year	County	Name of Mother	Year	County
1 Elijah Heskett		Non Cit	Eliza A Smith		Tobucksy
2 John Hammons		non citizen	No.1		
3 " "			N°1		
4					
5					
6					
7					
8		On 1896 roll Lizzie Heskett			
9		Husband of No1, John Hammons, is a non citizen			
10		Evidence of marriage filed April 24 1901			
11		No.2 Enrolled April 25, 1901			
12		N°2 Died Aug 19, 1901: proof of death filed Sept 9, 1902			
13		N°3 Born Aug. 18, 1902: enrolled Sept 9, 1902.			
14		For child of No.1 see NB (Apr 26-06) No. 809			
15		" " " " " " (Mar 3-05) " 837			
16			Date of Application for Enrollment.		
17	P.O. Crowder IT 3/25/05		Sept 15- 1899		

Choctaw By Blood Enrollment Cards 1898-1914

RESIDENCE: Tobucksy   **COUNTY.**   **Choctaw Nation**   **Choctaw Roll** *(Not Including Freedmen)*   **CARD No.**
POST OFFICE: Indianola   **FIELD No.** 4813

Dawes' Roll No.	NAME		Relationship to Person Named	AGE	SEX	BLOOD	Year	County	No.
13277	₁ Nale John	39	First Named	36	m	3/4	1893	Tobucksy	598
I.W. 588	₂ " Mary Isabelle	33	wife	29	f	IW			
13278	₃ " Benjamin C	13	Son	10	m	3/8	1893	"	599
13279	₄ " Joseph S	10	"	7	"	3/8	1893	"	600
13280	₅ " Elsie M	8	D	5	f	3/8			
13281	₆ " Daniel J	6	Son	2	m	3/8			
13282	₇ " Katey Gurtrue	3	Dau	4mo	F	3/8			
13283	₈ " William Lee	1	Son	2wks	M	3/8			
	9								
	10								
	11	ENROLLMENT OF NOS. 2 HEREON APPROVED BY THE SECRETARY OF INTERIOR FEB 8 1904							
	12								
	13								
	14								
	15	ENROLLMENT OF NOS. 1 3 4 5 6 7 & 8 HEREON APPROVED BY THE SECRETARY OF INTERIOR MAR 19 1903							
	16								
	17								

TRIBAL ENROLLMENT OF PARENTS

	Name of Father	Year	County	Name of Mother	Year	County
1	Ben Nale	Dead	Gaines	Margaret Nale	Dead	Gaines
2	Green Slayton		Non Cit	Margaret Slayton	Dead	Non Cit
3	No1			No2		
4	No1			No2		
5	No1			No2		
6	No1			No2		
7	No.1			No.2		
8	N⁰1			N⁰2		
9						
10	No1 on Tobucksy Co P R p 68 #598					
11	No3 " " " " " 599 as Ben Nale					
	No4 " " " " " 600 Joseph Do					
12	No.7 Enrolled June 23d, 1900					
13	Evidence of birth of N⁰5 received and filed Feby 28, 1902					
14	N⁰8 Born July 30, 1902: enrolled Aug 12, 1902			#1 to 6 inc
15	For child of N⁰ˢ 1&2 see NB (Apr 26, 1906) card No. 258			Date of Application for Enrollment.
16				Sept 15- 1899
17				

13

Choctaw By Blood Enrollment Cards 1898-1914

RESIDENCE: Atoka	COUNTY. Choctaw Nation	Choctaw Roll (Not Including Freedmen)	CARD NO.
POST OFFICE: Atoka			FIELD NO. 4814

Dawes' Roll No.	NAME	Relationship to Person First Named	AGE	SEX	BLOOD	TRIBAL ENROLLMENT Year	County	No.
I.W.265	1 Breedlove, Thomas 58	First Named	45	M	I.W.			
13284	2 " Susan 32	wife	29	f	Full	1896	Atoka	8331
	3							
	4							
	5							
	6							
	7	ENROLLMENT OF NOS. ~~~1~~~ HEREON APPROVED BY THE SECRETARY OF INTERIOR Dec. 30 1904						
	8							
	9							
	10							
	11							
	12	ENROLLMENT OF NOS. ~~~2~~~ HEREON APPROVED BY THE SECRETARY OF INTERIOR Mar. 19 1903						
	13							
	14							
	15							
	16							
	17							

TRIBAL ENROLLMENT OF PARENTS

	Name of Father	Year	County	Name of Mother	Year	County
1	Robt. Breedlove	dead	Non Cit	Mary Breedlove	Dead	Non Cit
2	Tecumseh Leader	"	Atoka	Salina Leader	"	Atoka
3						
4						
5	License and certificate dated					
6	Sept 4th 1899 see his testimony					
7						
8						
9	No.2 transferred from Card #64.					
10						
11	No 2 on 1896 roll as Susan Leader					
12	Nos 1&2 have separated 11/6/02					
13	No.2 is now the wife of Andrew Carney, Chick Card #279					
14					Date of Application for Enrollment.	
15	P.O. Foster, I.T.				Sept 15- 1899	
16						
17	P.O. Foster, I.T.	Ana. I.T.	10/14/'04			

14

Choctaw By Blood Enrollment Cards 1898-1914

| RESIDENCE: | Sans Bois | COUNTY. | | | | |
| POST OFFICE: | Texana[sic] | | | | | |

Choctaw Nation

Choctaw Roll (Not Including Freedmen)

CARD No. FIELD No. **4815**

Dawes' Roll No.	NAME	Relationship to Person	AGE	SEX	BLOOD	TRIBAL ENROLLMENT		
						Year	County	No.
13285	1 Johnson, Zeno	43 First Named	40	M	1/8	1896	San[sic] Bois	6427
13286	2 " Fount	6 S	3	"	1/16	1896	" "	6428
DEAD	3 " Harvey	DEAD "	1	"	1/16			
	4							
	5							
	6							
	7							
	8							
	9							
	10							
	11	No. 3 hereon dismissed under order of						
	12	the Commission to the Five Civilized						
	13	Tribes of March 31, 1905.						
	14							
	15	ENROLLMENT OF NOS. 1 and 2						
	16	APPROVED BY THE SECRETARY HEREON						
	17	OF INTERIOR Mar 19 1903						

TRIBAL ENROLLMENT OF PARENTS

	Name of Father	Year	County	Name of Mother	Year	County
1	Wᵐ M Johnson	Decd	Jack Forks	Susan Bumgarner		San[sic] Bois
2	No.1		San[sic] Bois	Nannie Johnson	Dead	Cherokee
3	No.1			Do Do		
4						
5						
6						
7						
8	As to marriage of parents					
9	of above children see testimony					
10	of Susan Bumgarner					
11	No.3 died February 17, 1900. Proof of death filed August 1, 1901.					
12						
13						
14						
15						
16					Date of Application for Enrollment.	
17					Sept 15 - 1899	

15

Choctaw By Blood Enrollment Cards 1898-1914

RESIDENCE: Cherokee Nation COUNTY.
POST OFFICE: Texanna

Choctaw Nation

Choctaw Roll (Not Including Freedmen)

CARD NO.
FIELD NO. 4816

Dawes' Roll No.	NAME	Relationship to Person	AGE	SEX	BLOOD	TRIBAL ENROLLMENT		
						Year	County	No.
13287	1 Bumgarner Susan 67	First Named	64	f	1/8	1896	San[sic] Bois	691
	2							
	3							
	4							
	5							
	6							
	7							
	8							
	9							
	10							
	11							
	12							
	13							
	14							
	15	ENROLLMENT OF NOS. ~~~~ 1 ~~~~ HEREON APPROVED BY THE SECRETARY OF INTERIOR MAR 19 1903						
	16							
	17							

TRIBAL ENROLLMENT OF PARENTS

	Name of Father	Year	County	Name of Mother	Year	County
1	Geo Walker	Dead	Atoka	Rebecca Walker	Dead	Atoka
2						
3						
4						
5						
6						
7	Father a Creek, she has					
8	been enrolled there until					
9	the last few years, enroll-ment was refused her.					
10	See above this. Never enrolled as a Creek by Dawes Com.					
11	On 1890 Creek Roll; Not on final Creek Roll					
12						
13						
14						
15					Date of Application for Enrollment.	
16						
17					Sept 15- 1899	

16

Choctaw By Blood Enrollment Cards 1898-1914

RESIDENCE: Cherokee Nation COUNTY. **Choctaw Nation** **Choctaw Roll** CARD No.
POST OFFICE: Starvilla[sic] (Not Including Freedmen) FIELD No. 4817

Dawes' Roll No.	NAME	Relationship to Person First Named	AGE	SEX	BLOOD	TRIBAL ENROLLMENT		
						Year	County	No.
13288	1 Bumgarner Samuel W[25]	First Named	22	M	1/8	1896	San[sic] Bois	692
	2							
	3							
	4							
	5							
	6							
	7							
	8							
	9							
	10							
	11							
	12							
	13							
	14							
	15							
	16							
	17							

ENROLLMENT
OF NOS. ~~13288~~ HEREON
APPROVED BY THE SECRETARY
OF INTERIOR MAR 19 1903

TRIBAL ENROLLMENT OF PARENTS

Name of Father	Year	County	Name of Mother	Year	County
1 Jno W Bumgarner		Cherokee	Susan Bumgarner		San[sic] Bois
2					
3					
4 On roll 1896 Sam Bumgarner					
5					
6					
7					
8 October 16/99 On 1894 Canadian					
9 ~~District Pay Roll of Cherokee~~					
10 ~~Nation No 154~~					
11 On Cherokee Card C2563 as Samuel Bumgarner: This Card Cancelled					
12					
13					
14					
15				Date of Application for Enrollment.	
16					
17 P.O. Texanna, I.T.				Sept 15- 99	

Choctaw By Blood Enrollment Cards 1898-1914

RESIDENCE: Tobucksy COUNTY.
POST OFFICE: McAlester

Choctaw Roll (Not Including Freedmen)

CARD NO.
FIELD NO. 4818

Dawes Roll No.	NAME	Relationship to Person First Named	AGE	SEX	BLOOD	TRIBAL ENROLLMENT		
						Year	County	No.
13289	1 McMurry, Rebecca ²⁴	Named	21	f	1/4	1896	Tobucksy	4015
13290	2 Fairlie, Nettie ⁷	d	4	f	1/8	1896	"	4016
13291	3 " John T ⁴	S	1	M	1/8			
13292	4 McMurry Evie ¹	Dau	2mo	F	1/8			
	5							
	6							
	7							
	8							
	9							
	10							
	11							
	12							
	13							
	14							
	15							
	16							
	17							

ENROLLMENT
OF NOS. 1 2 3 & 4 HEREON
APPROVED BY THE SECRETARY
OF INTERIOR MAR 19 1903

TRIBAL ENROLLMENT OF PARENTS

	Name of Father	Year	County	Name of Mother	Year	County
1	Jack Fulton		Tobucksy	Catherine Fulton		Tobucksy
2	Wm Fairlie		Non Citizen	No1		
3	Do Do		" "	No1		
4	Olive M McMurry		noncitizen	No1		
5						
6						
7						
8	See letter of R.B. Coleman as to enrollment of No1 and death of her husband					
9	Wm Fairlee[sic] , and her subsequent marriage to Olive M McMurry filed Aug 15, 1901.					
10	No4 Enrolled Aug 15, 1901 Evidence of marriage of parents of No4 requested. Received and filed Oct. 15, 1901.					
11	For child of No 1 see NB (March 3, 1905) #1276					
12						
13						
14						
15						
16						
17	P.O. Crowder City, IT 4/24/05					

#1 to 3 inc

Date of Application for Enrollment. Sept 15- 1899

18

Choctaw By Blood Enrollment Cards 1898-1914

RESIDENCE: Tobucksy
POST OFFICE: McAlester

COUNTY. **Choctaw Nation**

Choctaw Roll
(Not Including Freedmen)

CARD NO.
FIELD NO. 4819

Dawes' Roll No.	NAME		Relationship to Person First Named	AGE	SEX	BLOOD	TRIBAL ENROLLMENT		
							Year	County	No.
13293	₁ Cartledge Nancy	22		19	f	1/4	1896	Tobucksy	2322
13294	₂ " Bessie	6	d	3	f	1/8			
13295	₃ " Cecil	1	Son	1mo	m	1/8			
	4								
	5								
	6								
	7								
	8								
	9								
	10								
	11								
	12								
	13								
	14								
	15								
	16								
	17								

ENROLLMENT
OF NOS. 1 2 & 3 HEREON
APPROVED BY THE SECRETARY
OF INTERIOR MAR 9 1903

TRIBAL ENROLLMENT OF PARENTS

	Name of Father	Year	County	Name of Mother	Year	County
₁	Jack Fulton		Tobucksy	Catherine Fulton		Tobucksy
₂	Albert Cartledge		Non Cit	No1		
₃	" "		" "	No1		
4						
5						
6						
7			No.3 Enrolled Sept. 4, 1901			
8			For child of No.1 see NB (March 3,1905) #838			
9						
10						
11						
12						
13						
14						
15					#1&2	
16				Date of Application for Enrollment.		
17				Sept 15-	1899	

19

Choctaw By Blood Enrollment Cards 1898-1914

RESIDENCE: Tobucksy   COUNTY. **Chocta[...]on**   **Choctaw Roll** (Not Including Freedmen) CARD NO.

T OFFICE: McAlester   FIELD NO. **4820**

wes' l No.	NAME		Relationship to Person	AGE	SEX	BLOOD	TRIBAL ENROLLMENT		
							Year	County	No.
296	1 Fulton Catherine	44	First Named	41	f	1/2	1896	Tobucksy	4057
297	2 " John R	21	son	18	m	1/4	1896	"	4065
13298	3 Trohbe M L Elizabeth	16	D	13	f	1/4	1896	"	4058
13299	4 Fulton Aurilla	15	D	12	f	1/4	1896	"	4059
13300	5 " Jackson	8	S	5	m	1/4	1896	"	4062
13301	6 " Newton	8	S	5	m	1/4	1896	"	4061
13302	7 " Tilda	7	d	4	f	1/4	1896	"	4063
13303	8 Trohbe Charles Louis	1	Gr. son	1mo	m	1/8			
IW983	9 Fulton Jack	52	Hus	52	m	IW			
	10								
	11 ENROLLMENT								
	OF NOS. ~ 9 ~ HEREON								
	12 APPROVED BY THE SECRETARY								
	13 OF INTERIOR Sep 22 1904								
	14								
	15 ENROLLMENT								
	OF NOS. 1 2 3 4 5 6 7 & 8 HEREON								
	16 APPROVED BY THE SECRETARY								
	OF INTERIOR Mar 19 1903								
	17								

TRIBAL ENROLLMENT OF PARENTS

	Name of Father	Year	County	Name of Mother	Year	County
1	Silas Gardner	Dead		Elizabeth Gardner		Tobucksy
2	Jack Fulton		Non Cit	No1		
3	" "		" "	No1		
4	" "		" "	No1		
5	" "		" "	No1		
6	" "		" "	No1		
7	" "		" "	No1		
8	John C Trohbe		" "	No3		
9	James Fulton	Dead	" "	Nancy Fulton		noncitizen

10 Husband of No1 on Choctaw Card D972

11 No2 on 1896 roll John Fulton

12 No4 " " " Orilla Do (#4 died 3/11/04 see G.F. #15348-12 Homer A Metcalf claims to be husband of No4)

~~Full name of No3 is Mary Louisa Elizabeth Fulton~~

13 No3 is now the wife of John C Trohbe, non-citizen Jan 3, 1902. Evidence of marriage filed Feby 26, 1902

14 No8 Born Dec 1, 1901: enrolled Jan 3, 1902   #1 to 7 inc

15 No9 transferred from Choctaw D972 August 4, 1904

~~See decision of July 19, 1904~~   Date of Application for Enrollment.

16 For child of No2 see NB (Mar 3'05) #385   Sept 15th 1899

17 " " " No1 " " #386

No3 " #1111

20

Choctaw By Blood Enrollment Cards 1898-1914

CE: Indianola **Choctaw Nation** (Not Including Freedmen) FIELD No. 4821

	NAME		Relationship to Person First Named	AGE	SEX	BLOOD	TRIBAL ENROLLMENT		
							Year	County	No.
1	Choate James H	32	First Named	29	m	1/2	1896	Tobucksy	2343
2	" Ida	29	Wife	26	f	IW	1896	"	14395
3	" Corneal	5	Dau	2	f	1/4			
4	" Harry T		Son	7mo	m	1/4			
5	" Leslie R	1	son	3mo	m	1/4			
6	" Lors[sic] B	1	son	3mo	m	1/4			
7									
8	No. 4 HEREON DISMISSED UNDER								
9	ORDER OF THE COMMISSION TO THE FIVE								
10	CIVILIZED TRIBES OF MARCH 31, 1905.								
11	ENROLLMENT								
12	OF NOS. ~~~~ 2 ~~~~ HEREON APPROVED BY THE SECRETARY								
13	OF INTERIOR FEB -8 1904								
14									
15	ENROLLMENT								
16	OF NOS. 1, 3, 5 & 6 HEREON APPROVED BY THE SECRETARY								
17	OF INTERIOR MAR 19 1903								

TRIBAL ENROLLMENT OF PARENTS

	Name of Father	Year	County	Name of Mother	Year	County
1	Jno Choate	Dead	Tobucksy	Tennessee Choate	dead	Tobucksy
2	Geo H Pettus		Non Cit	Amanda J Pettus		Non Cit
3	No 1			No 2		
4	No.1			No.2		
5	No 1			No 2		
6	No 1			No 2		
7						
8						
9			Evidence of the birth of			
10			No 3 to be supplied Received and filed			
11			No.4 Enrolled July 17, 1900			
12			No 2 admitted by Dawes Commission in 1896 as an inter-			
13			married citizen: Choctaw case #768: no appeal			
14			N⁰4 Died Nov. 7,1900, proof of death filed Oct. 9, 1902			
15			Nos 5 and 6 placed hereon December 20,1902. Question as to exact date of the birth of these children			
16			N⁰2 admitted by Dawes Commission in 1896 as an intermarried citizen, Choctaw Case #768; no appeal			#1 to 3
17			For child of Nos 1&2 see NB (Apr 26'06) Card #79			Date of Application for Enrollment.
			" " " " " " " " (Mar 3 '05) " #652			Sept 6ᵗʰ 1899

12/24-1902 PO Tandy IT

Choctaw By Blood Enrollment Cards 1898-1914

RESIDENCE: Creek Nation COUNTY. **Choctaw Nation** Choctaw Roll
POST OFFICE: Eufaula, I.T. *(Not Including Freedmen)*

CARD NO.
FIELD NO. 4822

Dawes' Roll No.	NAME		Relationship to Person First Named	AGE	SEX	BLOOD	TRIBAL ENROLLMENT		
							Year	County	No.
13308	1 Nero, Jane	27	First Named	24	F	5/8	1896	Sans Bois	9563
13309	2 " Henry	6	Son	3	M	5/16	1896	" "	9564
13310	3 " Delia	4	Dau	1	F	5/16			
13311	4 " Hallie	2	Dau	2½	F	5/16			
	5								
	6								
	7								
	8								
	9								
	10								
	11								
	12								
	13								
	14								
	15	ENROLLMENT OF NOS. 1 2 3 & 4 HEREON APPROVED BY THE SECRETARY OF INTERIOR MAR 19 1903							
	16								
	17								

TRIBAL ENROLLMENT OF PARENTS

	Name of Father	Year	County	Name of Mother	Year	County
1	Todd Flack	Dead	Sans Bois	Melinda Flack	Dead	Sans Bois
2	Joseph Nero		Non Citz Col	No1		
3	" "		" " "	No1		
4	" "		" " "	No1		
5						
6						
7	3/20/19 For Birthday of No3 see Old Creek Card No 2219.					
8				See Creek A-16		
9	For child of No1 see NB (March 3,1905) #761					
10	No3 Affidavit of birth to be supplied: Received and filed May 6, 1901					
11	Joseph Nero: husband of No 1 and father of above children					
12	on Creek roll card #2383					
13	See evidence of Joseph Nero filed Aug 23, 1901					
14	Evidence of marriage between N°1 and father of children on this card received and filed Nov. 5, 1902					
15	Statement of Joseph Nero filed Nov. 5, 1902			Date of Application for Enrollment.		
16	No4 born May 24, 1900: enrolled December 16, 1902			Sept 16/99		
17						

Choctaw By Blood Enrollment Cards 1898-1914

RESIDENCE: Eagle COUNTY. **Choctaw Nation** Choctaw Roll CARD NO.
POST OFFICE: Bok Tuklo, I.T. (Not Including Freedmen) FIELD NO. 4823

Dawes' Roll No.	NAME	Relationship to Person First Named	AGE	SEX	BLOOD	TRIBAL ENROLLMENT		
						Year	County	No.
13312	1 Ward, Adeline²⁸	First Named	25	F	Full	1896	Eagle	13477
	2							
	3							
	4							
	5							
	6							
	7							
	8							
	9							
	10							
	11							
	12							
	13							
	14							
	15	ENROLLMENT OF NOS. 1 HEREON APPROVED BY THE SECRETARY OF INTERIOR MAR 9 1903						
	16							
	17							

TRIBAL ENROLLMENT OF PARENTS

	Name of Father	Year	County	Name of Mother	Year	County
1	Lyman Ward	Dead	Eagle	Silway Ward	Dead	Eagle
2						
3						
4						
5						
6	On 1896 roll as Adaline Ward					
7	For child of No 1 see NB (Apr 26-06) Card #667					
8						
9						
10						
11						
12						
13				Date of Application for Enrollment.		
14						
15				Oct 10/99		
16						
17						

Choctaw By Blood Enrollment Cards 1898-1914

RESIDENCE: Jackson COUNTY. **Choctaw Nation** Choctaw Roll CARD NO.
POST OFFICE: Bennington, I.T. *(Not Including Freedmen)* FIELD NO. **4824**

Dawes' Roll No.	NAME	Relationship to Person	AGE	SEX	BLOOD	Year	County	No.
13313	1 Robinson, Cyrus 36	First Named	33	M	Full	1896	Jackson	10885
13314	2 Annie DIED PRIOR TO SEPTEMBER 25, 2602	Wife	25	F	"	1896	"	1528
13315	3 " Newton 15	Son	12	M	"	1896	"	10886
13316	4 " Joel 8	"	5	"	"	1896		1529
DP	5 " Nattie	"	10	"	"			
DP	6 " John	"	7	"	"			
13317	7 " Willie May 3	Dau	5mo	F	"			
	8							
	9							
	10							
	11							
	12	Nos 5&6 Granted - Oct 30, 1906						
	13	under act of Apr. 26/06						
	14							
	15	ENROLLMENT						
	16	OF NOS. 1,2,3,4 & 7 HEREON APPROVED BY THE SECRETARY						
	17	OF INTERIOR Mar 10 1903						

TRIBAL ENROLLMENT OF PARENTS

	Name of Father	Year	County	Name of Mother	Year	County
1		Dead	Choctaw	Lucy Robinson	Dead	Jackson
2	Robinson Battiest	"	Jackson	Liney Battiest	"	"
3	No.1			Elsie Robinson		Choctaw
4	No.1			No.2		
5	No.1			Elsie Robinson		Choctaw
6	No.1			" "		"
7	No.1			No.2		
8						
9						
10	No.2 on 1896 roll as Annie Battiest					
11	No.4 " 1896 " " Joel "					
12	As to enrollment of these children, that					
13	is Nos. 5-6, see testimony of Moses Johnson No.7- Affidavit of birth to be					Date of Application for Enrollment
14	supplied. Filed Nov. 2/99					Oct 10/99
15	No.2 died July 12, 1902: Enrollment cancelled by Department July 8, 1904					
16	Nos. 5&6 transferred to Choctaw NB (Apr 26 '06) No. 1145 Oct 30,1906					
17						

Choctaw By Blood Enrollment Cards 1898-1914

COUNTY. **Choctaw Nation**

Choctaw Roll
(Not Including Freedmen)

CARD NO.
FIELD NO. **4825**

Dawes' Roll No.	NAME		Relationship to Person	AGE	SEX	BLOOD	TRIBAL ENROLLMENT		
							Year	County	No.
13318	₁ Noley, Lucy	24	First Named	21	F	Full	1893	Eagle	222
13319	₂ Wesley, Eliza	6	Dau	2	"	"			
DEAD	₃ " George DEAD		Son	1	M	"			
13320	₄ Tonahka, Wilson	1	Son	1	M	"			
	₅								
	₆								
	₇								
	₈								
	₉								
	10								
	11	No 3 hereon dismissed under order of							
	12	the Commission to the Five Civilized							
	13	Tribes of March 31, 1905.							
	14								
	15	ENROLLMENT							
	16	OF NOS. 1 2 & 4 HEREON APPROVED BY THE SECRETARY							
	17	OF INTERIOR Mar 19, 1903							

TRIBAL ENROLLMENT OF PARENTS

	Name of Father	Year	County	Name of Mother	Year	County
₁	Noley	Dead	Eagle	Siney Noley		Bok Tuklo
₂	Lenas Wesley		"	No.1		
₃	" "		"	No.1		
₄	Unknown			No.1		
₅						
₆						
₇						
8						
9						
10	No.1 On 1893 Pay Roll, Page 22, No. 222, Eagle Co					
11	No.4 Born Aug. 1, 1901. Enrolled Nov. 11, 1902.					
12	No.4 is illegitimate and was deserted by its mother					
13	See letter from Claude Denson filed herein, Nov.					#1 to 3 inc
14	No.3 died Aug. 12, 1901; proof of death filed Dec. 4, 1902.					Date of Application for Enrollment.
15	For child of No.1 see NB (Apr 26-06) card #849					Oct 10/99
16						
17						

Choctaw By Blood Enrollment Cards 1898-1914

RESIDENCE: Tobucksy COUNTY.
POST OFFICE: McAlester, I.T.

Choctaw Nation

Choctaw Roll
(Not Including Freedmen)

CARD NO.
FIELD NO. 4826

Dawes' Roll No.	NAME	Relationship to Person	AGE	SEX	BLOOD	TRIBAL ENROLLMENT		
						Year	County	No.
13321	1 King, Alice ⁱ³	First Named	10	F	Full	1896	Tobucksy	7489
	2							
	3							
	4							
	5							
	6							
	7							
	8							
	9							
	10							
	11							
	12							
	13							
	14							
	15	ENROLLMENT OF NOS. ~~~ 1 ~~~ HEREON						
	16	APPROVED BY THE SECRETARY						
	17	OF INTERIOR MAR 9 1903						

TRIBAL ENROLLMENT OF PARENTS

	Name of Father	Year	County	Name of Mother	Year	County
1	Leonidas King	Dead	Tobucksy		Dead	Tobucksy
2						
3						
4						
5						
6	On 1896 roll as Agnes King					
7						
8						
9						
10						
11						
12						
13						
14				Date of Application for Enrollment.		
15				Oct 10/99		
16						
17						

Choctaw By Blood Enrollment Cards 1898-1914

RESIDENCE: Tobucksy   COUNTY.
POST OFFICE: McAlester, I.T.

Choctaw Nation

Choctaw Roll
(Not Including Freedmen)

CARD NO.
FIELD NO. 4827

Dawes' Roll No.	NAME	Relationship to Person First Named	AGE	SEX	BLOOD	TRIBAL ENROLLMENT Year	County	No.
13322	1 Gardner, Josiah 53	First Named	50	M	Full	1896	Tobucksy	4700
13323	2 " Sallie 45	Wife	42	F	3/4	1896	"	4701
13324	3 Carter, Frances 23	Dau	20	"	Full	1896	"	4702
13325	4 Gardner, Jefferson 16	Son	13	M	7/8	1896	"	4703
13326	5 " Rena 13	Dau	10	F	7/8	1896	"	4704
13327	6 " Castine 8	Son	5	M	7/8	1896	"	4705
13328	7 Carter Ada 1	Son of No.3	9mo	M	Full			
8								
9								
10								
11								
12								
13								
14								

ENROLLMENT
OF NOS. 1 2 3 4 5 6 & 7 HEREON
APPROVED BY THE SECRETARY
OF INTERIOR   MAR 19 1903

TRIBAL ENROLLMENT OF PARENTS

	Name of Father	Year	County	Name of Mother	Year	County
1	Jackson Gardner	Dead	Blue	Mary Gardner	Dead	Blue
2	Me-she-mah-tubby	"	Tobucksy	Mary	"	Tobucksy
3	No 1			Sallie Gardner	"	"
4	No 1			No 2		
5	No 1			No 2		
6	No 1			No 2		
7	Jesse Carter		Choc Card 3232	No 3		
8						
9	Note 9-25-36 Sex of No.7 changed to "M" Dept D-9939 Sept 17-36 JDF					
10						
11	No.3 Now wife of Jesse Carter on Choctaw Card #3232: Evidence of marriage					
12	No.7 Born September 23rd 1901; Enrolled June 20th 1902					
13	For child of No3 see NB (Mar 3-05) Card #216				#1 to 6	
14					Date of Application for Enrollment.	
15					Oct 10/99	
16						
17						

Choctaw By Blood Enrollment Cards 1898-1914

| RESIDENCE: | Eagle | COUNTY | Choctaw Nation | | Choctaw Roll | CARD NO. | |
| POST OFFICE: | Eagletown, I.T. | | | | (Not Including Freedmen) | FIELD NO. | 4828 |

Dawes' Roll No.	NAME	Relationship to Person First Named	AGE	SEX	BLOOD	TRIBAL ENROLLMENT		
						Year	County	No.
13329	1 Jones, Melissa DIED PRIOR TO SEPTEMBER 25 1902	First Named	20	F	Full	1896	Eagle	6942
	2							
	3							
	4							
	5							
	6							
	7							
	8							
	9							
	10							
	11							
	12							
	13							
	14							
	15							
	16							
	17							

ENROLLMENT
OF NOS. 1 HEREON
APPROVED BY THE SECRETARY
OF INTERIOR MAR 19 1903

TRIBAL ENROLLMENT OF PARENTS

	Name of Father	Year	County	Name of Mother	Year	County
1	Ely Harris	Dead	Eagle		Dead	Eagle
2						
3						
4						
5						
6						
7			On 1896 roll as Malissie Jones			
8			No 1 died before Sept 25, 1902; Enrollment cancelled by Department May 2, 1906			
9						
10						
11						
12						
13					Date of Application for Enrollment.	
14						
15					Oct 10/99	
16						
17						

28

Choctaw By Blood Enrollment Cards 1898-1914

Dawes' Roll No.	NAME		Relationship to Person First Named	AGE	SEX	BLOOD	TRIBAL ENROLLMENT		
							Year	County	No.
13330	1 Munkus, Lillie	22		19	F	1/16	1896	Atoka	8849
13331	2 " Ether	5	Dau	2	"	1/32			
13332	3 " Joseph G	2	Son	2mo	M	1/32			
13333	4 " Estell D	1	Dau	6mo	F	1/32			
I.W. 689	5 " Beverly C	29	Hus	26	M	I.W.			
	6								
	7								
	8								
	9								
	10								
	11								
	12								
	13								
	14								
	15								
	16								
	17								

ENROLLMENT
OF NOS. 5 HEREON
APPROVED BY THE SECRETARY
OF INTERIOR MAR 26 1904

ENROLLMENT
OF NOS. 1 2 3 & 4 HEREON
APPROVED BY THE SECRETARY
OF INTERIOR MAR 9 1903

TRIBAL ENROLLMENT OF PARENTS

	Name of Father	Year	County	Name of Mother	Year	County
1	William Spam	Dead	Chick Dist	Lou Spam		Intermarried
2	Beverly C Munkus		white man	No1		
3	" " "		" "	No.1		
4	" " "		" "	Nº1		
5	Holiard Munkus	Dead	noncitizen	Harriet Munkus		noncitizen
6						
7						
8						
9	No1 on 1896 roll as Lillie Munker					
10						
11	As to marriage of parents of No2 ~~see testimony of A. Telle~~					
12						
13	Beverly C Munkus on Card No D510 No.3 Enrolled November 28th 1900				Date of Application for Enrollment.	
14	~~Nº4 Born Feby 27, 1902: enrolled Sept. 3, 1902~~					
15	No5 transferred from Choctaw card #D510 January 23,1904				Oct 10/99	
16	See decision of January 6, 1904					
17	For child of Nos 1&5 see NB (March 3,1905) #728					

Choctaw By Blood Enrollment Cards 1898-1914

RESIDENCE: Gaines COUNTY. **Choctaw Nation** Choctaw Roll CARD No.
POST OFFICE: Wilburton, I.T. *(Not Including Freedmen)* FIELD No. 4830

Dawes' Roll No.	NAME		Relationship to Person	AGE	SEX	BLOOD	TRIBAL ENROLLMENT		
							Year	County	No.
13334	1 Anderson, Robert	32	First Named	29	M	3/4	1896	Gaines	90
I.W. 590	2 " Rosie	20	Wife	19	F	I.W.			
13335	3 " Emmett	15	Son	12	M	7/8			91
13336	4 " Alfred	2	"	2	"	3/8			
	5								
	6								
	7								
	8								
	9								
	10	ENROLLMENT OF NOS. 2 HEREON APPROVED BY THE SECRETARY OF INTERIOR FEB -8 1904							
	11								
	12								
	13								
	14	ENROLLMENT OF NOS. 1 3 & 4 HEREON APPROVED BY THE SECRETARY OF INTERIOR MAR 19 1903							
	15								
	16								
	17								

TRIBAL ENROLLMENT OF PARENTS

	Name of Father	Year	County	Name of Mother	Year	County
1	Thos Anderson		Choctaw	Sinie Anderson		Choctaw
2	Sam Wheat	Dead	Non Citz	Martha Wheat		Non Citz
3	No 1			Lena Anderson	Dead	Gaines
4	No.1			No.2		
5						
6						
7						
8	Nos 1-3 were admitted by Choctaw					
9	Council Dec 8/91					
10	No.4 Born Sept. 1, 1900: Enrolled Dec. 24, 1902					
11	For child of Nos 1&2 see NB (Apr 26-06) Card #702 " children " " " " " (Mar 3-05) " #387					
12						
13						#1 to 3
14						Date of Application for Enrollment.
15						Oct 10/99
16	P.O. Atoka, I.T.					
17	Coalgate; No1 P.O. Bethel OK					

30

Choctaw By Blood Enrollment Cards 1898-1914

RESIDENCE:	Gaines	COUNTY.		CARD NO.
POST OFFICE:	Wilburton, I.T.	**Choctaw Nation**	**Choctaw Roll** (Not Including Freedmen)	FIELD NO. **4831**

Dawes' Roll No.	NAME	Relationship to Person First Named	AGE	SEX	BLOOD	TRIBAL ENROLLMENT		
						Year	County	No.
13337	₁ Willis, William ²²	First Named	19	M	Full	1893	Gaines	2
	₂							
	₃							
	₄							
	₅							
	₆							
	₇							
	₈							
	₉							
	10							
	11							
	12							
	13							
	14							
	15	ENROLLMENT OF NOS. ~~~~~ HEREON APPROVED BY THE SECRETARY						
	16	OF INTERIOR Mar 19-1903						
	17							

TRIBAL ENROLLMENT OF PARENTS

	Name of Father	Year	County	Name of Mother	Year	County
₁	Dixon Willis		Choctaw	Miley Willis		Choctaw
₂						
₃						
₄						
₅						
₆						
₇	On 1893 Pay Roll, Page 1, No.2					
₈	Gaines Co., as Willy Willis					
₉	Also on 1896 roll Page 179, No 3278					
10	as Willie Dickson, Gaines Co.					
11						
12						
13				Date of Application for Enrollment.		
14						Oct 9/99
15						
16						
17						

31

Choctaw By Blood Enrollment Cards 1898-1914

Choctaw Nation

Choctaw Roll (Not Including Freedmen)

CARD NO.
FIELD NO. 4832

Dawes' Roll No.	NAME		Relationship to Person	AGE	SEX	BLOOD	TRIBAL ENROLLMENT		
							Year	County	No.
13338	1 Colbert, Levi	39	First Named	36	M	Full	1896	Nashoba	2494
13339	2 " Winnie	29	Wife	26	F	"	1896	"	2495
13340	3 " Sina	12	Dau	9	"	"	1896	"	2498
13341	4 " Sillen	9	"	6	"	"	1896	"	2499
13342	5 " Philiston	6	Son	3	M	"	1896	"	2500
13343	6 " Sophia	DIED PRIOR TO SEPTEMBER 25, 1902	Dau	1/2	F	"			
	7								
	8								
	9								
	10								
	11								
	12								
	13								
	14								
	15	ENROLLMENT OF NOS. 1 2 3 4 5 and 6 HEREON							
	16	APPROVED BY THE SECRETARY OF INTERIOR MAR 19 1903							
	17								

TRIBAL ENROLLMENT OF PARENTS

	Name of Father	Year	County	Name of Mother	Year	County
1	Jonas Colbert	Dead	Nashoba	Sally Colbert	Dead	Nashoba
2	Tushka Billy	"	Eagle	Seliney Billy	"	Eagle
3	No 1			No 2		
4	No 1			No 2		
5	No 1			No 2		
6	No 1			No 2		
7						
8						
9	No 3 on 1896 roll as Sainey Colbert					
10	No 4 " 1896 " " Cellen "					
11	For child of Nos 1&2 see NB (March 3 1905) #921					
12						
13						
14						
15					Date of Application for Enrollment.	Oct 10/99
16						
17						

32

Choctaw By Blood Enrollment Cards 1898-1914

RESIDENCE: Nashoba COUNTY. **Choctaw Nation** **Choctaw Roll** CARD No.
POST OFFICE: Smithville, I.T. *(Not Including Freedmen)* FIELD No. **4833**

Dawes' Roll No.	NAME	Relationship to Person First Named	AGE	SEX	BLOOD	TRIBAL ENROLLMENT		
						Year	County	No.
13344	1 Bohanan, Watson		28	M	Full	1896	Nashoba	1118
13345	2 " Wysie 17	Wife	14	F	"	1896	"	2497
	3							
	4							
	5							
	6							
	7							
	8							
	9							
	10							
	11							
	12							
	13							
	14							
	15							
	16							
	17							

DIED PRIOR TO SEPTEMBER 25, 1902

ENROLLMENT
OF NOS. 1 and 2 HEREON
APPROVED BY THE SECRETARY
OF INTERIOR Mar 19 1903

TRIBAL ENROLLMENT OF PARENTS

	Name of Father	Year	County	Name of Mother	Year	County
1	Julius Bohanan	Dead	Nashoba	Sally Bohanan		Nashoba
2	Levi Colbert		"	Salena Colbert	Dead	"
3						
4						
5						
6						
7	No.2 on 1896 roll as Wysie Colbert					
8	No.1 died Aug - 1900: Enrollment cancelled by Department July 8, 1904					
9	For child of No.2 see NB (Apr 26-06) Card #596					
10						
11						
12						
13						
14					Date of Application for Enrollment.	
15					Oct 10/99	
16						
17						

33

Choctaw By Blood Enrollment Cards 1898-1914

RESIDENCE: Atoka COUNTY.
POST OFFICE: Atoka, I.T.

Choctaw Nation

Choctaw Roll
(Not Including Freedmen)

CARD NO.
FIELD NO. 4834

Dawes' Roll No.	NAME	Relationship to Person First Named	AGE	SEX	BLOOD	TRIBAL ENROLLMENT		
						Year	County	No.
~~13346~~	~~1 Jacob, Samillie~~ DIED PRIOR TO SEPTEMBER 25, 1902	~~First Named~~	~~26~~	~~F~~	~~Full~~	~~1893~~	~~Atoka~~	~~312~~
14906	2 " Sila 8	Dau	4	"	"			
	3							
	4							
	5							
	6							
	7							
	8							
	9							
	10							
	11							
	12							
	13							
	14							
	15							
	16							
	17							

ENROLLMENT
OF NOS. 1 HEREON
APPROVED BY THE SECRETARY
OF INTERIOR MAR 19 1903

ENROLLMENT
OF NOS. 2 HEREON
APPROVED BY THE SECRETARY
OF INTERIOR MAY 21 1903

TRIBAL ENROLLMENT OF PARENTS

	Name of Father	Year	County	Name of Mother	Year	County
1	~~Amos Yahamby~~	~~Dead~~	~~Atoka~~	~~Daisy Yahamby~~	~~Dead~~	~~Atoka~~
2	Jonas Frazier		"	No1		
3						
4						
5						
6						
7			No.1 died June 5, 1901. Enrollment cancelled by Department May 2, 190?			
8			No1 on 1893 Pay Roll, Page 30, No			
9			312, Atoka Co., as Somelie Frazier			
10			No2 Affidavit of birth to be			
11			supplied: Received and filed March 14, 1903			
12						
13			No2 "Duplicate of Susan Frazier Choctaw 15053			
14			Not entitled to land or money under No 14906"			
15			Dept Authy D-1470-43 4-16-43 JDF	Date of Application for Enrollment.	Oct 10/99	
16						
17						

34

Choctaw By Blood Enrollment Cards 1898-1914

RESIDENCE: Jackson COUNTY. **Choctaw Nation** Choctaw Roll CARD NO.
POST OFFICE: Jackson, I.T. (Not Including Freedmen) FIELD NO. 4835

Dawes' Roll No.	NAME	Relationship to Person First Named	AGE	SEX	BLOOD	TRIBAL ENROLLMENT		
						Year	County	No.
13347	1 LeFlore, Louisa ⁱ⁹	First Named	16	F	3/4	1896	Jackson	8144
15851	2 Billy, Rossie	Dau	1	F	7/8			
	3							
	4							
	5							
	6							
	7							
	8							
	9	ENROLLMENT OF NOS. 1 HEREON						
	10	APPROVED BY THE SECRETARY						
	11	OF INTERIOR MAR 19 1903						
	12							
	13	ENROLLMENT OF NOS. 2 HEREON						
	14	APPROVED BY THE SECRETARY						
	15	OF INTERIOR JUN 12 1905						
	16							
	17							

TRIBAL ENROLLMENT OF PARENTS

	Name of Father	Year	County	Name of Mother	Year	County
1	Colbert LeFlore	Dead	Jackson	Siney LeFlore	Dead	Jackson
2	Walton Billy	1896	Blue	No.1		
3						
4						
5						
6						
7	On 1896 roll as Louiser LeFlore					
8	No.1 is the wife of Walton Billy, Choctaw care #3461: March 25, 1905					
9	No.2 was born March 13, 1902: application received and name placed on this card March 25, 1905 under provision of act of Congress approved					
10	March 3, 1905.					
11	For child of No.1 see NB (March 3,1905) #1047					
12						
13						
14					#1	
15				Date of Application for Enrollment.	Oct 10/99	
16						
17						

35

Choctaw By Blood Enrollment Cards 1898-1914

RESIDENCE: Blue COUNTY.
POST OFFICE: Bennington I.T.

Choctaw Nation

Choctaw Roll (Not Including Freedmen)

CARD NO.
FIELD NO. **4836**

Dawes' Roll No.	NAME	Relationship to Person First Named	AGE	SEX	BLOOD	TRIBAL ENROLLMENT		
						Year	County	No.
13348	1 Robinson, William 43		40	M	Full	1896	Blue	10941
13349	2 DIED PRIOR TO SEPTEMBER 25, 1902 Lucy	Wife	22	F	"	1896	Jackson	13844
13350	3 DIED PRIOR TO SEPTEMBER 25, 1902 Susan	Dau	1mo	"	"			
	4							
	5							
	6							
	7							
	8							
	9							
	10							
	11							
	12							
	13							
	14							
	15							
	16							
	17							

ENROLLMENT OF NOS. 1, 2 & 3 HEREON APPROVED BY THE SECRETARY OF INTERIOR Mar 19 1903

TRIBAL ENROLLMENT OF PARENTS

	Name of Father	Year	County	Name of Mother	Year	County
1	Te-sha-ho-tubby	Dead	Blue	Ah-no-le-huna	Dead	Blue
2	John White	"	Jakson	Elic White	"	Jackson
3	No.1			No.2		
4						
5						
6						
7						
8						
9						
10		No.1 on 1896 roll as Wm Robinson				
		No.2 " 1896 " " Lucy White				
11		No.3 affidavit of birth to be supplied. Filed Dec. 14/99				
12		No.1 in penitentiary - Nov 12-1902				
13						
14	No.2 died June 25,1902: No.3 died May 27,1902: Enrollment cancelled by Department Sept 16, 1904					
15					Date of Application for Enrollment.	
16					Oct 11/99	
17	PO Tatunis, I.T. 3/1903					

Choctaw By Blood Enrollment Cards 1898-1914

RESIDENCE: Red River COUNTY.
POST OFFICE: Kullituklo, I.T.
Choctaw Nation
Choctaw Roll
(Not Including Freedmen)
CARD NO.
FIELD NO. 4837

Dawes' Roll No.	NAME	Relationship to Person	AGE	SEX	BLOOD	TRIBAL ENROLLMENT		
						Year	County	No.
13351	1 Jacob, Melissa 43	First Named	40	F	Full	1896	Nashoba	8620
	2							
	3							
	4							
	5							
	6							
	7							
	8							
	9							
	10	ENROLLMENT						
	11	OF NOS. ~~~ 1 ~~~ HEREON APPROVED BY THE SECRETARY						
	12	OF INTERIOR MAR 19 1903						
	13							
	14							
	15							
	16							
	17							

TRIBAL ENROLLMENT OF PARENTS

	Name of Father	Year	County	Name of Mother	Year	County
1			Choctaw			Choctaw
2						
3						
4						
5	No.1 on 1896 roll as Melissa Momintubbi					
6	No.1 also On 1893 Pay Roll, Page 39, No. 324					
7	Red River Co					
8	No other information could be ascer-					
9	tained					
10						
11						
12						
13						
14				Date of Application for Enrollment.	Oct 11/99	
15						
16						
17						

Choctaw By Blood Enrollment Cards 1898-1914

RESIDENCE: Gaines   COUNTY.   **Choctaw Nation**   **Choctaw Roll**   CARD No.

POST OFFICE: Wilburton, I.T.   *(Not Including Freedmen)*   FIELD No. **4838**

Dawes' Roll No.	NAME	Relationship to Person First Named	AGE	SEX	BLOOD	TRIBAL ENROLLMENT Year	County	No.
13352	1 Colbert, Lena 51	48	F	Full		1896	Tobucksy	2347
13353	2 King, Sibbie 23	Niece	20	"	"	1893	Gaines	265
13354	3 " Jackson 21	Nephew	18	M	"	1896	Tobucksy	7491
13355	4 " Joel 12	G.S.	9	"	"	1893	Gaines	304
	5							
	6							
	7							
	8							
	9	ENROLLMENT						
	10	OF NOS. 1 2 3 & 4 HEREON APPROVED BY THE SECRETARY						
	11	OF INTERIOR Mar 19 1903						
	12							
	13							
	14							
	15							
	16							
	17							

TRIBAL ENROLLMENT OF PARENTS

	Name of Father	Year	County	Name of Mother	Year	County
1	Na-ho-yubbee	Dead	Skullyville	Sophie		Tobucksy
2	John King	"	Gaines	No-wa-yo-key	Dead	"
3	" "	"	"	"		"
4	Leonidas King	"	"	Elizabeth King		"
5						
6						
7						
8						
9	No.1 on 1896 roll as Kaneyona Colbert					
10	No.2 " 1893 Pay Roll, Page 28, No. 265					
11	Gaines County as Isabelle King					
12	No.4 on 1893 Pay Roll Page 32 No. 304 Gaines Co					
13	No.2 "Died prior to September 25, 1902 not entitled to land or money"					Date of Application for Enrollment.
14	See copy of Indian Office Letter of November 9, 1907. (I.T. 82861-1907)					
15						Oct 11/99
16						
17	No.2 Blanco I.T. 11/1/04					

38

Choctaw By Blood Enrollment Cards 1898-1914

RESIDENCE: Bok Tuklo   COUNTY. **Choctaw Nation**   **Choctaw Roll** *(Not Including Freedmen)*   CARD NO.
POST OFFICE: Lukfata, I.T.   FIELD NO. 4839

Dawes' Roll No.	NAME	Relationship to Person First Named	AGE	SEX	BLOOD	TRIBAL ENROLLMENT		
						Year	County	No.
DEAD. 1	Tokubbee, Lizzie		15	F	Full	1893	Bok Tuklo	272
2								
3								
4								
5								
6								
7								
8								
9								
10								
11								
12								
13								
14								
15	No. 1 HEREON DISMISSED UNDER							
16	ORDER OF THE COMMISSION TO THE FIVE CIVILIZED TRIBES OF MARCH 31, 1905.							
17								

CANCELLED

Applicant died prior to ratification of Choctaw Chickasaw

TRIBAL ENROLLMENT OF PARENTS

	Name of Father	Year	County	Name of Mother	Year	County
1	Bill Tokubbee	Dead	Bok Tuklo	Easter Tokubbee	Dead	Bok Tuklo
2						
3						
4						
5						
6						
7		On 1893 Pay Roll, Page 44, No 272,.				
8		Bok Tuklo Co., as Lessie Tuckubbee, also				
9		on 1896 roll as Lizzie Tukobbe, Page 317,				
10		No 12179, Bok Tuklo Co.				
11		No1 died Jany 12, 1900: proof of death filed Dec 13, 1902				
12						
13						
14					Date of Application for Enrollment.	
15					Oct 11/99	
16						
17						

Choctaw By Blood Enrollment Cards 1898-1914

RESIDENCE: Tobucksy   COUNTY.

POST OFFICE: Kiowa, I.T.

Choctaw Nation

Choctaw Roll
(Not Including Freedmen)

CARD NO.

FIELD NO. 4840

Dawes' Roll No.	NAME	Relationship to Person	AGE	SEX	BLOOD	TRIBAL ENROLLMENT		
						Year	County	No.
13356	1 Cobb, Silas 53	First Named	50	M	Full	1896	Gaines	2277
	2							
	3							
	4							
	5							
	6							
	7							
	8							
	9							
	10							
	11							
	12							
	13							
	14							
	15							
	16							
	17							

ENROLLMENT
OF NOS. 1 HEREON
APPROVED BY THE SECRETARY
OF INTERIOR MAR 19 1903

TRIBAL ENROLLMENT OF PARENTS

	Name of Father	Year	County	Name of Mother	Year	County
1	A-la-tubbee	Dead	Gaines	Sophia		Tobucksy
2						
3						
4						
5						
6						
7						
8						
9						
10						
11						
12						
13						
14				Date of Application for Enrollment.		
15				Oct 11/99		
16	P.O. Bango[sic], I.T.					
17						

40

Choctaw By Blood Enrollment Cards 1898-1914

RESIDENCE: Tobucksy COUNTY. **Choctaw Nation** **Choctaw Roll** CARD NO.
POST OFFICE: Kiowa, I.T. *(Not Including Freedmen)* FIELD NO. 4841

Dawes' Roll No.	NAME	Relationship to Person First Named	AGE	SEX	BLOOD	TRIBAL ENROLLMENT		
						Year	County	No.
13357	1 Olasechubbe, Sophie	DIED PRIOR TO SEPTEMBER 25, 1902	70	F	Full	1896	Tobucksy	9920
	2							
	3							
	4							
	5							
	6							
	7							
	8							
	9	ENROLLMENT OF NOS. 1 HEREON						
	10	APPROVED BY THE SECRETARY						
	11	OF INTERIOR MAR 19 1903						
	12							
	13							
	14							
	15							
	16							
	17							

TRIBAL ENROLLMENT OF PARENTS

	Name of Father	Year	County	Name of Mother	Year	County
1		Dead	Choctaw		Dead	Choctaw
2						
3						
4						
5						
6						
7	On 1896 roll as Sopha Olasechubbe					
8	No. 1 died before Sept. 25, 1902. Enrollment cancelled by Department May 2, 1906					
9						
10						
11						
12						
13				Date of Application for Enrollment.		
14						
15				Oct 11/99		
16						
17						

41

Choctaw By Blood Enrollment Cards 1898-1914

RESIDENCE: Towson COUNTY.
POST OFFICE: Garvin, I.T.

Choctaw Nation *(Not Including Freedmen)*

Choctaw Roll

CARD NO.

FIELD NO. 4842

Dawes' Roll No.	NAME		Relationship to Person	AGE	SEX	BLOOD	TRIBAL ENROLLMENT		
							Year	County	No.
13358	1 Cruttes, Anna B	22	First Named	19	F	1/2	1896	Towson	2462
	2								
	3								
	4								
	5								
	6								
	7								
	8	ENROLLMENT							
	9	OF NOS. 1 HEREON APPROVED BY THE SECRETARY							
	10	OF INTERIOR MAR 19 1903							
	11								
	12								
	13								
	14								
	15								
	16								
	17								

TRIBAL ENROLLMENT OF PARENTS

	Name of Father	Year	County	Name of Mother	Year	County
1	E.S. Cruettes[sic]		Non Citz	Sarah Cruttes	Dead	Kiamitia
2						
3						
4						
5						
6						
7						
8	On 1896 roll as Anna B. Cruette					
9	For child of No1 see NB (Apr 26 '06) Chickasaw Card #98					
10						
11						
12						
13					Date of Application for Enrollment.	
14						
15					Oct 12/99	
16						
17						

Choctaw By Blood Enrollment Cards 1898-1914

| RESIDENCE: Sugar Loaf | COUNTY. | Choctaw Nation | Choctaw Roll | CARD NO. |
| POST OFFICE: Wister, I.T. | | | (Not Including Freedmen) | FIELD NO. 4843 |

Dawes' Roll No.	NAME		Relationship to Person	AGE	SEX	BLOOD	TRIBAL ENROLLMENT		
							Year	County	No.
13359	1 Wade, Willis	23	First Named	20	M	1/2	1896	Sugar Loaf	12865
	2								
	3								
	4								
	5								
	6								
	7								
	8								
	9								
	10								
	11								
	12								
	13								
	14								
	15								
	16								
	17								

ENROLLMENT
OF NOS. 1 HEREON
APPROVED BY THE SECRETARY
OF INTERIOR MAR 19 1903

TRIBAL ENROLLMENT OF PARENTS

	Name of Father	Year	County	Name of Mother	Year	County
1	Simon Wade	Dead	Sans Bois	Mary Ann Peter	Dead	Skullyville
2						
3						
4						
5						
6						
7			For children of No1 see NB (March 3 1905) #1303			
8						
9						
10						
11						
12						
13						
14						
15				Date of Application for Enrollment.	Oct 12/99	
16						
17	P.O. Atoka, I.T.					

43

Choctaw By Blood Enrollment Cards 1898-1914

RESIDENCE: Gaines   COUNTY. **Choctaw Nation**   **Choctaw Roll** *(Not Including Freedmen)*   CARD NO.
POST OFFICE: Wilburton, I.T.   FIELD NO. **4844**

Dawes' Roll No.	NAME	Relationship to Person First Named	AGE	SEX	BLOOD	TRIBAL ENROLLMENT		
						Year	County	No.
13360	1 Anderson, Minnie ⁱ⁸		15	F	3/4	1896	Gaines	88
	2							
	3							
	4							
	5							
	6							
	7							
	8							
	9	ENROLLMENT OF NOS. ~~~ 1 ~~~ HEREON APPROVED BY THE SECRETARY						
	10	OF INTERIOR Mar. 19 1903						
	11							
	12							
	13							
	14							
	15							
	16							
	17							

TRIBAL ENROLLMENT OF PARENTS

	Name of Father	Year	County	Name of Mother	Year	County
1	Andrew Anderson		Tobucksy	Eliza Anderson		Tobucksy
2						
3						
4						
5						
6			No. 1 is duplicate of Minnie Anderson No. 1 on Choctaw Card #370			
7			Enrollment cancelled by Department January 24, 1907 (I.T.D. 806-1907)			
8			D.C. #5525-1907			
9						
10						
11						
12						
13					Date of Application for Enrollment.	
14						
15					Oct 13/99	
16						
17						

44

Choctaw By Blood Enrollment Cards 1898-1914

RESIDENCE: Jacks Fork   COUNTY. **Choctaw Nation**   **Choctaw Roll**   CARD NO.
POST OFFICE: Stringtown, I.T.   *(Not Including Freedmen)*   FIELD NO. 4845

Dawes' Roll No.	NAME	Relationship to Person First Named	AGE	SEX	BLOOD	TRIBAL ENROLLMENT Year	TRIBAL ENROLLMENT County	TRIBAL ENROLLMENT No.
13361	1 Bond, Harrison²¹	First Named	18	M	Full	1896	Jacks Fork	1884
	2							
	3							
	4							
	5							
	6							
	7							
	8							
	9							
	10							
	11							
	12							
	13							
	14							
	15							
	16							
	17							

ENROLLMENT
OF NOS. 1 HEREON
APPROVED BY THE SECRETARY
OF INTERIOR MAR 19 1903

TRIBAL ENROLLMENT OF PARENTS

Name of Father	Year	County	Name of Mother	Year	County
1 Tambe Bond		Jacks Fork	Narcissa Bond	Dead	Jacks Fork
2					
3					
4					
5					
6					
7					
8					
9					
10					
11					
12					
13					
14				Date of Application for Enrollment.	
15				Oct 13/99	
16					
17					

45

Choctaw By Blood Enrollment Cards 1898-1914

RESIDENCE: Blue COUNTY.
POST OFFICE: Academy, I.T.

Choctaw Nation

Choctaw Roll
(Not Including Freedmen)

CARD NO.
FIELD NO. 4846

Dawes' Roll No.	NAME		Relationship to Person First Named	AGE	SEX	BLOOD	TRIBAL ENROLLMENT		
							Year	County	No.
13362	1 Wright, Peter	20	First Named	17	M	Full	1896	Sans Bois	12714
	2								
	3								
	4								
	5								
	6								
	7								
	8								
	9								
	10								
	11	ENROLLMENT OF NOS. 1 HEREON APPROVED BY THE SECRETARY OF INTERIOR MAR 19 1903							
	12								
	13								
	14								
	15								
	16								
	17								

TRIBAL ENROLLMENT OF PARENTS

	Name of Father	Year	County	Name of Mother	Year	County
1	John Wright	Dead	Nashoba		Dead	
2						
3						
4						
5						
6						
7						
8						
9						
10			Duplicate of Card D 511			
11						
12						
13					Date of Application for Enrollment.	
14						
15					Oct 13/99	
16						
17						

Choctaw By Blood Enrollment Cards 1898-1914

RESIDENCE: Gaines COUNTY.
POST OFFICE: Wilburton, I.T.

Choctaw Nation

Choctaw Roll
(Not Including Freedmen)

CARD NO.
FIELD NO. 4847

Dawes' Roll No.	NAME	Relationship to Person First Named	AGE	SEX	BLOOD	TRIBAL ENROLLMENT		
						Year	County	No.
1	Ward, Pianna	Named	5	F	1/2	1896	Gaines	12982
2								
3								
4								
5								
6								
7								
8								
9								
10								
11								
12								
13								
14								
15								
16								
17								

CANCELLED

TRIBAL ENROLLMENT OF PARENTS

	Name of Father	Year	County	Name of Mother	Year	County
1	Henry Ward		Chick Roll	Judie Ward	Dead	Gaines
2						
3						
4						
5						
6						
7		Living with Jackson James,				
8		Wilburton, I.T.				
9						
10						
11		Duplicate of Card 459				
12						
13					Date of Application for Enrollment.	
14					Oct 13/99	
15						
16						
17						

Choctaw By Blood Enrollment Cards 1898-1914

RESIDENCE: Chickasaw Nation ~~COUNTY.~~
POST OFFICE: Johnson, I.T.

Choctaw Nation

Choctaw Roll
(Not Including Freedmen)

CARD NO.
FIELD NO. 4848

Dawes' Roll No.	NAME	Relationship to Person First Named	AGE	SEX	BLOOD	TRIBAL ENROLLMENT		
						Year	County	No.
Denied 1	Byars, William E	Named	20	M	1W			
2	" Sallie V	Wife	17	F	1/16	1896	Chick Dist	6193
Denied 3	" David Levi	Son	2m	M	1/32			
4								
5								
6								
7								
8								
9								
10								
11								
12								
13								
14								
15								
16								
17								

#2 DISMISSED
MAR 18 1905

Decision of Commission of April 3, 1905
refusing Nos 1 and 3 affirmed by Department May 18, 1905 (I.T.D. #3702-1905)
DAC. #23912-1905

TRIBAL ENROLLMENT OF PARENTS

	Name of Father	Year	County	Name of Mother	Year	County
1	W. L. Byars		Non Citz	Addie Byars		Non Citz
2	D. M. Hyden		Choctaw	Dicey J Hyden	Dead	" "
3	No.1			No2		
4						
5						
6	No2 denied in 96 Case #1344					
7	No2 was admitted by U.S. Court, Southern Dist, December 22/97, Case					
8	No 141 as Sallie Hyden. On 1896					
9	roll as Sallie Hyden					
10	Judgment of US Ct admitting Nos 1 and 2 vacated and set aside by Decree of Choctaw Chickasaw Cit Court Decr 17 02					
11	No1- as to marriage see his testimony.					
12	No3 Enrolled January 22, 1901					
13	No appeal to C.C.C.C.					
14	No.2 [illegible]			Date of Application for Enrollment.		
15				Oct 20/99		
16						
17						

48

Choctaw By Blood Enrollment Cards 1898-1914

RESIDENCE: Sans Bois COUNTY. **Choctaw Nation** **Choctaw Roll** CARD No.
POST OFFICE: Featherstone, I.T. *(Not Including Freedmen)* FIELD No. 4849

Dawes' Roll No.	NAME	Relationship to Person First Named	AGE	SEX	BLOOD	TRIBAL ENROLLMENT		
						Year	County	No.
13364	1 Davis, Tom 31	First Named	28	M	Full	1896	Sans Bois	3156
	2							
	3							
	4							
	5							
	6							
	7							
	8							
	9							
	10	ENROLLMENT						
	11	OF NOS. 1 HEREON APPROVED BY THE SECRETARY						
	12	OF INTERIOR MAR 19 1903						
	13							
	14							
	15							
	16							
	17							

TRIBAL ENROLLMENT OF PARENTS

	Name of Father	Year	County	Name of Mother	Year	County
1		Dead	Choctaw		Dead	Choctaw
2						
3						
4						
5						
6						
7	In penitentiary at Ft Leavenworth					
8	No 1 is now husband of Rosa Drake on Choctaw card #2979					
9	Evidence of marriage filed December 15, 1902					
10	For child of No. 1 see NB (March 3, 1905) #792					
11						
12						
13					Date of Application for Enrollment.	
14						
15					Nov 14/99	
16						
17						

49

RESIDENCE:	Sans Bois	COUNTY.					Choctaw Roll	CARD No.	
POST OFFICE:	Whitefield, I.T.	**Choctaw Nation**					(Not Including Freedmen)	FIELD No. 4850	

Dawes' Roll No.	NAME		Relationship to Person First Named	AGE	SEX	BLOOD	TRIBAL ENROLLMENT		
							Year	County	No.
13365 1	Folsom, Daniel	28	Named	25	M	1/2	1896	Sans Bois	3918
13366 2	" May B	9	Dau	6	F	1/4	1896	" "	3919
13367 3	" Daniel Jr	7	Son	4	M	1/4	1896	"	3867
4									
5									
6									
7									
8									
9									
10	ENROLLMENT OF NOS. 1 2 & 3 HEREON APPROVED BY THE SECRETARY								
11	OF INTERIOR MAR 19 1903								
12									
13									
14									
15									
16									
17									

TRIBAL ENROLLMENT OF PARENTS

	Name of Father	Year	County	Name of Mother	Year	County
1	Elias Folsom		Sans Bois		Dead	Choctaw
2	No 1			Viney Folsom		white woman
3	No 1			" "		" "
4						
5						
6						
7						
8	Nos 1 and 2 duplications of Nos 1 and 3 on Choctaw					
9	12952 - 2953 No3 erroneous enrollment Cancellation					
10	mental letter of Feb 3 1904 (D.C. #4186-1904)					
11	No 1 on 1896 roll as Daniel Folsum					
12						
13						
14					Date of Application for Enrollment.	
15					Nov 14/99	
16						
17						

Choctaw By Blood Enrollment Cards 1898-1914

RESIDENCE: Sans Bois   COUNTY. **Choctaw Nation**   **Choctaw Roll** *(Not Including Freedmen)*   CARD NO.

POST OFFICE: Stigler, I.T.   FIELD NO. **4851**

Dawes' Roll No.	NAME	Relationship to Person First Named	AGE	SEX	BLOOD	TRIBAL ENROLLMENT Year	County	No.
13368	1 Nail, Salina 27	First Named	24	F	1/2	1896	Sans Bois	9549
13369	2 " Mary 2	Dau	9mo	F	1/2			
13370	3 " Amanda 4	"	2	F	1/2			
	4							
	5							
	6							
	7							
	8							
	9							
	10							
	11							
	12							
	13							
	14							
	15							
	16							
	17							

> ENROLLMENT OF NOS. 1, 2 & 3 HEREON APPROVED BY THE SECRETARY OF INTERIOR Mar 19 1903

TRIBAL ENROLLMENT OF PARENTS

Name of Father	Year	County	Name of Mother	Year	County
1 Wilson James		Choctaw	Maulsey Williams		Choctaw
2 Richard Nail	1896	Sans Bois	No.1		
3 " "			No.1		
4					
5					
6					
7					
8					

9   No.1 is the wife of Richard Nail on Choctaw Card #2844. See letter of

10   No.2 Enrolled Oct. 5, 901

11   No.3 transferred to this card from Choctaw Card #4752. See notation

   No.3 Died Oct. 7, 1902, proof of death filed Dec. 30, 1902

12   No.1 on Tobucksy Co Payroll P. 100 Nº 839 as Sissie James

13   For child of No.1 see NB (Apr 26, 1906) Card No. 213   #1

14   " " " " " (Mar 3 1905) " " 1352   Date of Application for Enrollment.

15   Nov 14/99

16

17   P.O. Ryan, I.T. 4/25/05

Choctaw By Blood Enrollment Cards 1898-1914

RESIDENCE: Sans Bois COUNTY.
POST OFFICE: Iron Bridge, I.T.

Choctaw Nation
Choctaw Roll
(Not Including Freedmen)

CARD NO.
FIELD NO. 4852

Dawes' Roll No.	NAME		Relationship to Person	AGE	SEX	BLOOD	TRIBAL ENROLLMENT		
							Year	County	No.
15593	1 McCann, Jane	36	First Named	33	F	Full	1896	Sans Bois	10088
	2								
	3								
	4								
	5								
	6								
	7								
	8								
	9								
	10								
	11								
	12								
	13								
	14								
	15								
	16								
	17								

ENROLLMENT
OF NOS. ~~~ 1 ~~~ HEREON
APPROVED BY THE SECRETARY
OF INTERIOR SEP 22 1904

TRIBAL ENROLLMENT OF PARENTS

	Name of Father	Year	County	Name of Mother	Year	County
1	Pona, or John Hall	dead	Choctaw	Ishtemahona	Dead	Choctaw
2						
3						
4						
5						
6						
7						
8						
9	On 1896 roll as Jane Pong[sic]					
10	See testimony of Nº1 taken at Atoka I.T. May 13, 1904					
11						
12						
13						
14						
15				Date of Application for Enrollment.	Nov 14/99	
16						
17						

Choctaw By Blood Enrollment Cards 1898-1914

Choctaw Nation

Choctaw Roll *(Not Including Freedmen)*

CARD No. FIELD No. 4853

Dawes' Roll No.	NAME	Relationship to Person	AGE	SEX	BLOOD	TRIBAL ENROLLMENT Year	County	No.
15962	1 Pope, Judy ^16	First Named	13	F	Full	1896	Sans Bois	11097
15692	2 " Mitchell ^2	Son	3	M	"			
	3							
	4							
	5							
	6							
	7							
	8							
	9	ENROLLMENT OF NOS. ~~~1~~~ HEREON APPROVED BY THE SECRETARY OF INTERIOR NOV 27 1905						
	10							
	11	ENROLLMENT OF NOS. ~~2~~ HEREON APPROVED BY THE SECRETARY OF INTERIOR DEC 22 1904						
	12							
	13							
	14							
	15							
	16							
	17							

TRIBAL ENROLLMENT OF PARENTS

Name of Father	Year	County	Name of Mother	Year	County
1 Alex Sexton	Dead	Choctaw	Rhoda Sexton	Dead	Choctaw
2 Noel Pope	1896	Sans Bois	Nº1		
3					
4					
5					
6					

7 No.1 is a duplication of No.3 on Choctaw freedman card #786

8 No.1 is now the wife of Noel Pope on Choctaw Card #3087. Evidence of marriage filed Oct 19, 1901

9 Nº2 Born Oct 3, 1900. Application for enrollment first received March 10 1901 and

10 returned for identification of the mother and evidence of marriage

11 Nº2 Enrolled September 2 1904

12 Noel Pope, father of No.2, on final roll, No. 9004

13 For child of No1 see NB (Apr 26-06) Card #508

Nº1 GRANTED

OCT 5- 1905

Nov 14/99

53

Choctaw By Blood Enrollment Cards 1898-1914

RESIDENCE: Sans Bois COUNTY.
POST OFFICE: Sans Bois, I.T.

Choctaw Nation

Choctaw Roll
(Not Including Freedmen)

CARD NO.
FIELD NO. 4854

Dawes' Roll No.	NAME	Relationship to Person First Named	AGE	SEX	BLOOD	TRIBAL ENROLLMENT Year	TRIBAL ENROLLMENT County	TRIBAL ENROLLMENT No.
1	Thompson, Sealy 41		38	F	Full	1896	Sans Bois	11834
2								
3								
4								
5								
6								
7								
8								
9								
10								
11								
12								
13								
14								
15								
16								
17								

DISMISSED

AUG 18 1906

TRIBAL ENROLLMENT OF PARENTS

	Name of Father	Year	County	Name of Mother	Year	County
1		Dead	Choctaw		Dead	Choctaw
2						
3						
4						
5						
6						
7	No.1 died before September 25, 1902. Proof of death filed August 18, 1906					
8						
9						
10						
11						
12						
13						
14					Date of Application for Enrollment.	
15					Nov 14/99	
16						
17						

54

Choctaw By Blood Enrollment Cards 1898-1914

RESIDENCE: Sans Bois	COUNTY. **Choctaw Nation**	**Choctaw Roll**	CARD No.
POST OFFICE: Sans Bois, I.T.		(Not Including Freedmen)	FIELD No. 4855

Dawes' Roll No.	NAME		Relationship to Person	AGE	SEX	BLOOD	TRIBAL ENROLLMENT		
							Year	County	No.
13373	1 Wyatt, Lourena	12	First Named	9	F	1/4	1896	Sans Bois	12708
	2								
	3								
	4								
	5								
	6								
	7								
	8								
	9								
	10								
	11								
	12								
	13								
	14								
	15								
	16								
	17								

ENROLLMENT
OF NOS. 1 HEREON
APPROVED BY THE SECRETARY
OF INTERIOR MAR 19 1903

TRIBAL ENROLLMENT OF PARENTS

	Name of Father	Year	County	Name of Mother	Year	County
1			Non Citz	Fannie Riddle	Dead	Choctaw
2						
3						
4						
5						
6	On 1896 roll as Lucinda Wyatt					
7						
8						
9						
10						
11						
12						
13					Date of Application for Enrollment.	
14						
15					Nov 14/99	
16						
17						

Choctaw By Blood Enrollment Cards 1898-1914

RESIDENCE:	Gaines	COUNTY.							
POST OFFICE:	Hartshorne, IT	**Choctaw Nation**					**Choctaw Roll** *(Not Including Freedmen)*	CARD No. FIELD No. 4856	

Dawes' Roll No.	NAME		Relationship to Person	AGE	SEX	BLOOD	TRIBAL ENROLLMENT		
							Year	County	No.
13374	1 Cooper, Willis	27	First Named	24	M	3/4	1896	Sans Bois	2054
	2								
	3								
	4								
	5								
	6								
	7								
	8								
	9								
	10								
	11	ENROLLMENT OF NOS. 1 HEREON APPROVED BY THE SECRETARY OF INTERIOR MAR 19 1903							
	12								
	13								
	14								
	15								
	16								
	17								

TRIBAL ENROLLMENT OF PARENTS

Name of Father	Year	County	Name of Mother	Year	County
1 Thompson Cooper	Dead	Choctaw	Ontishuna	Dead	Choctaw
2					
3					
4					
5					
6					
7	Wife and child on Card 4307				
8	Nº1 is separated from wife on Choc. Card #4307				
9					
10					
11					
12					
13				Date of Application for Enrollment.		
14	P.O. Mess, Arbo J. T. I.T.			Nov 14/99		
15						
16						
17 P.O. San[sic] Bois, I.T.						

RESIDENCE:	Tobucksy	COUNTY.					**Choctaw Roll**		CARD No.	
POST OFFICE:	South McAlester, I.T.		**Choctaw Nation**				*(Not Including Freedmen)*		FIELD No.	4857

Dawes' Roll No.	NAME	Relationship to Person First Named	AGE	SEX	BLOOD	TRIBAL ENROLLMENT		
						Year	County	No.
1	Arnold, Martha	Named	77	F	1/2		D	
2								
3								
4								
5								
6								
7								
8								
9								
10								
11								
12								
13								
14								
15								
16								
17								

TRIBAL ENROLLMENT OF PARENTS

	Name of Father	Year	County	Name of Mother	Year	County
1	James Hall	Dead	Non Citz	Nancy Hall	Dead	Choctaw
2						
3						
4						
5						
6						
7						
8						

9 No. 1 denied by Commission in 1896, case No. 495

10 Admitted by U.S. Court, Central

Dist. Nov 11/99. As to residence, see No.3 So McAlester [sic]

11 his testimony

12 Judgements of U.S. Court admitting No.1 vacated and set aside by Decree of Choctaw Chickasaw Citizenship Court Dec 17/02

13 No.1 now in C.C.C.C. Case #97

14 No.1 Petition to reopen denied by the Department May 2, 190[?]

conformity with opinion of Asst. Atty. General in case of [illegible] West et al

15 Jan 24 1907 Motion for rehearing forwarded Department

Feb 14 1907 " " denied by "

16 March 2, 1907 Parties hereon [remander illegible]

17

Date of Application for Enrollment.

Nov 14/99

Choctaw By Blood Enrollment Cards 1898-1914

RESIDENCE: **Skullyville** COUNTY. **Choctaw Nation**
POST OFFICE: **Bokoshe, I.T.**

Choctaw Roll *(Not Including Freedmen)*

CARD NO.
FIELD NO. **4858**

Dawes' Roll No.	NAME	Relationship to Person	AGE	SEX	BLOOD	TRIBAL ENROLLMENT		
						Year	County	No.
I.W. 1354 1	James, Elizabeth M ★ 41	First Named	38	F	I.W.			
2								
3								
4								
5								
6								
7								
8								
9								
10								
11								
12								
13								
14	ENROLLMENT							
15	OF NOS. 1 HEREON APPROVED BY THE SECRETARY							
16	OF INTERIOR Mar 14 1905							
17								

TRIBAL ENROLLMENT OF PARENTS

	Name of Father	Year	County	Name of Mother	Year	County
1	James Arnold	Dead	Non Citz	Martha Arnold		Choctaw
2						
3						
4						
5						
6						
7	Testimony as to Intermarried status taken Nov. 9" 04					
8	No.1 denied by Commission in 1896 Case No. 495					
9	Admitted by U.S. Court, Central Dist. Nov 11/99 Case No.3 As to residence					
10	see testimony of Martha Arnold in her					
11	own enrollment.					
12	Judgment of U.S.C. admitting No1 vacated and set aside by Decree of Choctaw Chickasaw Citizenship Court Dec' 17'02					
13	No.1 is wife of Silas W James, Choc Card #2638 No.1 now in C.C.C. Case #97					
14	★ No.1 denied as a citizen by blood by C.C.C.C. Case #97 in Oct. 25,04 as				Date of Application for Enrollment.	
15	"Elizabeth James (nee Arnold) or Elizabeth M James (nee Arnold)				Nov 14/99	
16						
17	P.O. Box 552 So. McAlester I.T.					

58

Choctaw By Blood Enrollment Cards 1898-1914

RESIDENCE: Tobucksy COUNTY. **Choctaw Nation** Choctaw Roll CARD No.
POST OFFICE: South McAlester, I.T. *(Not Including Freedmen)* FIELD No. 4859

Dawes' Roll No.	NAME	Relationship to Person First Named	AGE	SEX	BLOOD	TRIBAL ENROLLMENT		
						Year	County	No.
1	Arnold, Frank J	Named	45	M	1/4		D	
2	" James F	Son	21	"	1/8		D	
3								
4								
5								
6								
7								
8								
9								
10								
11								
12								
13								
14								
15								
16								
17								

TRIBAL ENROLLMENT OF PARENTS

	Name of Father	Year	County	Name of Mother	Year	County
1	James Arnold	Dead	Non Citz	Martha Arnold		Choctaw
2	No 1			Harriet F Arnold		Non Citz
3						
4						
5						
6						
7						
8						

Nos1 and 2 denied by Commission in 1896 case No. 495
Admitted by U.S. Court, Central Dist,
Nov 11/99, Case No3 As to residence, see
testimony of No1

No.1 is the husband of Harriet F Arnold on Choctaw card #R.4

Date of Application for Enrollment.
Nov 14/99

Choctaw By Blood Enrollment Cards 1898-1914

RESIDENCE: Tobucksy COUNTY. **Choctaw Nation** Choctaw Roll CARD NO.
POST OFFICE: South McAlester, I.T. *(Not Including Freedmen)* FIELD NO. 4860

Dawes' Roll No.	NAME	Relationship to Person First Named	AGE	SEX	BLOOD	TRIBAL ENROLLMENT		
						Year	County	No.
1	Arnold, Woodson H	First Named	44	M	1/4		D	
2								
3								
4								
5								
6								
7								
8								
9								
10								
11								
12								
13								
14								
15								
16								
17								

Watermark: No.1 Denied by C.C.C.C. as "Woodson H Arnold or Woodson H Arnold" / C.C.C.C. Case 497 Oct. 25 '04 / DENIED CITIZENSHIP BY THE CHOCTAW AND CHICKASAW CITIZENSHIP COURT

TRIBAL ENROLLMENT OF PARENTS

	Name of Father	Year	County	Name of Mother	Year	County
1	James Arnold	Dead	Byon Citz	Martha Arnold		Choctaw
2						
3						
4						
5						
6						
7						
8						

No1 denied by Commission in 1896 case 495
Admitted by U.S. Court, Central Dist,
Nov 11/99, Case No3   As to residence, see
testimony of No1
Judgement of U.S. C't admitting No1 vacated and set aside by Decree of C'' C.C., Dec' 17 '02
No.1 is the husband of Kitty Arnold on Choctaw card #R.7
Not now in C.C.C.C. Case #97

Date of Application for Enrollment.
Nov 14/99

60

Choctaw By Blood Enrollment Cards 1898-1914

RESIDENCE: Tobucksy COUNTY. **Choctaw Nation** Choctaw Roll CARD NO.
POST OFFICE: Celestine, I.T. (Not Including Freedmen) FIELD NO. 4861

Dawes' Roll No.	NAME	Relationship to Person First Named	AGE	SEX	BLOOD	TRIBAL ENROLLMENT		
						Year	County	No.
1	Arnold, Jones N	Named	40	M	1/4		D	
2	" Roscoe C	Son	12	"	1/8		D	
3								
4								
5								
6								
7								
8								
9								
10								
11								
12								
13								
14								
15								
16								
17								

C.C.C.C. Case #97 Oct. 25 '04

DENIED CITIZENSHIP BY THE CHOCTAW AND CHICKASAW CITIZENSHIP COURT

TRIBAL ENROLLMENT OF PARENTS

	Name of Father	Year	County	Name of Mother	Year	County
1	James Arnold	Dead Non Citz		Martha Arnold		Choctaw
2	No1			Julia A Arnold		Non Citz
3						
4						
5						
6						
7						
8						
9						

Nos1&2

Nos 1 and 2 denied by Commission in 1896 case 495
Admitted by U.S. Court, Central Dist,
Nov 11/99, Case No3   As to residence, see
testimony of No1

No.1 is the husband of Julia Arnold on Choctaw card #R.5

Nos 1 and 2 Petition to reopen denied by the Department May 2, 1906 in conformity with opinion of Ass't Atty General in Case of Loula West, et al
Aug 9, 1906 - Motion for reopening forwarded Dept
Nov 28, 1906   "   "   "   "   Denied by   "
Jan 24, 1907 Motion for rehearing forwarded Department

Date of Application for Enrollment
Nov 14/99

Choctaw By Blood Enrollment Cards 1898-1914

| RESIDENCE: | Tobucksy | COUNTY. | | | | | | | |
| POST OFFICE: | South McAlester, I.T. | | | | | | | | FIELD NO. 4862 |

Choctaw Nation — Choctaw Roll *(Not Including Freedmen)* — CARD NO. — FIELD NO. 4862

Dawes' Roll No.	NAME	Relationship to Person First Named	AGE	SEX	BLOOD	TRIBAL ENROLLMENT Year	County	No.
1	Arnold, James E	Named	36	M	1/4		D	
2	" Lizzie	Dau	15	F	1/8		D	
3	" Hugh	Son	14	M	1/8		D	
4	" Arthur W	"	10	"	1/8		D	
5	" Tottie	"	6	"	1/8		D	
6	" Hazel	Dau	3 wks	F	1/8		D	
7								

Nº6 - DISMISSED

NOV 29 1904

10. No5 Denied by C.C.C.C. as "Lottie Arnold or Tottie Arnold"
11. Nos 1,2,3,4 and 5 Petition to reopen denied by the
    Department May 2, 1906 in conformity with opinion of
12. Asst Atty General in case of Loula West, et al.
13.

14.
15.
16. Nos 1,2,4,5 — DENIED CITIZENSHIP BY THE CHOCTAW AND CHICKASAW CITIZENSHIP COURT

No.3 No mention is made of No3 in Decree of C.C.C.C.   C.C.C.C. Case #97 Oct 25'04

			TRIBAL ENROLLMENT OF PARENTS			
	Name of Father	Year	County	Name of Mother	Year	County
1	James Arnold	Dead	Non Citz	Martha Arnold		Choctaw
2	No 1			Cordelia Arnold		Non Citz
3	No 1			" "		" "
4	No 1			" "		" "
5	No 1			" "		" "
6	No. 1			" "		" "
7						
8						
9						

10. Nos 1 to 5 inclusive denied by Commission in 1896,
    All admitted by U.S. Court, Central
11. Dist., Nov 11/99 Case No.   As to
    residence see testimony of No1
12. No.6 Enrolled January 3, 1901
13. No.1 is the husband of Cordelia D. Arnold on Choctaw

Judgment [of] U.S. Court admitting No vacated and set aside by Decree of Choctaw Chickasaw Citizenship Court Dec 17/02

Nos 1,2,4,5 and 6 [...] C.C.C.C. Case #97

Date of Application for Enrollment.
Nov 14/99.

Choctaw By Blood Enrollment Cards 1898-1914

RESIDENCE: **Tobucksy** COUNTY. **Choctaw Nation** **Choctaw Roll** CARD NO.

POST OFFICE: **South McAlester, I.T.** (Not Including Freedmen) FIELD NO. **4863**

Dawes' Roll No.	NAME	Relationship to Person First Named	AGE	SEX	BLOOD	TRIBAL ENROLLMENT Year	TRIBAL ENROLLMENT County	TRIBAL ENROLLMENT No.
1	Arnold, Park E	Named	31	M	1/4			
2								
3								
4								
5								
6								
7								
8								
9								
10								
11								
12								
13								
14								
15								
16								
17								

No. 1 - Denied Citizenship By The Choctaw And Chickasaw Citizenship Court

C.C.C.C. Case #97 Oct 25 '04

TRIBAL ENROLLMENT OF PARENTS

	Name of Father	Year	County	Name of Mother	Year	County
1	James Arnold	Dead	Non Citz	Martha Arnold		Choctaw
2						
3						
4						
5						
6						

No. 1 denied by Commission in 1896, Case No 4
Admitted by U.S. Court, Central
Dist, Nov 11/99, Case No.3   As to
residence see his testimony
Judgment of U.S. Ct admitting No1 vacated and set aside by Decree of Choctaw Chickasaw Citizenship Court Dec 17'02
No1 now in C.C.C.C. Case #97

Petition to reopen denied by the Department, May 2, 1906 in conformity with opinion of
Asst Atty General in Case of Loula West et al.

Date of Application for Enrollment.

Nov 14/99

Choctaw By Blood Enrollment Cards 1898-1914

RESIDENCE: Gaines
POST OFFICE: Wilburton, I _(Not including Freedmen)_ FIELD NO. 4864

Dawes' Roll No.	NAME		Relationship to Person	AGE	SEX	BLOOD	TRIBAL ENROLLMENT		
							Year	County	No.
13375	1 Battles, William E	25	First Named	22	M	3/4	1896	Gaines	826
13376	2 " Henry Franklin	1	Son	1½ mo	M	3/8			
I.W. 1430	3 " Martha		Wife	19	F	I.W.			
	4								
	5								
	6								
	7								
	8								
	9	ENROLLMENT OF NOS. 1 & 2 HEREON							
	10	APPROVED BY THE SECRETARY OF INTERIOR MAR 19 1903							
	11								
	12								
	13								
	14	ENROLLMENT							
	15	OF NOS. 3 HEREON APPROVED BY THE SECRETARY							
	16	OF INTERIOR JUN 12 1905							
	17								

TRIBAL ENROLLMENT OF PARENTS

	Name of Father	Year	County	Name of Mother	Year	County
1	Frank Battles		Non Citz	Susan Battles		Gaines
2	Nº1			Marthy[sic] Battles		white woman
3	Wm Helton		non citz	Lizzie Helton		non-citz
4						
5						
6						
7						
8						
9						
10	On 1896 roll as Wm Ed Battles					
11	Nº1 is now the husband of Martha Battles a non-citizen: evidence of marriage filed March 14,1902					
12	Nº2 Born Jany 26, 1902; enrolled March 14, 1902 No.3 originally listed for enrollment on Choctaw card #D-976 - Dec 24, 1901:					
13	transferred to this card May 15,1905. See decision April 22, 1905					
14					#1	
15					Date of Application for Enrollment.	Nov 14/99
16						
17			Gowen			

64

Choctaw By Blood Enrollment Cards 1898-1914

RESIDENCE: Blue COUNTY.
POST OFFICE: Bok Chito, I.T.

Choctaw Nation

Choctaw Roll
(Not Including Freedmen)

CARD NO.
FIELD NO. 4865

Dawes' Roll No.	NAME	Relationship to Person First Named	AGE	SEX	BLOOD	TRIBAL ENROLLMENT		
						Year	County	No.
13377	1 Martin, Mary 41	First Named	38	F	Full	1896	Blue	8803
	2							
	3							
	4							
	5							
	6							
	7							
	8							
	9	ENROLLMENT OF NOS. 1 HEREON						
	10	APPROVED BY THE SECRETARY OF INTERIOR MAR 19 1903						
	11							
	12							
	13							
	14							
	15							
	16							
	17							

TRIBAL ENROLLMENT OF PARENTS

	Name of Father	Year	County	Name of Mother	Year	County
1	Davis Noah	Dead	Blue	Winnie Noah	Dead	Blue
2						
3						
4						
5						
6						
7						
8						
9						
10						
11						
12						
13						
14						
15						
16						
17						

Date of Application for Enrollment.

Nov 14/99

Choctaw By Blood Enrollment Cards 1898-1914

RESIDENCE: Gaines COUNTY. **Choctaw Nation** **Choctaw Roll** CARD NO.
POST OFFICE: Damon, I.T. *(Not Including Freedmen)* FIELD NO. 4866

Dawes' Roll No.	NAME		Relationship to Person	AGE	SEX	BLOOD	TRIBAL ENROLLMENT		
							Year	County	No.
13378	1 Carr, Sophia	35	First Named	32	F	1/2	1896	Gaines	2284
	2								
	3								
	4								
	5								
	6								
	7								
	8								
	9	ENROLLMENT OF NOS. 1 HEREON							
	10	APPROVED BY THE SECRETARY OF INTERIOR Mar 19 1903							
	11								
	12								
	13								
	14								
	15								
	16								
	17								

TRIBAL ENROLLMENT OF PARENTS

	Name of Father	Year	County	Name of Mother	Year	County
1	John Carr	Dead	Gaines	Eliza Carr	Dead	Gaines
2						
3						
4						
5						
6						
7	On 1896 roll as Sophy Carr					
8						
9						
10						
11						
12						
13					Date of Application for Enrollment.	
14						
15					Nov 14/99	
16						
17						

66

Choctaw By Blood Enrollment Cards 1898-1914

RESIDENCE: Gaines COUNTY. **Choctaw Nation** Choctaw Roll ~~D NO.~~

POST OFFICE: Hartshorne, I.T. (Not Including Freedmen) D NO. 4867

Dawes' Roll No.	NAME	Relationship to Person First Named	AGE	SEX	BLOOD	TRIBAL ENROLLMENT		
						Year	County	No.
1	~~James, Benjamin~~ DIED PRIOR TO SEPTEMBER 25, 1902		~~31~~	~~M~~	~~Full~~	~~1896~~	~~Gaines~~	~~6593~~
2								
3								
4								
5								
6								
7								
8								
9	No. 1 HEREON DISMISSED UNDER							
10	ORDER OF THE COMMISSION TO THE FIVE CIVILIZED TRIBES OF MARCH 31, 1905.							
11								
12								
13								
14								
15								
16								
17								

TRIBAL ENROLLMENT OF PARENTS

	Name of Father	Year	County	Name of Mother	Year	County
1	Joseph James		Gaines		Dead	Gaines
2						
3						
4						
5	No.1 is son of No.1 on Choctaw card No. 1					
6						
7	No.1 Died in April, 1901 Proof of death filed February 20, 1905 See also testimony of Joseph James of February 10, 1905					
8						
9						
10						
11						
12						
13					Date of Application for Enrollment.	
14						
15					Nov 14	
16						
17						

Not Died prior to September 25 1902

CANCELLED

Choctaw By Blood Enrollment Cards 1898-1914

RESIDENCE:	Gaines	COUNTY.						CARD NO. 4868
POST OFFICE:	Vireton, I.T.		**Choctaw Nation**			Choctaw Roll *(Not Including Freedmen)*		FIELD NO. 486

Dawes' Roll No.	NAME		Relationship to Person First Named	AGE	SEX	BLOOD	TRIBAL ENROLLMENT		
							Year	County	No.
13380	1 Jones, Samuel	44	First Named	41	M	3/4	1896	Gaines	6630
13381	2 " Rebecca	35	Wife	32	F	3/4	1896	"	6631
13382	3 " Robert	20	Son	17	M	3/4	1896	"	6632
13383	4 " Edmund	10	"	7	"	3/4	1896	"	6633
15852	5 " Missie		Dau	4	F	3/4			
15853	6 " Minnie		"	2	F	3/4			
	7								
	8								
	9 ENROLLMENT OF NOS. 1 2 3 & 4 HEREON APPROVED BY THE SECRETARY OF INTERIOR MAR 19 1903								
	10								
	11								
	12								
	13 ENROLLMENT OF NOS. ~~ 5 and 6 ~~ HEREON APPROVED BY THE SECRETARY OF INTERIOR JUN 12 1905								
	14								
	15								
	16								
	17								

TRIBAL ENROLLMENT OF PARENTS

	Name of Father	Year	County	Name of Mother	Year	County
1	Jimson Jones	Dead	Gaines	Sophia Jones	Dead	Gaines
2	Billy LeFlore	"	Tobucksy	Mary LeFlore	"	"
3	No1			No2		
4	No1			No2		
5	No1			No2		
6	No1			No2		
7						
8						
9						
10	No5 was born May 5, 1898					
11	No6 " " Jan. 31, 1901					
12	Application for enrollment of Nos 5 and 6 received March 4, 1905 under Act of Congress approved March 3, 1905					
13	For child of No3 see NB (March 3,1905) #1224					
14	" " " No2 " " " " " #1333			Date of Application for Enrollment.		
15				Nov 14/99		
16						
17						

68

Choctaw By Blood Enrollment Cards 1898-1914

RESIDENCE: Gaines   COUNTY. **Choctaw Nation**   **Choctaw Roll**   CARD NO.
POST OFFICE: Kiowa, I.T.   *(Not Including Freedmen)*   FIELD NO. 4869

Dawes' Roll No.	NAME	Relationship to Person	AGE	SEX	BLOOD	TRIBAL ENROLLMENT		
						Year	County	No.
13384	1 Logan, Clemiake ⁵⁹	First Named	56	F	Full	1896	Gaines	7823
	2							
	3							
	4							
	5							
	6							
	7							
	8							
	9							
	10							
	11							
	12							
	13							
	14							
	15							
	16							
	17							

ENROLLMENT
OF NOS. ~~1~~ HEREON
APPROVED BY THE SECRETARY
OF INTERIOR MAR 19 1903

TRIBAL ENROLLMENT OF PARENTS

Name of Father	Year	County	Name of Mother	Year	County
1 Flo-mo-tubbee	Dead	Gaines		Dead	Gaines
2					
3					
4					
5					
6					
7					
8					
9					
10					
11					
12					
13					
14					
15					
16					
17					

Date of Application for Enrollment.
Nov 14/99

Choctaw By Blood Enrollment Cards 1898-1914

RESIDENCE: Gaines COUNTY. **Choctaw Nation**   Choctaw Roll   CARD No.
POST OFFICE: Hartshorne, I.T.   *(Not Including Freedmen)*   FIELD No. **4870**

Dawes' Roll No.	NAME	Relationship to Person	AGE	SEX	BLOOD	TRIBAL ENROLLMENT Year	County	No.
13385	1 Murphy, Robinson 18	First Named	15	M	3/4	1896	Gains[sic]	8535
16052	2 " Trase[sic]	Dau	2	F	3/8			
	3							
	4							
	5							
	6							
	7							
	8							
	9							
	10							
	11							
	12							
	13							
	14							
	15							
	16							
	17							

ENROLLMENT OF NOS. ~~1~~ HEREON APPROVED BY THE SECRETARY OF INTERIOR Mar 19 1903

ENROLLMENT OF NOS. ~~2~~ HEREON APPROVED BY THE SECRETARY OF INTERIOR Aug 22 1906

No2 Granted July 10- 1906

TRIBAL ENROLLMENT OF PARENTS

	Name of Father	Year	County	Name of Mother	Year	County
1	David Murphy	Dead	Gaines	Caroline Murphy	Dead	Gaines
2	No.1			Celin Murphy	Chic Roll 5003	Choctaw
3						
4						
5						
6						
7						
8						
9						
10						
11						
12						
13						
14						
15						
16						
17						

Application was made for the enrollment of No.2 December 24, 1902
Mother of No.2 is said to be a Choctaw but has not been
identified upon the records of the Commission. No.2 placed
~~have on May 26, 1905. She is identified (as Sillin Willis) upon the~~
~~1893 Chickasaw pay roll (Ieshatubby Roll)~~
For child of No.1 see NB (March 3, 1905) #117

Date of Application for Enrollment.
For No.1 Nov 14/99

70

Choctaw By Blood Enrollment Cards 1898-1914

RESIDENCE: Gaines COUNTY.
POST OFFICE: Blanco I.T. June 9 '04 **Choctaw Nation** Choctaw Roll *(Not Including Freedmen)* CARD NO. FIELD NO. 4871

Dawes' Roll No.	NAME	Relationship to Person	AGE	SEX	BLOOD	TRIBAL ENROLLMENT		
						Year	County	No.
15594	1 McCoy, Simon 18	First Named	15	M	Full	1896	Gaines	9151
	2							
	3							
	4							
	5							
	6							
	7							
	8							
	9							
	10							
	11							
	12							
	13							
	14							
	15							
	16							
	17							

ENROLLMENT
OF NOS. 1 HEREON
APPROVED BY THE SECRETARY
OF INTERIOR SEP 22 1904

TRIBAL ENROLLMENT OF PARENTS

	Name of Father	Year	County	Name of Mother	Year	County
1	Charles McCoy	Dead		Sallie McCoy	Dead	
2						
3						
4						
5						
6						
7						
8						
9			No other information could be			
10			obtained			
11			See testimony of Nº 1 and Isom Pickens of June 9 1904			
12						
13						
14				Date of Application for Enrollment		
15				Nov 14/99		
16	P.O. Blanco, I.T.					
17	c/o Isom Pickens	12/24/02				

71

Choctaw By Blood Enrollment Cards 1898-1914

RESIDENCE: Gaines   COUNTY. **Choctaw Nation**   **Choctaw Roll**   CARD No.

POST OFFICE: Damon   *(Not Including Freedmen)*   FIELD No. 4872

Dawes' Roll No.	NAME	Relationship to Person	AGE	SEX	BLOOD	TRIBAL ENROLLMENT Year	County	No.
13386	1 Taylor, James 51	First Named	48	M	Full	1896	Gaines	11978
13387	2 " Susan 42	Wife	39	F	1/2	1896	"	11979
13388	3 Samuel DIED PRIOR TO SEPTEMBER 25, 1902	Son	14	M	3/4	1896	"	11980
13389	4 Anderson, Emeline 18	Dau	15	F	3/4	1896	"	11981
13390	5 Taylor, Lillie 10	"	7	"	3/4	1896	"	11983
13391	6 Salina DIED PRIOR TO SEPTEMBER 25, 1902	"	4	"	3/4	1896	"	11984
13392	7 " Frances 4	"	1	"	3/4			
	8							
	9							
	10	ENROLLMENT OF NOS. 1 2 3 4 5 6 & 7 HEREON						
	11	APPROVED BY THE SECRETARY OF INTERIOR MAR 19 1903						
	12							
	13							
	14	For child of No.4 see NB (Apr 26 06) Card #397						
	15	" " " " " " (Mar 3 '05) " #860						
	16							
	17							

TRIBAL ENROLLMENT OF PARENTS

	Name of Father	Year	County	Name of Mother	Year	County
1	Ea-ho-nubbee	Dead	Gaines	Pis-ta-hoke	Dead	Gaines
2	John Carr	"	"	Eliza Carr	"	"
3	No1			No2		
4	No1			No2		
5	No1			No2		
6	No1			No2		
7	No1			No2		
8						
9						
10	No.2 on 1896 roll as Lucy Taylor					
11	No.3 " 1896 " " Sam Taylor					
12	No.4 is now wife of Reason Anderson, Choctaw card #1865 evidence of marriage filed Dec 13, 1902.					
13	No.3 died July 31, 1899; No.6 died Oct 19, 1901; Enrollment cancelled by					
14	Department July 8, 1904			Date of Application for Enrollment		
15						Nov 14/99
16						
17	P.O. Tuskahoma, I.T. 4/11/05					

72

Choctaw By Blood Enrollment Cards 1898-1914

RESIDENCE: Gaines COUNTY.
POST OFFICE: Hartshorne, I.T.

Choctaw Nation

Choctaw Roll
(Not Including Freedmen)

CARD NO.
FIELD NO. 4873

Dawes' Roll No.	NAME	Relationship to Person First Named	AGE	SEX	BLOOD	TRIBAL ENROLLMENT Year	County	No.
13393	1 Bonaparte, Wyme 29		26	F	3/4	1896	Gaines	12944
13394	2 Williams Luena 14	Dau	11	"	3/4	1896	"	12945
13395	3 " Lizzie 12	"	9	"	3/4	1896	"	12946
13396	4 " Susan 6	"	3	"	3/4			
13397	5 Bonaparte, Oscar 2	Son	3mo	M	3/4			
	6							
	7							
	8							
	9							
	10							
	11	ENROLLMENT OF NOS. 1 2 3 4 & 5 HEREON						
	12	APPROVED BY THE SECRETARY						
	13	OF INTERIOR MAR 19 1903						
	14							
	15							
	16							
	17							

TRIBAL ENROLLMENT OF PARENTS

	Name of Father	Year	County	Name of Mother	Year	County
1	Adam Thompson	Dead	Chickasaw	Permelia Thompson	Dead	Gaines
2	Moses Williams	"	Gaines	No1		
3	" "	"	"	No1		
4	" "	"	"	No1		
5	Nabert Bonaparte			No.1		
6						
7						
8	No.1 is now wife of Nabert Bonaparte on Choc Card #4496					
9						
10						
11	No. 5 Born Sept 23, 1902; Enrolled Dec 23, 1902					
12						
13						#1 to 4
14						Date of Application for Enrollment.
15						Nov 14/99
16						
17						

Choctaw By Blood Enrollment Cards 1898-1914

RESIDENCE: Gaines   COUNTY. **Choctaw Nation**   **Choctaw Roll** (Not Including Freedmen)   CARD No.
POST OFFICE: Kiowa, I.T.   FIELD No. 4874

	NAME		Relationship to Person	AGE	SEX	BLOOD	TRIBAL ENROLLMENT		
							Year	County	No.
1	Wilkins, Sallie	41	First Named	38	F	Full	1896	Gaines	12956
2	" John	14	Son	11	M	"	1896	"	12957
3									
4									
5									
6									
7									
8									
9	ENROLLMENT								
10	OF NOS. 1 & 2 HEREON APPROVED BY THE SECRETARY								
11	OF INTERIOR MAR 19 1903								
12									
13									
14									
15									
16									
17									

TRIBAL ENROLLMENT OF PARENTS

	Name of Father	Year	County	Name of Mother	Year	County
1		Dead	Gaines	Aba-lun-na	Dead	Gaines
2	Solomon Wilkins	"	"	No1		
3						
4						
5						
6						
7						
8		No1 on 1896 roll as Sallie Wilkin				
9		No2 " 1896 " " John "				
10						
11						
12						
13				Date of Application fzor Enrollment.		
14						
15				Nov 14/99		
16						
17						

Choctaw By Blood Enrollment Cards 1898-1914

RESIDENCE: Gaines   COUNTY. **Choctaw Nation**   **Choctaw Roll** CARD NO.
POST OFFICE: Kiowa, I.T.   *(Not Including Freedmen)*   FIELD NO. 4875

Dawes' Roll No.	NAME	Relationship to Person	AGE	SEX	BLOOD	TRIBAL ENROLLMENT		
						Year	County	No.
14948	1 Worcestor, Alfred 25	First Named	27	M	3/4	1896	Gaines	12958
	2							
	3							
	4							
	5							
	6							
	7							
	8	ENROLLMENT						
	9	OF NOS. ~~~ 1 ~~~ HEREON APPROVED BY THE SECRETARY						
	10	OF INTERIOR OCT 15 1903						
	11							
	12							
	13							
	14							
	15							
	16							
	17							

TRIBAL ENROLLMENT OF PARENTS

	Name of Father	Year	County	Name of Mother	Year	County
1	Abel Worcester[sic]	Dead	Gaines	Eliz. Worcester	Dead	Gaines
2						
3						
4						
5						
6						
7	See testimony of June 3, 1903					
8	For child of No1 see Chickasaw NB (March 3 1905) #108					
9						
10						
11						
12						
13						
14						
15				Date of Application for Enrollment.	Nov 14/99	
16						
17	P.O. Blanco I.T.					

75

Choctaw By Blood Enrollment Cards 1898-1914

RESIDENCE: Cedar COUNTY. **Choctaw Nation** **Choctaw Roll** CARD NO.
POST OFFICE: Tushkahomma[sic], I.T. *(Not Including Freedmen)* FIELD NO. 4876

Dawes' Roll No.	NAME		Relationship to Person	AGE	SEX	BLOOD	TRIBAL ENROLLMENT		
							Year	County	No.
13401	1 Ben, James	25	First Named	22	M	Full	1896	Cedar	1062
	2								
	3								
	4								
	5								
	6								
	7								
	8								
	9								
	10								
	11								
	12								
	13								
	14								
	15								
	16								
	17								

ENROLLMENT
OF NOS. 1 HEREON
APPROVED BY THE SECRETARY
OF INTERIOR MAR 19 1903

TRIBAL ENROLLMENT OF PARENTS

	Name of Father	Year	County	Name of Mother	Year	County
1	German Ben	Dead	Cedar	Lucy Ben		Cedar
2						
3						
4						
5						
6						
7						
8	No.1 is now husband of Narcissa Bohanan on Choctaw Card #1949					
9	For child of No.1 see NB (March 3,1905) #1258					
10						
11						
12						
13						
14						
15				Date of Application for Enrollment.	Nov 15/99	
16						
17						

Choctaw By Blood Enrollment Cards 1898-1914

RESIDENCE: Cedar COUNTY. **Choctaw Nation**   **Choctaw Roll** CARD No.
POST OFFICE: Tushkahomma[sic], I.T.   *(Not Including Freedmen)*   FIELD No. 4877

Dawes' Roll No.	NAME	Relationship to Person First Named	AGE	SEX	BLOOD	TRIBAL ENROLLMENT		
						Year	County	No.
DP	1 Betsy 70	First Named	67	F	Full	1896	Cedar	1069
	2							
	3							
	4							
	5							
	6							
	7							
	8							
	9							
	10							
	11							
	12							
	13							
	14							
	15							
	16							
	17							

DISMISSED
JAN 30 1907

TRIBAL ENROLLMENT OF PARENTS

	Name of Father	Year	County	Name of Mother	Year	County
1		Dead	Choctaw		Dead	Choctaw
2						
3						
4						
5						
6						
7						
8						
9						
10						
11						
12						
13					Date of Application for Enrollment.	
14						
15					Nov 15/99	
16						
17						

Choctaw By Blood Enrollment Cards 1898-1914

RESIDENCE: Cedar COUNTY. **Choctaw Nation** **Choctaw Roll** CARD NO.
POST OFFICE: Thushkahomma[sic], I.T. *(Not Including Freedmen)* FIELD NO. **4878**

Dawes' Roll No.	NAME		Relationship to Person	AGE	SEX	BLOOD	TRIBAL ENROLLMENT		
							Year	County	No.
13403	₁ Cooper, Thomas	33	First Named	30	M	Full	1896	Cedar	2450
13404	₂ " Emily	27	Wife	24	F	"	1896	"	3707
	₃								
	₄								
	₅								
	₆								
	₇								
	₈	ENROLLMENT							
	₉	OF NOS. 1 & 2 HEREON							
	₁₀	APPROVED BY THE SECRETARY OF INTERIOR Mar 10 1903							
	₁₁								
	₁₂								
	₁₃								
	₁₄								
	₁₅								
	₁₆								
	₁₇								

TRIBAL ENROLLMENT OF PARENTS

	Name of Father	Year	County	Name of Mother	Year	County
₁	Gilbert Cooper	Dead	Cedar			Cedar
₂		"	"			"
₃						
₄						
₅						
₆						
₇	No.2 on 1896 roll as Emily					
₈						
₉	3/18/19 Nos 1&2 are duplicates of of[sic] Nos. 1&2 on Choctaw Card No. 1936					
₁₀						
₁₁						
₁₂						
₁₃					Date of Application for Enrollment.	
₁₄						
₁₅					Nov 15/99	
₁₆						
₁₇						

78

Choctaw By Blood Enrollment Cards 1898-1914

RESIDENCE: Cedar COUNTY. **Choctaw Nation** Choctaw Roll CARD NO.
POST OFFICE: Doaksville, I.T. *(Not Including Freedmen)* FIELD NO. 4879

Dawes' Roll No.	NAME	Relationship to Person First Named	AGE	SEX	BLOOD	TRIBAL ENROLLMENT Year	County	No.
13405	1 Elapashabbe, Barnett 18	First Named	15	M	Full	1896	Cedar	3720
	2							
	3							
	4							
	5							
	6							
	7							
	8							
	9							
	10							
	11							
	12							
	13							
	14							
	15							
	16							
	17							

ENROLLMENT
OF NOS. 1 HEREON
APPROVED BY THE SECRETARY
OF INTERIOR MAR 19 1903

TRIBAL ENROLLMENT OF PARENTS

	Name of Father	Year	County	Name of Mother	Year	County
1	Elapashabbe	Dead	Cedar		Dead	Cedar
2						
3						
4						
5						
6	On 1896 roll as Burnett Elaposhabbe					
7	For child of No.1 see NB (March 3 1905) #1400					
8						
9						
10						
11						
12						
13						
14				Date of Application for Enrollment.		
15				Date of Application for Enrollment. Nov 15/99		
16						
17	P.O. Corinne IT 4/4/05					

79

Choctaw By Blood Enrollment Cards 1898-1914

RESIDENCE: Gaines   COUNTY. **Choctaw Nation**   **Choctaw Roll**   CA▓▓▓
POST OFFICE: Wilburton, I.T.   *(Not Including Freedmen)*   FIELD NO. 4880

Dawes' Roll No.	NAME		Relationship to Person First Named	AGE	SEX	BLOOD	TRIBAL ENROLLMENT		
							Year	County	No.
▓▓▓	1 Wade, Simeon	47	Named	44	M	Full	1896	Gaines	12961
	2 " Anne	43	Wife	40	F	"	1896	"	12962
14909	3 " Esiah	16	Son	13	M	"	1896	"	12963
14910	4 " Rhoda	12	Dau	9	F	"	1896	"	12964
	5								
	6								
	9								
	10								
	11								
	12								
	13								
	14								
	15								
	16								
	17								

ENROLLMENT
OF NOS. 1, 2, 3, and 4   HEREON
APPROVED BY THE SECRETARY
OF INTERIOR   MAY 21 1903

TRIBAL ENROLLMENT OF PARENTS

	Name of Father	Year	County	Name of Mother	Year	County
1	Hoparkentubbee	Dead	Gaines		Dead	Gaines
2		"	"		"	"
3	No 1			No 2		
4	No 1			No 2		
5						
6						
7						
8						
9						
10						
11						
12						
13						
14						Date of Application for Enrollment.
15						Nov 14/99
16						
17						

Choctaw By Blood Enrollment Cards 1898-1914

RESIDENCE: Tobucksy   COUNTY.   **Choctaw Nation**   **Choctaw Roll** *(Not Including Freedmen)*   CARD NO.
POST OFFICE: Kiowa, I.T.   FIELD NO. 4881

Dawes' Roll No.	NAME	Relationship to Person First Named	AGE	SEX	BLOOD	TRIBAL ENROLLMENT		
						Year	County	No.
13410 3410	1 McCann, Bicy		57	F	Full	1896	Tobucksy	9220
	2							
	3							
	4							
	5							
	6							
	7							
	8							
	9							
	10							
	11							
	12							
	13							
	14							
	15							
	16							
	17							

ENROLLMENT OF NOS. 1 HEREON APPROVED BY THE SECRETARY OF INTERIOR MAR 19 1903

TRIBAL ENROLLMENT OF PARENTS

	Name of Father	Year	County	Name of Mother	Year	County
1	Ea-lo-ma	Dead	Tobucksy		Dead	Tobucksy
2						
3						
4						
5						
6			On 1896 roll as Basie McCann			
7					2, 1906	
8						
9						
10						
11						
12						
13						
14				Date of Application for Enrollment.		
15				Nov 14/99		
16						
17						

Choctaw By Blood Enrollment Cards 1898-1914

RESIDENCE: Tobucksy	COUNTY.	Choctaw Nation	Choctaw Roll (Not Including Freedmen)	CARD NO.
POST OFFICE: Kiowa, I.T.				FIELD NO. 4882

Dawes' Roll No.	NAME	Relationship to Person First Named	AGE	SEX	BLOOD	TRIBAL ENROLLMENT		
						Year	County	No.
13411	1 Wilkins, Micey[sic] 25	First Named	22	F	Full	1896	Tobucksy	13016
13412	2 " Henry 5	Son	2	M	"			
	3							
	4							
	5							
	6							
	7							
	8							
	9							
	10							
	11							
	12	ENROLLMENT						
	13	OF NOS. 1 & 2 HEREON APPROVED BY THE SECRETARY						
	14	OF INTERIOR MAR 19 1903						
	15							
	16							
	17							

TRIBAL ENROLLMENT OF PARENTS

Name of Father	Year	County	Name of Mother	Year	County
1 War-ka-che	Dead	Sans Bois	Sophie Warkeche[sic]		Sans Bois
2 Jefferson Wilkins	"	Tobucksy	No1		
3					
4					
5					
6					
7					
8	Nº1 is now wife of William P Anderson, Choc Card #3281				
9					
10					
11					
12					
13					
14					
15			Date of Application for Enrollment.	Nov 14/99	
16					
17					

Choctaw By Blood Enrollment Cards 1898-1914

RESIDENCE: Jacks Fork   COUNTY. **Choctaw Nation**   **Choctaw Roll** CARD NO.
POST OFFICE: Antlers, I.T.   *(Not Including Freedmen)*   FIELD NO. **4883**

Dawes' Roll No.	NAME	Relationship to Person First Named	AGE	SEX	BLOOD	TRIBAL ENROLLMENT		
						Year	County	No.
13413	1 Billy, Eliza	DIED PRIOR TO SEPTEMBER 25 1902	15	F	Full	1896	Jacks Fork	1944
	2							
	3							
	4							
	5							
	6							
	7							
	8							
	9							
	10	ENROLLMENT OF NOS. 1 HEREON APPROVED BY THE SECRETARY OF INTERIOR MAR 19 1903						
	11							
	12							
	13							
	14							
	15							
	16							
	17							

TRIBAL ENROLLMENT OF PARENTS

	Name of Father	Year	County	Name of Mother	Year	County
1	Peter Billy	Dead	Jacks Fork			Jacks Fork
2						
3						
4						
5						
6						
7						
8						
9						
10						
11						
12						
13						
14						Date of Application for Enrollment.
15						Nov 15/99
16						
17						

Choctaw By Blood Enrollment Cards 1898-1914

RESIDENCE: Jacks Fork   COUNTY. **Choctaw Nation**   **Choctaw Roll**   CARD NO.
POST OFFICE: Antlers, I.T.   *(Not Including Freedmen)*   FIELD NO. 4884

Dawes' Roll No.	NAME	Relationship to Person	AGE	SEX	BLOOD	TRIBAL ENROLLMENT		
						Year	County	No.
13414	1 Jefferson, Elsie 22	First Named	19	F	Full	1896	Jacks Fork	7359
	2							
	3							
	4							
	5							
	6							
	7							
	8							
	9							
	10							
	11							
	12	ENROLLMENT OF NOS. 1 HEREON						
	13	APPROVED BY THE SECRETARY						
	14	OF INTERIOR MAR 19 1903						
	15							
	16							
	17							

TRIBAL ENROLLMENT OF PARENTS

	Name of Father	Year	County	Name of Mother	Year	County
1	Gilbert Jefferson		Cedar			Jacks Fork
2						
3						
4						
5						
6						
7						
8						
9						
10						
11						
12						
13	No. 1 is duplicate of Elsie James, Choctaw card #1801 approved				Date of Application for Enrollment.	
14	roll #5111. Enrollment cancelled under Departmental					
15	instructions of November 10, 1905 (I.T.D. 12170-1905) D.C. 51587				Nov 15/99	
16						
17						

84

Choctaw By Blood Enrollment Cards 1898-1914

RESIDENCE: Jacks Fork	Choctaw Nation
POST OFFICE: Antlers, I.T.	

Choctaw Roll (Not Including Freedmen)

CARD NO.
FIELD NO. 4885

Dawes' Roll No.	NAME	Relationship to Person First Named	AGE	SEX	BLOOD	TRIBAL ENROLLMENT		
						Year	County	No.
1	Matona ⁷⁸		75	F	Full	1896	Jacks Fork	8896
2								
3								
4								
5								
6								
7								
8								
9								
10								
11								
12								
13								
14								
15								
16								
17								

TRIBAL ENROLLMENT OF PARENTS

	Name of Father	Year	County	Name of Mother	Year	County
1		Dead	Choctaw		Dead	Choctaw
2						
3						
4						
5						
6						
7			On 1896 roll as Matena			
8						
9						
10						
11						
12						
13					Date of Application for Enrollment.	
14						
15					Nov 15/99	
16						
17						

CANCELLED

Duplicate of Montena Tom, No. 1726, Choctaw roll card No. 1726.

APR 27 1905

Choctaw By Blood Enrollment Cards 1898-1914

RESIDENCE:	Jacks Fork	COUNTY.							CARD NO.	
POST OFFICE:	Antlers, I.T.	**Choctaw Nation**				Choctaw Roll *(Not Including Freedmen)*			FIELD NO. 4886	

Dawes' Roll No.	NAME		Relationship to Person	AGE	SEX	BLOOD	TRIBAL ENROLLMENT		
							Year	County	No.
13416	1 Patterson, John	26	First Named	23	M	Full	1896	Jacks Fork	10598
	2								
	3								
	4								
	5								
	6								
	7								
	8	ENROLLMENT							
	9	OF NOS. ~1~ HEREON APPROVED BY THE SECRETARY							
	10	OF INTERIOR MAR 19 1903							
	11								
	12								
	13								
	14								
	15								
	16								
	17								

TRIBAL ENROLLMENT OF PARENTS

	Name of Father	Year	County	Name of Mother	Year	County
1	Simon Patterson	Dead	Jacks Fork		Dead	Jacks Fork
2						
3						
4						
5						
6						
7	On 1896 roll as John Petterson					
8						
9	In penitentiary at Detroit, Mich					
10						
11						
12						
13						
14					Date of Application for Enrollment.	
15					Nov 15/99	
16						
17						

RESIDENCE: Cherokee Nation COUNTY. **Choctaw Nation** Choctaw Roll CARD NO.
POST OFFICE: (Not Including Freedmen) FIELD NO. **4887**

Dawes' Roll No.	NAME	Relationship to Person	AGE	SEX	BLOOD	TRIBAL ENROLLMENT		
						Year	County	No.
13417	1 Folsom, Levi F ⁴⁸	First Named	45	M	1/2	1896	Tobucksy	4066
	2							
	3							
	4							
	5							
	6							
	7							
	8							
	9							
	10							
	11							
	12							
	13							
	14							
	15							
	16							
	17							

ENROLLMENT
OF NOS. ~~~~~ 1 ~~~~~ HEREON
APPROVED BY THE SECRETARY
OF INTERIOR MAR 19 1903

TRIBAL ENROLLMENT OF PARENTS

	Name of Father	Year	County	Name of Mother	Year	County
1	Ward Folsom	Dead	Skullyville	Eliza Folsom	Dead	Skullyville
2						
3						
4						
5						
6						
7	On 1896 troll as Levi F Fulsom					
8						
9	Residence, Going Snake Dist.,					
10	Cherokee Nation					
11						
12						
13						
14						
15					Nov 15/99	
16					Date of Application for Enrollment.	
17						

Choctaw By Blood Enrollment Cards 1898-1914

RESIDENCE:	Gaines	COUNTY.							
POST OFFICE:	Hartshorne, I.T.	**Choctaw Nation**				Choctaw Roll (Not Including Freedmen)		CARD NO. FIELD NO. 4888	

Dawes' Roll No.	NAME		Relationship to Person	AGE	SEX	BLOOD	TRIBAL ENROLLMENT		
							Year	County	No.
13418	1 Garvin, Lewis	20	First Named	17	M	Full	1896	Tobucksy	4706
	2								
	3								
	4								
	5								
	6								
	7								
	8								
	9								
	10	ENROLLMENT							
	11	OF NOS. 1 HEREON APPROVED BY THE SECRETARY							
	12	OF INTERIOR MAR 19 1903							
	13								
	14								
	15								
	16								
	17								

TRIBAL ENROLLMENT OF PARENTS

	Name of Father	Year	County	Name of Mother	Year	County
1	Lewis Garvin	Dead	Tobucksy	Rhoda Bond		Tobucksy
2						
3						
4						
5						
6						
7						
8						
9						
10						
11						
12						
13						
14					Date of Application for Enrollment.	
15					Nov 15/99	
16						
17						

Died prior to September 25, 1902 not entitled to land or money
(See Indian Office letter Nov. 2, 1910)

Choctaw By Blood Enrollment Cards 1898-1914

POST OFFICE: McAlester, I.T.　　　**ctaw Nation**　Choctaw Roll (Not Including Freedmen)　FIELD NO. 4889

Dawes' Roll No.	NAME	Relationship to Person First Named	AGE	SEX	BLOOD	TRIBAL ENROLLMENT		
						Year	County	No.
13419	1 LeFlore, Lucy ⁴⁷	First Named	44	F	1/2	1896	Tobucksy	7853
13420	2 " Alexander ¹⁵	Son	12	M	1/4	1896	"	7854
13421	3 " Watson ¹²	"	9	"	1/4	1896	"	7855
13422	4 " Cornelius ¹⁰	Son	7	M	1/4	1896	"	7856
	5							
	6							
	7							
	8							
	9							
	10							
	11							
	12							
	13							
	14							
	15							
	16							
	17							

ENROLLMENT
OF NOS. 1 2 3 & 4 HEREON
APPROVED BY THE SECRETARY
OF INTERIOR MAR 19 1903

TRIBAL ENROLLMENT OF PARENTS

	Name of Father	Year	County	Name of Mother	Year	
1		Dead	Choctaw	Lucy LeFlore		Tobucksy
2	Austin LeFlore		Freedman	No 1		
3	" "		"	No 1		
4	" "		"	No 1		
5						
6						
7	Husband of N⁰1 and father of children on this card is					
8	Austin Leflore on Choctaw Freedman Card #1158.					
9	No4 Name "Cornelius" Sex "Male" Change made under Departmental					
10	instructions of October 21, 1904 (ITD #10732-1904 DC #41067-1904)					
11						
12						
13					Date of Application for Enrollment.	
14						
15					Nov 15/99	
16						
17						

Choctaw By Blood Enrollment Cards 1898-1914

RESIDENCE: Chickasaw Nation ~~COUNTY.~~ **Choctaw Nation**   Choctaw Roll   CARD NO.
POST OFFICE: Fitzhugh, I.T.   (Not Including Freedmen)   FIELD NO. 4890

Dawes' Roll No.	NAME	Relationship to Person First Named	AGE	SEX	BLOOD	TRIBAL ENROLLMENT Year	County	No.
13423	1 Nail, Sophronia	12	9	F	Full	1896	Tobucksy	7604
	2							
	3							
	4							
	5							
	6							
	7							
	8							
	9							
	10							
	11							
	12							
	13							
	14							
	15							
	16							
	17							

ENROLLMENT
OF NOS. 1 HEREON
APPROVED BY THE SECRETARY
OF INTERIOR MAR 19 1903

TRIBAL ENROLLMENT OF PARENTS

	Name of Father	Year	County	Name of Mother	Year	County
1	Joe Nail	Dead	Tobucksy	Vicey Steward		Tobucksy
2						
3						
4						
5						
6						
7						
8						
9						
10	On 1896 roll as Sophrony Nail					
11						
12	Nº 1 is duplicate of Sophronia E Nail, Choctaw card Nº 467					
13	approved roll of Choctaw by blood Nº 889					
	Enrollment of Nº 1 cancelled by Secretary of Interior September 2, 1904					
14	see Departmental letter of that date. (I.T.D. 6948-1904; DC 32928-1904					
15				Date of Application for Enrollment.	Nov 15/99	
16						
17						

Choctaw By Blood Enrollment Cards 1898-1914

RESIDENCE: Atoka COUNTY.
POST OFFICE: Boggy Depot, IT
Choctaw Nation
Choctaw Roll
(Not Including Freedmen)
CARD NO.
FIELD NO. 4891

Dawes' Roll No.	NAME	Relationship to Person	AGE	SEX	BLOOD	TRIBAL ENROLLMENT		
						Year	County	No.
13424	1 Byington Melina ⁵¹	First Named	48	F	Full	1896	Atoka	1798
13425	2 " , Benjamin ²²	Son	19	M	"	1896	"	1799
	3							
	4							
	5							
	6							
	7							
	8							
	9							
	10							
	11							
	12							
	13							
	14							
	15							
	16							
	17							

ENROLLMENT
OF NOS. 1 & 2 HEREON
APPROVED BY THE SECRETARY
OF INTERIOR MAR 19 1903

TRIBAL ENROLLMENT OF PARENTS

	Name of Father	Year	County	Name of Mother	Year	County
1		Dead	Choctaw		Dead	Choctaw
2	Thompson Byington	"	Atoka	No1		
3						
4						
5						
6						
7	No1 on 1896 roll as Bolinda Byington					
8	No2 " 1896 " " Benjamin "					
9						
10	N°2 is now the husband of Elizabeth Foster on Choctaw card #3823 Sept 1, 1902					
11	For child of No.2 see Chickasaw NB (March 3, 1905) 4549					
12						
13						
14						
15				Date of Application for Enrollment.	Nov 15/99	
16						
17						

Choctaw By Blood Enrollment Cards 1898-1914

RESIDENCE: Wade COUNTY.
POST OFFICE: Tushkahomma[sic], I.T. **Choctaw Nation** **Choctaw Roll** *(Not Including Freedmen)* CARD NO.
FIELD NO. 4892

Dawes' Roll No.	NAME	Relationship to Person First Named	AGE	SEX	BLOOD	TRIBAL ENROLLMENT		
						Year	County	No.
DP	1 Frazier, Lizzie ²⁴		21	F	Full	1896	Cedar	4120
	2							
	3							
	4							
	5							
	6							
	7							
	8							
	9							
	10							
	11							
	12							
	13							
	14							
	15							
	16							
	17							

DISMISSED
JAN 30 1907

TRIBAL ENROLLMENT OF PARENTS

	Name of Father	Year	County	Name of Mother	Year	County
1		Dead	Cedar		Dead	Cedar
2						
3						
4						
5						
6						
7						
8						
9						
10						
11						
12						
13						
14						
15				Date of Application for Enrollment.	Nov 15/99	
16						
17						

Choctaw By Blood Enrollment Cards 1898-1914

RESIDENCE: Cedar   COUNTY. **Choctaw Nation**   **Choctaw Roll**   CARD NO.
POST OFFICE: Doaksville, I.T.   *(Not Including Freedmen)*   FIELD NO. 4893

Dawes' Roll No.	NAME	Relationship to Person	AGE	SEX	BLOOD	TRIBAL ENROLLMENT		
						Year	County	No.
13427	1 Henderson, Lena 20	First Named	17	F	Full	1896	Cedar	5414
	2							
	3							
	4							
	5							
	6							
	7							
	8							
	9	ENROLLMENT OF NOS. 1 HEREON						
	10	APPROVED BY THE SECRETARY OF INTERIOR MAR 19 1903						
	11							
	12							
	13							
	14							
	15							
	16							
	17							

TRIBAL ENROLLMENT OF PARENTS

	Name of Father	Year	County	Name of Mother	Year	County
1	Arcabus Henderson	Dead	Cedar		Dead	Cedar
2						
3						
4						
5						
6						
7	On 1896 roll as Leney Henderson					
8						
9						
10						
11						
12						
13						
14				Date of Application for Enrollment.	Nov 15/99	
15						
16						
17						

93

Choctaw By Blood Enrollment Cards 1898-1914

RESIDENCE: **Nashoba** COUNTY. **Choctaw Nation** **Choctaw Roll** CARD NO.
POST OFFICE: **Alikchi, I.T.** *(Not Including Freedmen)* FIELD NO. **4894**

Dawes' Roll No.	NAME	Relationship to Person First Named	AGE	SEX	BLOOD	TRIBAL ENROLLMENT		
						Year	County	No.
DP	₁ Harrison, Willy 30	Named	27	M	Full	1896	Cedar	5458
	₂ " Margaret 31	Wife	28	F	"	1896	"	5459
	3							
	4							
	5	DISMISSED						
	6	JAN 30 1907						
	7							
	8							
	9							
	10							
	11							
	12							
	13							
	14							
	15							
	16							
	17							

TRIBAL ENROLLMENT OF PARENTS

	Name of Father	Year	County	Name of Mother	Year	County
1		Dead	Nashoba		Dead	Nashoba
2			Choctaw			Choctaw
3						
4						
5						
6						
7						
8						
9						
10						
11						
12						
13						
14						
15				Date of Application for Enrollment.	Nov 15/99	
16						
17						

Choctaw By Blood Enrollment Cards 1898-1914

RESIDENCE: Cedar COUNTY. **Choctaw Nation** **Choctaw Roll** CARD NO.
POST OFFICE: Doaksville, I.T. *(Not Including Freedmen)* FIELD NO. 4895

Dawes' Roll No.	NAME	Relationship to Person First Named	AGE	SEX	BLOOD	TRIBAL ENROLLMENT		
						Year	County	No.
DP 1	Incy	7	4	F	Full	1896	Cedar	6259
2								
3								
4								
5								
6								
7								
8								
9								
10								
11								
12								
13								
14								
15								
16								
17								

DISMISSED JAN 30 1907

TRIBAL ENROLLMENT OF PARENTS

	Name of Father	Year	County	Name of Mother	Year	County
1		Dead	Choctaw		Dead	Choctaw
2						
3						
4						
5						
6						
7						
8						
9						
10						
11						
12						
13						
14						
15				Date of Application for Enrollment.	Nov 15/99	
16						
17						

95

Choctaw By Blood Enrollment Cards 1898-1914

RESIDENCE: Cedar COUNTY. **Choctaw Nation** **Choctaw Roll** CARD No.
POST OFFICE: Kosoma[sic], I.T. *(Not Including Freedmen)* FIELD No. **4896**

Dawes' Roll No.	NAME	Relationship to Person	AGE	SEX	BLOOD	TRIBAL ENROLLMENT		
						Year	County	No.
15500	1 Locke, Nellie ⁷	First Named	4	F	1/2	1896	Cedar	7916
	2							
	3							
	4							
	5							
	6							
	7							
	8							
	9	ENROLLMENT						
	10	OF NOS. ~~~~ 1 ~~~~ HEREON APPROVED BY THE SECRETARY						
	11	OF INTERIOR May 9 1904						
	12							
	13							
	14							
	15							
	16							
	17							

TRIBAL ENROLLMENT OF PARENTS

	Name of Father	Year	County	Name of Mother	Year	County
1	Henry Holland		white man	Eliza Ann McKinney		Choctaw
2						
3						
4						
5	No.1 lives with Elisha Locke					
6	See statement of Stowick Emer filed April 7, 1904					
7						
8						
9						
10						
11						
12						
13						
14						
15				Date of Application for Enrollment. Nov 15/99		
16						
17						

96

Choctaw By Blood Enrollment Cards 1898-1914

RESIDENCE: Cedar COUNTY.
POST OFFICE: Doaksville I.T.

Choctaw Nation

Choctaw Roll
(Not Including Freedmen)

CARD NO.
FIELD NO. 4897

Dawes' Roll No.	NAME		Relationship to Person	AGE	SEX	BLOOD	TRIBAL ENROLLMENT		
							Year	County	No.
13432	₁ Mullin, Celie	16	First Named	13	F	Full	1896	Cedar	8597
	2								
	3								
	4								
	5								
	6								
	7								
	8								
	9								
	10								
	11								
	12								
	13								
	14								
	15								
	16								
	17								

ENROLLMENT
OF NOS. 1
APPROVED BY THE SECRETARY HEREON
OF INTERIOR MAR 9 1903

TRIBAL ENROLLMENT OF PARENTS

	Name of Father	Year	County	Name of Mother	Year	County
1	Jas Mullin	Dead	Cedar		Dead	Cedar
2						
3						
4						
5						
6						
7						
8						
9						
10						
11						
12						
13						
14				Date of Application for Enrollment.		
15				Nov 15/99		
16						
17						

Choctaw By Blood Enrollment Cards 1898-1914

RESIDENCE: Cedar COUNTY.
POST OFFICE: Doaksville, I.T.

Choctaw Nation

Choctaw Roll
(Not Including Freedmen)

CARD No.
FIELD No. 4898

Dawes' Roll No.	NAME	Relationship to Person First Named	AGE	SEX	BLOOD	TRIBAL ENROLLMENT		
						Year	County	No.
1	Rose, Levi 31		28	M	Full	1896	Cedar	10779
2	" Lydie 40	Wife	37	F	"	1896	"	10780
3								
4								
5								
6								
7								
8								
9								
10								
11								
12								
13								
14								
15								
16								
17								

DISMISSED
JAN 30 1907

TRIBAL ENROLLMENT OF PARENTS

	Name of Father	Year	County	Name of Mother	Year	County
1	Wallen Rose	Dead	Cedar		Dead	Cedar
2		"	"		"	"
3						
4						
5						
6						
7						
8						
9						
10						
11						
12						
13						
14						
15						
16						
17						

Date of Application for Enrollment.

Nov 15/99

Choctaw By Blood Enrollment Cards 1898-1914

RESIDENCE: Cedar COUNTY.
POST OFFICE: Doaksville, I.T.

Choctaw Nation

Choctaw Roll
(Not Including Freedmen)

CARD NO.
FIELD NO. 4899

Dawes' Roll No.	NAME	Relationship to Person First Named	AGE	SEX	BLOOD	TRIBAL ENROLLMENT		
						Year	County	No.
1	Tims, Phoebe ⁵³		50	F	Full	1896	Cedar	12093
2								
3								
4								
5								
6								
7								
8								
9								
10								
11								
12								
13								
14								
15								
16								
17								

DISMISSED

JAN 30 1907

TRIBAL ENROLLMENT OF PARENTS

	Name of Father	Year	County	Name of Mother	Year	County
1		Dead	Cedar		Dead	Cedar
2						
3						
4						
5						
6						
7	On 1896 roll as Phoebe Tim[sic]					
8						
9						
10						
11						
12						
13						
14						Date of Application for Enrollment.
15						Nov 15/99
16						
17						

Choctaw By Blood Enrollment Cards 1898-1914

RESIDENCE:	COUNTY.	Choctaw Nation	Choctaw Roll (Not Including Freedmen)	CARD NO.
POST OFFICE:				FIELD NO. 4900

Dawes' Roll No.	NAME	Relationship to Person First Named	AGE	SEX	BLOOD	TRIBAL ENROLLMENT Year	County	No.
DP	1 Wesley, Selina 43		40	F	Full	1896	Cedar	13143
	2							
	3							
	4	DISMISSED						
	5	JAN 30 1907						
	6							
	7							
	8							
	9							
	10							
	11							
	12							
	13							
	14							
	15							
	16							
	17							

TRIBAL ENROLLMENT OF PARENTS

	Name of Father	Year	County	Name of Mother	Year	County
1		Dead	Choctaw		Dead	Choctaw
2						
3						
4						
5						
6						
7		No other information could be				
8		obtained				
9						
10						
11						
12						
13					Date of Application for Enrollment.	
14						
15					Nov 15/99	
16						
17						

100

Choctaw By Blood Enrollment Cards 1898-1914

RESIDENCE Cedar COUNTY. **Choctaw Nation** **Choctaw Roll** CARD NO.
POST OFFICE Doaksville, I.T. *(Not Including Freedmen)* FIELD NO. 4901

Dawes' Roll No.	NAME		Relationship to Person	AGE	SEX	BLOOD	TRIBAL ENROLLMENT		
							Year	County	No.
13437	1 Charley, Mary	22	First Named	19	F	Full	1896	Towson	6796
13438	2 " Michal[sic]	1	Son	9mo	M	"			
15795	3 " David	21	Husb	21	M	"	1893	Cedar	253
	4								
	5								
	6								
	7								
	8								
	9	ENROLLMENT OF NOS. 1 & 2 HEREON APPROVED BY THE SECRETARY OF INTERIOR MAR 19 1903							
	10								
	11								
	12								
	13	ENROLLMENT OF NOS. 3 HEREON APPROVED BY THE SECRETARY OF INTERIOR MAR 15 1905							
	14								
	15								
	16								
	17								

TRIBAL ENROLLMENT OF PARENTS

	Name of Father	Year	County	Name of Mother	Year	County
1	Thos. Jefferson	Dead	Towson	Suffey Jefferson	Dead	Towson
2	David Charley		Choctaw	Nº1		
3	Silas Brown	Dead	"	Silwe	Dead	Cedar
4						
5						
6						
7						
8						
9						
10	On 1896 roll as Mary Jefferson					
11						
12	Husband on Card D-525					
13	Nº2 Born Aug. 10, 1901; Enrolled May 20 1902					
13	Evidence of marriage of parents of Nº2 filed May 20, 1902					
14	Nº3 on 1893 pay roll as David Brown, orphan			#1		
15	As to residence see testimony of Robert S Frazier			Date of Application for Enrollment.		
16	Nº3 transferred from Choctaw card #D 525 Dec 19, 1904			Nov 16 '99		
17	For child of Nos 1&3 see NB (March 3,1905) #1473					

Choctaw By Blood Enrollment Cards 1898-1914

RESIDENCE:	COUNTY.						CARD NO.
POST OFFICE:	**Choctaw Nation**			**Choctaw Roll** *(Not Including Freedmen)*		FIELD NO.	4902

Dawes' Roll No.	NAME	Relationship to Person First Named	AGE	SEX	BLOOD	TRIBAL ENROLLMENT		
						Year	County	No.
DP✓	1 Davis, Matthew 54		51	M	Full	1896	Bok Tuklo	3400
	2							
	3							
	4	DISMISSED						
	5	JAN 30 1907						
	6							
	7							
	8							
	9							
	10							
	11							
	12							
	13							
	14							
	15							
	16							
	17							

TRIBAL ENROLLMENT OF PARENTS

	Name of Father	Year	County	Name of Mother	Year	County
1						
2						
3						
4						
5	No other information could be obtained					
6						
7						
8						
9						
10						
11						
12						
13						
14					Date of Application for Enrollment.	
15						
16					Nov 15/99	
17						

RESIDENCE:		COUNTY.		Choctaw Roll	CARD NO.		
POST OFFICE:		Choctaw Nation		(Not Including Freedmen)	FIELD NO. 4903		

Dawes' Roll No.	NAME	Relationship to Person First Named	AGE	SEX	BLOOD	TRIBAL ENROLLMENT		
						Year	County	No.
✓ 1	Mitihaya, Mandy ³⁰		27	F	Full	1896	Bok Tuklo	8639
2								
3								
4								
5								
6								
7								
8								
9								
10								
11								
12								
13								
14								
15								
16								
17								

TRIBAL ENROLLMENT OF PARENTS

	Name of Father	Year	County	Name of Mother	Year	County
1						
2						
3						
4						
5		No other information could be obtained				
6						
7		No1 died in spring of 1900 Proof of death filed June 9, 1906				
8						
9		No1 is duplicate of Silmy Mintihaya, No.2 on Choctaw card				
10		No. 1014 Roll 2687				
11						
12						
13					Date of Application	
14					for Enrollment.	
15					Nov 16/99	
16						
17						

CANCELLED

103

Choctaw By Blood Enrollment Cards 1898-1914

	Creek Nation COUNTY. **Choctaw Nation**	Choctaw Roll (Not Including Freedmen)	CARD NO.
CE:	Ft Gibson I.T.		FIELD NO. 4904

NAME	Relationship to Person	AGE	SEX	BLOOD	TRIBAL ENROLLMENT		
					Year	County	No.
1 Tekobbe, Sam 14	First Named	11	M	Full	1896	Bok Tuklo	12207
2							
3							
4							
5							
6							
7							
8							
9							
10							
11	ENROLLMENT						
12	OF NOS. ~1~ HEREON APPROVED BY THE SECRETARY						
13	OF INTERIOR DEC -2 1904						
14							
15							
16							
17							

TRIBAL ENROLLMENT OF PARENTS

Name of Father	Year	County	Name of Mother	Year	County
1 Bob Tekobbe	1896	Boktuklo[sic]	Learna Bond	1896	Eagle
2					
3					
4					
5					
6					
7	No other information could be obtained				
8	Father of Nº1 is Bob Tekobbe Choctaw card #1383				
9	Mother of Nº1 is Learna Bond deceased Choctaw card #717				
10	Nº1 is deaf and dumb. He is attending school for the Deaf and Dumb at Fort Gibson Ind Ter				
	See testimony of Bob Tekobbe, Sept 21, 1904.				
11					
12					
13					
14					
15				Date of Application for Enrollment.		
16				Nov 16/99		
17						

Choctaw By Blood Enrollment Cards 1898-1914

RESIDENCE: **Tobucksy**   COUNTY. **Choctaw Nation**   **Choctaw Roll** *(Not Including Freedmen)*   CARD NO.   FIELD NO. **4905**

POST OFFICE: **McAlester**

Dawes' Roll No.	NAME		Relationship to Person Named	AGE	SEX	BLOOD	TRIBAL ENROLLMENT		
							Year	County	No.
15796	1 Bell, Daniel	61	First Named	58	M	Full	1896	Tobucksy	870
15797	2 " Eliza	43	Wife	40	F	"	1896	"	871
15798	3 " Frances	9	Dau	6	"	"	1896	"	873
	4								
	5								
	6								
	7								
	8								
	9								
	10								
	11								
	12								
	13								
	14								
	15								
	16								
	17								

ENROLLMENT
OF NOS. 1, 2 and 3 HEREON
APPROVED BY THE SECRETARY
OF INTERIOR MAR 15 1905

TRIBAL ENROLLMENT OF PARENTS

	Name of Father	Year	County	Name of Mother	Year	County
1		Dead	Choctaw		Dead	Choctaw
2		"	"		"	"
3	No 1			No 2		
4						
5						
6						
7						
8	See testimony of S.S. Lawrance, R.B. Coleman, Jonas Sexton and					
9	Daniel Bell of January 3, 7 and 9, 1905					
10						
11						
12						
13					Date of Application for Enrollment.	
14						
15					Nov 17/99	
16						
17						

Choctaw By Blood Enrollment Cards 1898-1914

RESIDENCE: Tobucksy COUNTY.
POST OFFICE: MᶜAlester, I.T.

Choctaw Nation

Choctaw Roll
(Not Including Freedmen)

CARD NO.
FIELD NO. **4906**

Dawes' Roll No.	NAME	Relationship to Person First Named	AGE	SEX	BLOOD	TRIBAL ENROLLMENT		
						Year	County	No.
DEAD	1 Archibald, Allen 51		48	M	Full	1893	Tobac	23
	2							
	3 No. 1 hereon dismissed under order							
	4 of the Commission to the Five Civilized							
	5 Tribes of March 31, 1905.							
	6							
	7							
	8							
	9							
	10							
	11							
	12							
	13							
	14							
	15							
	16							
	17							

ENROLLMENT OF PARENTS

	Name of Father	Year	County		Name of Mother	Year	County
1	Anderson Archibald	Dead	Blue			Dead	Blue
2							
3							
4							
5							
6							
7							
8	On 1893 Pay Roll, Page 3, No. 23						
9	Tobucksy Co.						
10	No.1 Died in Muskogee Jail last week; March 20, 1902 Proof of death of No. 1 received and filed Feb. 4, 1903.						
11							
12							
13							
14						Date of Application for Enrollment.	
15							
16						Nov 17/99	
17							

Choctaw By Blood Enrollment Cards 1898-1914

RESIDENCE: Tobucksy COUNTY. **Choctaw Nation** **Choctaw Roll** *(Not Including Freedmen)* CARD NO.
POST OFFICE: McAlester, I.T. FIELD NO. 4907

Dawes' Roll No.	NAME	Relationship to Person First Named	AGE	SEX	BLOOD	TRIBAL ENROLLMENT		
						Year	County	No.
1	Brown, Sibillie 28		25	F	Full	1896	bucksy	906
2								
3								
4								
5								
6								
7								
8								
9								
10								
11								
12								
13								
14								
15								
16								
17								

No. 1 is a duplicate of Isabinga [Illegible] No2 on Choctaw card #4090 final roll of citizens by blood of the Choctaw Nation No. 11456

OCT 20 1905

CANCELLED

TRIBAL ENROLLMENT OF PARENTS

	Name of Father	Year	County	Name of Mother	Year	County
1	Benj. Wade	Dead	Tobucksy		Dead	Tobucksy
2						
3						
4						
5						
6						
7						
8						
9						
10						
11						
12						
13						
14						
15						
16						
17						

See testimony of Alfred Noah of February 14, 1905

Date of Application for Enrollment.
Nov 17/99

RESIDENCE: Tobucksy   COUNTY. **Choctaw Nation**   Choctaw Roll   CARD NO.
POST OFFICE: McAlester, I.T.   *(Not Including Freedmen)*   FIELD NO. 4908

Dawes' Roll No.	NAME	Relationship to Person First Named	AGE	SEX	BLOOD	TRIBAL ENROLLMENT		
						Year	County	No.
DEAD 1	Sealy, Martha 46	First Named	43	F	Full	1896	Tobucksy	2383
Void 2	" Furnetia 12	Dau	9	"	"	1896	"	2384
3								
4								
5								
6								
	No. 1 HEREON DISMISSED UNDER ORDER OF THE COMMISSION TO THE FIVE CIVILIZED TRIBES OF MARCH 31, 1905.							
9								
10	No. 2 is duplicate of No. 4 on							
11	Chickasaw card #316. Enroll-							
12	ment hereon cancelled							
13	Jan 26 1905. See testimony							
	of Jan 16 1905							
14								
15								
16								
17								

TRIBAL ENROLLMENT OF PARENTS

	Name of Father	Year	County	Name of Mother	Year	County
1		Dead	Tobucksy		Dead	Tobucksy
2				No 1		
3						
4						
5						
6						
7						
8						
9		Surname on 1896 roll as Cealy				
10						
11		No 1 died in March 1900. Proof of death filed January 23, 1905				
12						
13						
14					Date of Application for Enrollment.	
15					Nov 17/99	
16						
17						

Choctaw By Blood Enrollment Cards 1898-1914

RESIDENCE: Tobucksy	COUNTY.					CARD NO.
POST OFFICE: McAlester, I.T.	**Choctaw Nation**		**Choctaw Roll** *(Not Including Freedmen)*			FIELD NO. 4909

Dawes' Roll No.	NAME		Relationship to Person	AGE	SEX	BLOOD	TRIBAL ENROLLMENT		
							Year	County	No.
15799	₁ Fisher, Sillin	43	First Named	40	F	Full	1896	Tobucksy	4002
15800	₂ " George	8	Son	5	M	"	1896	"	4004
	3								
	4								
	5								
	6								
	7								
	8								
	9								
	10								
	11								
	12								
	13	ENROLLMENT OF NOS. 1 and 2 HEREON							
	14	APPROVED BY THE SECRETARY OF INTERIOR MAR 15 1905							
	15								
	16								
	17								

TRIBAL ENROLLMENT OF PARENTS

	Name of Father	Year	County	Name of Mother	Year	County
₁	Wilson Coley	Dead	Choctaw	Jincy Coley	Dead	Choctaw
₂	Israel Fisher	"	Tobucky[sic]	No1		
3						
4						
5						
6						
7	No1 on 1896 roll as Cillin Fisher					
8						
9	See testimony of S.S. Lawrance, Sillin Fisher and Jonas Sexton					
10	of January 3 and 9, 1905					
11	No.1 is now living with David Wade, Choctaw card #4922 1/9/05					
12						
13						
14					Date of Application for Enrollment.	
15						
16					Nov 17/99	
17						

109

Choctaw By Blood Enrollment Cards 1898-1914

RESIDENCE: Tobucksy	COUNTY.	**Choctaw Nation**	Choctaw Roll	NO.
POST OFFICE: McAlester, I.T.			(Not Including Freedmen) FIELD NO. 49	

Dawes' Roll No.	NAME		Relationship to Person First Named	AGE	SEX	BLOOD	TRIBAL ENROLLMENT		
							Year	County	No.
13450	1 Frazier, Wilson	29	First Named	26	M	Full	1896	Tobucksy	4024
13451	2 " Lucy	38	Wife	35	F	"	1896	"	4025
	3								
	4								
	5								
	6								
	7								
	8								
	9								
	10								
	11	ENROLLMENT							
	12	OF NOS. 1 & 2 HEREON APPROVED BY THE SECRETARY							
	13	OF INTERIOR MAR 19 1903							
	14								
	15								
	16								
	17								

TRIBAL ENROLLMENT OF PARENTS

	Name of Father	Year	County	Name of Mother	Year	County
1	Daniel Frazier	Dead	Sans Bois	Amy Wade		Tobucksy
2			Choctaw		Dead	Choctaw
3						
4						
5						
6						
7	For child of No2 see NB (Apr 26-06) Card #842					
8						
9						
10						
11						
12						
13						
14						
15						
16				Date of Application for Enrollment	Nov 17/99	
17						

Choctaw By Blood Enrollment Cards 1898-1914

RESIDENCE: Tobucksy	COUNTY. **Choctaw Nation**	Choctaw Roll (Not Including Freedmen)	CARD NO.
∪ST OFFICE: Mc Alester, I.T.			FIELD NO. 4⁹

Dawes' Roll No.	NAME	Relationship to Person First Named	AGE	SEX	BLOOD	TRIBAL ENROLLMENT Year	County	No.
'911	1 Hokey, Eliza	10	7	F	Full	1896	Tobucksy	5330
	2							
	3 ENROLLMENT							
	4 OF NOS. ~~ 1 ~~ HEREON APPROVED BY THE SECRETARY							
	5 OF INTERIOR MAY 21 1903							
	6							
	7							
	8							
	9							
	10							
	11							
	12							
	13							
	14							
	15							
	16							
	17							

TRIBAL ENROLLMENT OF PARENTS

	Name of Father	Year	County	Name of Mother	Year	
1	Davis Hokey	Dead	Tobucksy			Tobucksy
2						
3						
4						
5						
6						
7		On 1896 roll as Diciy[sic] Hokey				
8						
9						
10						
11		No1 is duplicate of No3 on Choctaw roll card No 4922 approved roll #14830				
12		Enrollment cancelled by Departmental authority of May 25, 1906 (I.T.D.				
13		9210 - 1906) DC 21520 - 1906				
14					Date of Application for Enrollment.	
15					Nov 17/99	
16						
17						

RESIDENCE: Tobucksy COUNTY. **Choctaw Nation** Choctaw Roll CARD No.
POST OFFICE: McAlester, I.T. *(Not Including Freedmen)* FIELD No. **4912**

Dawes' Roll No.	NAME	Relationship to Person	AGE	SEX	BLOOD	TRIBAL ENROLLMENT		
						Year	County	No.
13453	1 Harris, Simpson 45	First Named	42	M	Full	1896	Tobucksy	5375
13454	2 " Emeline 8	Dau	5	F	"	1896	"	5376
13455	3 " Robert 24	Son	21	M	"	1896	"	5377
15861	4 " Susan	Wife	45	F	"	1896	Gaines	3273
	5							
ZENSHIP CERTIFICATE								
D FOR NO 6 OCT 3 1904		ENROLLMENT						
	7	OF NOS. 1 2 & 3 HEREON						
	8	APPROVED BY THE SECRETARY						
		OF INTERIOR MAR 19 1903						
SHIP CERTIFICATE	9							
OR NO 10 and 2								
APR 29 1905	11							
	12	ENROLLMENT						
		OF NOS. ~~~ 4 ~~~ HEREON						
	13	APPROVED BY THE SECRETARY						
		OF INTERIOR JUN 12 1905						
SHIP CERTIFICATE	15							
FOR NO	~ 4 ~							
P 12 1907	16							
	17							

TRIBAL ENROLLMENT OF PARENTS

	Name of Father	Year	County	Name of Mother	Year	County
1		Dead	Choctaw		Dead	Choctaw
2	No.1			Susan Harris		Tobucksy
3	No.1			" "		"
4	Jesse McCoy	Dead				
5						
6						
7						
8						
9	No.4 transferred from Choctaw card D881, February 20, 1905. See testimony					
10	of February 9 and 10, 1905.					
11						
12						
13						
14						
15						
16						
17						Nov 17/99

Choctaw By Blood Enrollment Cards 1898-1914

RESIDENCE: Tobucksy COUNTY.
POST OFFICE: McAlester, I.T.

Choctaw Nation

Choctaw Roll
(Not Including Freedmen)

CARD NO.
FIELD NO. **4913**

Dawes' Roll No.	NAME	Relationship to Person	AGE	SEX	BLOOD	TRIBAL ENROLLMENT		
						Year	County	No.
15991	1 James, Sealy 41	First Named	38	M	Full	1896	Tobucksy	2357
	2							
	3							
	4							
	5							
	6							
	7							
	8 Granted Apr 24, 1906							
	9							
	10 ENROLLMENT							
	11 OF NOS. ~~~~ 1 ~~~~ HEREON APPROVED BY THE SECRETARY							
	12 OF INTERIOR JUN 16 1906							
	13							
	14							
	15							
	16							
	17							

TRIBAL ENROLLMENT OF PARENTS

	Name of Father	Year	County	Name of Mother	Year	County
1		Dead	Choctaw		Dead	Choctaw
2						
3						
4						
5	On 1896 Roll as Cealy Campbell					
6						
7						
8						
9	Notify Eddlemen & Graham Ardmore, I.T. 4/20/05					
10						
11						
12						
13						
14						
15						
16						
17						Nov 17/99

RESIDENCE:	Tobucksy	COUNTY.							
POST OFFICE:	McAlester, I.T.								

Choctaw Nation

Choctaw Roll (Not Including Freedmen)

CARD NO. FIELD NO. 4914

Dawes' Roll No.	NAME	Relationship to Person First Named	AGE	SEX	BLOOD	TRIBAL ENROLLMENT		
						Year	County	No.
DEAD	1 Jackson, Lewis	First Named	39	M	Full	1896	Tobucksy	6661
13457	2 " Asie 46	Wife	43	F	"	1896	"	6662
	3							
	4							
	5							
	6							
	7							
	8							
	9							
	10							
	11							
	12							
	13							
	14							
	15							
	16							
	17							

ENROLLMENT
OF NOS. 2 HEREON
APPROVED BY THE SECRETARY
OF INTERIOR MAR 19 1903

No. 1 HEREON DISMISSED UNDER
ORDER OF THE COMMISSION TO THE FIVE
CIVILIZED TRIBES OF MARCH 31, 1905.

TRIBAL ENROLLMENT OF PARENTS

	Name of Father	Year	County	Name of Mother	Year	County
1			Choctaw			Choctaw
2			"			"
3						
4						
5						
6						
7			No1 died January 11, 1902. Proof of death filed January 23, 1905.			
8						
9			No1 on 1896 roll as Lewis Johnson			
10			No.2 also on 1896 Choctaw census roll: page 163 No. 6640 as Mollie Jackson. Error			
11						
12						
13						
14						Date of Application for Enrollment.
15						Nov 17/99
16						
17						

Choctaw By Blood Enrollment Cards 1898-1914

RESIDENCE: Tobucksy COUNTY. **Choctaw Nation**

POST OFFICE: McAlester, I.T.

Choctaw Roll (Not Including Freedmen) 4915

Dawes' Roll No.	NAME		Relationship to Person First Named	AGE	SEX	BLOOD	TRIBAL ENROLLMENT		
							Year	County	No.
15638	1 James, Sallissie	51		48	F	Full	1896	Tobucksy	6674
	2 Jackson, Andy	13	Son	10	M	"	1896	"	6675
	3								
	4								
	5								
	6								
	7								
	8								
	9	ENROLLMENT OF NOS. ~~~ 1 ~~~ HEREON							
	10	APPROVED BY THE SECRETARY OF INTERIOR OCT 21 1904							
	11								
	12								
	13								
	14								
	15								
	16								
	17								

TRIBAL ENROLLMENT OF PARENTS

	Name of Father	Year	County	Name of Mother	Year	County
1			Choctaw			Choctaw
2	Jackson		"	No1		
3						
4						
5						
6						
7						
8						
9						
10						
11						
12						
13					Date of Application for Enrollment.	
14						
15					Nov 17/99	
16						
17						

Choctaw By Blood Enrollment Cards 1898-1914

RESIDENCE:	Tobucksy	COUNTY.	**Choctaw Nation**			taw Roll	CARD NO.	
POST OFFICE:	McAlester					(Not ... ding Freedmen)	FIELD NO. 4916	

Dawes' Roll No.	NAME		Relationship to Person	AGE	SEX	BLOOD	TRIBAL ENROLLMENT		
							Year	County	No.
15595	1 Lacey, Frank	23	First Named	20	M	1/4	1896	Tobucksy	7884
	2								
	3								
	4								
	5								
	6								
	7								
	8								
	9								
	10								
	11								
	12								
	13								
	14	ENROLLMENT							
	15	OF NOS. ~~~ 1 ~~~ HEREON							
	16	APPROVED BY THE SECRETARY OF INTERIOR SEP 22 1904							
	17								

TRIBAL ENROLLMENT OF PARENTS

	Name of Father	Year	County	Name of Mother	Year	County
1	Elias P Lacey		Non Citz	Annie Lacey	Dead	Bky--lue
2						
3						
4						
5						
6		On 1893 Blue County pay roll as Frank Lucy #1230 Page 29				
7	April 20" 24: Testimony of No1, Elias P Lacey and Josiah Beames taken.					
8						
9						
10						
11						
12						
13					Date of Application for Enrollment.	
14						
15					Nov 17/99	
16						
17	Bokchito I.T. 4/20/04					

116

RESIDENCE: Tobucksy COUNTY.
POST OFFICE: McAlester, I.T.

Choctaw Nation

Choctaw Roll
(Not Including Freedmen)

CARD NO.
FIELD NO. **4917**

Dawes' Roll No.	NAME		Relationship to Person First Named	AGE	SEX	BLOOD	TRIBAL ENROLLMENT		
							Year	County	No.
✓	Nail, George	19		16	M	Full	1896	Tobucksy	9606
2									
3									
4									
5									
6									
7									
8									
9									
10									
11									
12									
13									
14									
15									
16									
17									

TRIBAL ENROLLMENT OF PARENTS

	Name of Father	Year	County	Name of Mother	Year	County
1			Choctaw			Choctaw
2						
3						
4						
5						
6						
7	On 1896 roll as Gregoma Nail					
8						
9						
10						
11						
12						
13						
14						
15						
16						
17						

Date of Application for Enrollment.
Nov 17/99

117

Choctaw By Blood Enrollment Cards 1898-1914

RESIDENCE: Tobucksy COUNTY.		Choctaw Nation				Choctaw Roll (Not Including Freedmen)		CARD No. FIELD No. 4918	
POST OFFICE: McAlester, I.T.									

Dawes' Roll No.	NAME		Relationship to Person	AGE	SEX	BLOOD	TRIBAL ENROLLMENT		
							Year	County	No.
15639	1 Pusley, Alinton	34	First Named	31	M	Full	1896	Tobucksy	10222
	2								
	3								
	4								
	5								
	6								
	7								
	8	ENROLLMENT							
	9	OF NOS. ~~~~ 1 ~~~~ HEREON							
		APPROVED BY THE SECRETARY							
	10	OF INTERIOR OCT 21 1904							
	11								
	12								
	13								
	14								
	15								
	16								
	17								

TRIBAL ENROLLMENT OF PARENTS

	Name of Father	Year	County	Name of Mother	Year	County
1	Tom Pusley	Dead	Choctaw	Jincy Pusley	Dead	Choctaw
2						
3						
4						
5						
6						
7	On 1896 roll as Allington Pusley					
8	" 1893 " " " " Tobucksy Co, page 75, No 634					
9	" 1885 " " Allenton " Atoka Co, No. 1091					
10						
11						
12						
13						Date of Application for Enrollment.
14						
15						Nov 17/99
16						
17						

118

Choctaw By Blood Enrollment Cards 1898-1914

RESIDENCE: Tobucksy COUNTY. **Choctaw Nation** **Choctaw Roll** CARD No.
POST OFFICE: McAlester, I.T. *(Not Including Freedmen)* FIELD No. 4919

Dawes' Roll No.	NAME	Relationship to Person First Named	AGE	SEX	BLOOD	TRIBAL ENROLLMENT		
						Year	County	No.
DEAD	1 Elashubbee, Sim		41	M	Full	1896	Tobucksy	10224
	2							
	3							
	4							
	5							
	6							
	7							
	8							
	9							
	10							
	11							
	12	No. 1 HEREON DISMISSED UNDER						
	13	ORDER OF THE COMMISSION TO THE FIVE						
	14	CIVILIZED TRIBES OF MARCH 31, 1905.						
	15							
	16							
	17							

TRIBAL ENROLLMENT OF PARENTS

	Name of Father	Year	County	Name of Mother	Year	County
1	Ok-la-hubbee	Dead	Tobucksy	Lemsie	Dead	Choctaw
2						
3						
4						
5						
6						
7						
8						
9						
10	On 1896 roll as Sim Paxton					
11	See letter of D. D. Anderson filed Jany 23, 1903					
12	See testimony taken Jan 7, 9 and 18, 1905 February 14 ns 17, 1905					
13	No1 died in November 1901. See testimony above referred to					
14					Date of Application for Enrollment.	
15					Nov 17/99	
16						
17						

Choctaw By Blood Enrollment Cards 1898-1914

RESIDENCE: Tobucksy COUNTY. **Choctaw Nation**   **Choctaw Roll** CARD No.
POST OFFICE: McAlester, I.T.   *(Not Including Freedmen)*   FIELD No. 4920

Dawes' Roll No.		NAME		Relationship to Person	AGE	SEX	BLOOD	TRIBAL ENROLLMENT		
								Year	County	No.
13463	1	Peabody, Jonas	48	First Named	45	M	Full	1896	Tobucksy	10225
13464	2	" Sallie	39	Wife	36	F	"	1896	"	10226
DEAD	3	" Reuben	20	Son	17	M	"	1896	"	10227
13465	4	" Charles (DIED PRIOR TO SEPTEMBER 25, 1902)		"	12	"	"	1896	"	10228
13466	5	" Frank	13	"	10	"	"	1896	"	10229
	6									
	7									
	8									
	9									
	10									
	11									
	12									
	13									
	14									
	15									
	16									
	17									

ENROLLMENT
OF NOS. 1 2 4 & 5   HEREON
APPROVED BY THE SECRETARY
OF INTERIOR

No. 3 HEREON DISMISSED UNDER
ORDER OF THE COMMISSION TO THE FIVE
CIVILIZED TRIBES OF MARCH 31, 1905.

TRIBAL ENROLLMENT OF PARENTS

	Name of Father	Year	County	Name of Mother	Year	County
1		Dead	Choctaw		Dead	Choctaw
2		"	"		"	"
3	No1			No2		
4	No1			No2		
5	No1			No2		
6						
7						
8						
9	No3 died in December 1900 Proof of death filed January 23 1905					
10						
11						
12						
13					Date of Application for Enrollment.	
14						
15					Nov 17/99	
16						
17						

Choctaw By Blood Enrollment Cards 1898-1914

Choctaw Nation Choctaw Roll CARD No. 4921

Dawes' Roll No.	NAME	Relationship to Person First Named	AGE	SEX	BLOOD	TRIBAL ENROLLMENT		
						Year	County	No.
15801	1 Pickens, Nelson 27	First Named	24	M	Full	1896	Tobucksy	10258
16058	2 " , Malinda	Wife	17	F	"			
	3							
	4							
	5							
	6							
	7							
	8							
	9							
	10	ENROLLMENT OF NOS. ~~~ 2 ~~~ HEREON APPROVED BY THE SECRETARY OF INTERIOR AUG 22 1906						
	11							
	12							
	13	ENROLLMENT OF NOS. 1 HEREON APPROVED BY THE SECRETARY OF INTERIOR MAR 15 1905						
	14							
	15							
	16							
	17							

TRIBAL ENROLLMENT OF PARENTS

	Name of Father	Year	County	Name of Mother	Year	County
1	Thompson Pickens	Dead	Choctaw	Bessie Pickens	Dead	Choctaw
2	Daniel Bell		"			
3						
4						
5						
6	No.1 on 1893 Pay Roll, Gaines County, page 63, No. 598, as Nelson Pickens					
7	See testimony taken Jan. 3, 7, 9, and 16, 1905					
8						
9	For child of No1 see NB (Apr 26-06) Card #726					
10						
11	No.3 placed hereon under provisions of the Act of Congress					
12						#1
13	No2 enrolled by special provision of Act of Congress				Date of Application for Enrollment.	
14	June 21-1906 (34 stats 325)					
15					Nov 17/99	
16						
17						

121

Choctaw By Blood Enrollment Cards 1898-1914

RESIDENCE: Tobucksy   COUNTY. **Choctaw Nation**   **Choctaw Roll** CARD No.
POST OFFICE: McAlester, I.T.   *(Not Including Freedmen)* FIELD No. 4922

Dawes' Roll No.	NAME		Relationship to Person	AGE	SEX	BLOOD	TRIBAL ENROLLMENT		
							Year	County	No.
13468	1 Wade, David	42	First Named	39	M	Full	1896	Tobucksy	12987
13469	2 " Mamie	36	Wife	33	F	"	1896	"	12988
14830	3 Hokey. Eliza	10	Dau of N°2	10	F	"	1893	"	41/375
15944	4 Wade, Louisa		Dau	1	F	"			
	5								
	6								
	7								
	8								
	9	ENROLLMENT OF NOS. 1 & 2 HEREON APPROVED BY THE SECRETARY OF INTERIOR MAR 19 1903							
	10								
	11								
	12	ENROLLMENT OF NOS. 3 HEREON APPROVED BY THE SECRETARY OF INTERIOR MAY 20 1903							
	13								
	14								
	15	ENROLLMENT OF NOS. ~~~ 4 ~~~ HEREON APPROVED BY THE SECRETARY OF INTERIOR NOV 24 1905							
	16								
	17								

TRIBAL ENROLLMENT OF PARENTS

	Name of Father	Year	County	Name of Mother	Year	County
1	Isha-tubbee	Dead	Choctaw		Dead	Choctaw
2	Louie Nelson	dead	Choctaw	Mahaley Nelson	dead	"
3	Davis Hokey	dead	"	N°2		
4	No 1			Sillin Wade		Choctaw
5						
6						
7		N°2 on Tobucksy Co pay roll page 41 #373 as Mymie Hokey				
8		N°3 on Tobucksy Co pay roll page 41 #374 as Lizzie Hokes				
9		N°3 Enrolled Dec 22, 1902. See sworn statement of her mother of that date				
10						
11						
12						
13		No4 was born Oct 6, 1901: application received March 4, 1905 #1 & 2				
14		under Act of Congress approved March 3, 1905			Date of Application for Enrollment.	
15		Mother of No4 on Choctaw card No 4909, as Sillin Fisher.			Nov 17/99	
16						
17						

122

Choctaw By Blood Enrollment Cards 1898-1914

RESIDENCE: Tobucksy COUNTY. **Choctaw Nation** Choctaw Roll CARD NO.
POST OFFICE: McAlester, I.T. *(Not Including Freedmen)* FIELD NO. 4923

Dawes' Roll No.	NAME	Relationship to Person	AGE	SEX	BLOOD	TRIBAL ENROLLMENT		
						Year	County	No.
15802	1 Williams, Loring 27	First Named	24	M	Full	1896	Tobucksy	12990
	2							
	3							
	4							
	5							
	6							
	7							
	8							
	9							
	10							
	11							
	12							
	13							
	14							
	15							
	16							
	17							

ENROLLMENT
OF NOS. 1 HEREON
APPROVED BY THE SECRETARY
OF INTERIOR MAR 15 1905

TRIBAL ENROLLMENT OF PARENTS

	Name of Father	Year	County	Name of Mother	Year	County
1	Aaron Williams	Dead	Choctaw	Melissa Williams	Dead	Choctaw
2						
3						
4						
5						
6	No.1 on 1893 Pay Roll, Tobucksy County, page 98, No. 828					
7						
8						
9						
10						
11						
12						
13						
14					Date of Application for Enrollment.	
15					Nov 17/99	
16						
17	PO [Illegible] IT 7/25/07					

123

Choctaw By Blood Enrollment Cards 1898-1914

RESIDENCE: Tobucksy COUNTY.
POST OFFICE: McAlester, I.T.

Choctaw Nation

Choctaw Roll
(Not Including Freedmen)

CARD No.
FIELD No. 4924

Dawes' Roll No.	NAME		Relationship to Person	AGE	SEX	BLOOD	TRIBAL ENROLLMENT		
							Year	County	No.
13471	1 Wade, Bible	36	First Named	33	M	Full	1896	Tobucksy	12992
13472	2 " Nicey	26	Wife	23	F	"	111896	"	12993
	3								
	4								
	5								
	6								
	7								
	8								
	9	ENROLLMENT OF NOS. 1 & 2 HEREON							
	10	APPROVED BY THE SECRETARY							
	11	OF INTERIOR MAR 19 1903							
	12								
	13								
	14								
	15								
	16								
	17								

TRIBAL ENROLLMENT OF PARENTS

	Name of Father	Year	County	Name of Mother	Year	County
1	Wade	Dead	Choctaw		Dead	Choctaw
2	Lewis Jackson		"	Salissie	Dead	"
3						
4						
5						
6						
7						
8						
9						
10						
11						
12						
13					Date of Application for Enrollment.	
14						
15					Nov 17/99	
16						
17						

Choctaw By Blood Enrollment Cards 1898-1914

RESIDENCE: Tobucksy COUNTY. **Choctaw Nation** Choctaw Roll CARD NO.
POST OFFICE: McAlester, I.T. (Not Including Freedmen) FIELD NO. 4925

Dawes' Roll No.	NAME	Relationship to Person First Named	AGE	SEX	BLOOD	TRIBAL ENROLLMENT		
						Year	County	No.
1	Kachafixico, Selina ⁵¹	First Named	48	F	Full	1896	Tobucksy	7479
2								
3								
4								
5								
6								
7								
8								
9								
10								
11								
12								
13								
14								
15								
16								
17								

DISMISSED

OCT 6- 1905

TRIBAL ENROLLMENT OF PARENTS

	Name of Father	Year	County	Name of Mother	Year	County
1		Dead	Choctaw		Dead	Choctaw
2						
3						
4						
5						
6						
7	Is not No.1 a duplicate of Salina Fixeco, on Creek roll card #2794:					
8	field No. 2909: approved roll of Creek citizens by blood No. 8127					
9	No.1 also on 1893 Choctaw based District payment					Dec. 16, 1904
10	roll, Tobucksy County, page 54: No. 481 as					
11	Salina Kahachafichico payment receipted for by Louis Hancock					
12						
13	See testimony of S S Lawrance of January 3, 1905					
14	and R.B. Coleman of January 7, 1905					
15						Nov 17/99
16	No1 is enrolled as a citizen of the Creek Nation Creek Indian Card #2909					
17	Roll #8127					

Date of Application for Enrollment.

Choctaw By Blood Enrollment Cards 1898-1914

RESIDENCE: Tobucksy COUNTY. **Choctaw Nation** Choctaw Roll CARD NO.
POST OFFICE: McAlester, I.T. (Including Freedmen) FIELD NO. 4926

Dawes' Roll No.	NAME		Relationship to Person First Named	AGE	SEX	BLOOD	TRIBAL ENROLLMENT		
							Year	County	No.
13474	1 Kate John	31	First Named	28	M	Full	1896	Tobucksy	7505
13475	2 " Mearey	26	Wife	23	F	"	1896	"	7506
	3								
	4								
	5								
	6								
	7								
	8	ENROLLMENT OF NOS. 1 & 2 HEREON							
	9	APPROVED BY THE SECRETARY							
	10	OF INTERIOR MAR 19 1903							
	11								
	12								
	13								
	14								
	15								
	16								
	17								

TRIBAL ENROLLMENT OF PARENTS

	Name of Father	Year	County	Name of Mother	Year	County
1	Byington Kate		Tobucksy	Rhoda Bond		Tobucksy
2	Johnson Noel		"	Lucy Noel		"
3						
4						
5						
6						
7			N°2 also on 1893 payroll, p. 55, N°494 as Mary Kate			
8						
9						
10						
11						
12						
13						
14					Date of Application for Enrollment.	
15					Nov 17/99	
16						
17						

126

Choctaw By Blood Enrollment Cards 1898-1914

RESIDENCE: Red River	COUNTY. Choctaw Nation	Choctaw Roll	CARD NO.
POST OFFICE: Garvin, I.T.		(Not Including Freedmen)	FIELD NO. **4927**

Dawes' Roll No.	NAME	Relationship to Person First Named	AGE	SEX	BLOOD	TRIBAL ENROLLMENT Year	County	No.
13476	1 Tullihela, Willie 24	First Named	21	M	Full	1896	Red River	5690
	2							
	3							
	4							
	5							
	6							
	7							
	8							
	9							
	10							
	11							
	12							
	13							
	14							
	15							
	16							
	17							

ENROLLMENT
OF NOS. 1 HEREON
APPROVED BY THE SECRETARY
OF INTERIOR Mar 19 1903

TRIBAL ENROLLMENT OF PARENTS

	Name of Father	Year	County	Name of Mother	Year	County
1						
2						
3						
4						
5						
6	On 1896 roll as Willie Haley					
7	No.1 is husband of Siney Willis on Choc #4273					
8						
9	For child of No.1 see NB (Mar 3-05) Card #94					
10						
11						
12						
13						
14						
15				Date of Application for Enrollment. Nov 17/99		
16						
17						

127

Choctaw By Blood Enrollment Cards 1898-1914

RESIDENCE: Red River COUNTY. **Choctaw Nation** Choctaw Roll CARD No.
POST OFFICE: Kullituklo, I.T. *(Not Including Freedmen)* FIELD No. 4928

Dawes' Roll No.	NAME Jones		Relationship to Person	AGE	SEX	BLOOD	TRIBAL ENROLLMENT		
							Year	County	No.
1	James, Arison	30	First Named	27	M	Full	1896	Red River	7026
2									
3									
4									
5									
6									
7									
8									
9									
10									
11									
12									
13									
14									
15									
16									
17									

TRIBAL ENROLLMENT OF PARENTS

	Name of Father	Year	County	Name of Mother	Year	County
1	Simpson Luke	Dead	Bok Tuklo	Mehatima	Dead	Bok Tuklo
2						
3						
4						
5						
6						
7						
8			On 1896 roll as Arison Jones			
9						
10			No 1 is duplicate of Isin Ontontabi, No.1 on Choctaw card No 909 approved roll No 2440			
11						
12						
13					Date of Application for Enrollment.	
14						
15					Nov 17/99	
16						
17						

CANCELLED

JUL 12 1906

Duplicate of No 1 on Choctaw card No 909

Choctaw By Blood Enrollment Cards 1898-1914

RESIDENCE: Red River   COUNTY. **Choctaw Nation**   **Choctaw Roll**   CARD NO.

POST OFFICE: Garvin, I.T.   (Not Including Freedmen)   FIELD NO. 4929

Dawes' Roll No.	NAME	Relationship to Person First Named	AGE	SEX	BLOOD	TRIBAL ENROLLMENT		
						Year	County	No.
✓	1 Jones, Colbert	10 First Named	7	M	Full	1896	Red River	7027
	2							
	3							
	4							
	5							
	6							
	7							
	8							
	9							
	10							
	11							
	12							
	13							
	14							
	15							
	16							
	17							

TRIBAL ENROLLMENT OF PARENTS

	Name of Father	Year	County	Name of Mother	Year	County
1						
2						
3						
4						
5						
6						
7						
8						
9						
10						
11						
12						
13					Date of Application for Enrollment.	
14						
15					Nov 17/99	
16						
17						

129

RESIDENCE:	Red River	COUNTY.							
POST OFFICE:	Garvin, I.T.		**Choctaw Nation** *(Not Including Freedmen)*				Choctaw Roll	CARD NO. FIELD NO. 4930	

Dawes' Roll No.	NAME	Relationship to Person	AGE	SEX	BLOOD	TRIBAL ENROLLMENT		
						Year	County	No.
✓	1 Wilson, Sarah 26	First Named	23	F	Full	1896	Red River	7028
	2							
	3							
	4							
	5							
	6							
	7							
	8							
	9							
	10							
	11							
	12							
	13							
	14							
	15							
	16							
	17							

OCT 20 1905

CANCELLED

TRIBAL ENROLLMENT OF PARENTS

	Name of Father	Year	County	Name of Mother	Year	County
1						
2						
3						
4						
5						
6						
7						
8		On 1896 roll as Sarah Jones				
9		No.1 is a duplicate of Sarah Pisachubbi, No.2 on Choctaw card #1273				
10		final roll of citizens by blood of the Choctaw Nation No. 3471				
11						
12					Date of Application for Enrollment.	
13					Nov 17/99	
14						
15						
16						
17						

Choctaw By Blood Enrollment Cards 1898-1914

	RESIDENCE:	Red River		COUNTY.							

RESIDENCE: Red River   **COUNTY.**   **Choctaw Nation**   **Choctaw Roll** *(Not Including Freedmen)*   CARD NO.

POST OFFICE: Garvin, I.T.   FIELD NO. **4931**

Dawes' Roll No.	NAME	Relationship to Person First Named	AGE	SEX	BLOOD	TRIBAL ENROLLMENT		
						Year	County	No.
DP✓ 1	Tullihela, Isaac ²⁴	First Named	21	M	Full	1896	Red River	12316
5/4/06 2								
3								
4								
5								
6								
7								
8								
9								
10								
11								
12								
13								
14								
15								
16								
17								

TRIBAL ENROLLMENT OF PARENTS

	Name of Father	Year	County	Name of Mother	Year	County
1						
2						
3						
4						
5						
6						
7						
8			In penitentiary			
9						
10			On 1896 roll as Isaac Tullehely			
11			Nº1 is step son of Nancy Haley Choctaw card #D138 1591⁹			
12						
13						
14						Date of Application for Enrollment.
15			DISMISSED			Nov 17/99
16			JUN 21 1906			
17						

131

Choctaw By Blood Enrollment Cards 1898-1914

RESIDENCE: Red River   COUNTY. **Choctaw Nation**   **Choctaw Roll**   CARD NO.
POST OFFICE: Garvin, I.T.   *(Not Including Freedmen)*   FIELD NO. **4932**

Dawes' Roll No.		NAME		Relationship to Person First Named	AGE	SEX	BLOOD	TRIBAL ENROLLMENT		
								Year	County	No.
DEAD	1	Willie, Ansie	DEAD		54	F	Full	1896	Red River	13649
13481	2	" Sayanis	29	Dau	26	"	"	1896	" "	13650
13482	3	" Susanna	22	"	19	"	"	1896	" "	13651
13483	4	" Willis	22	Son	19	M	"	1896	" "	13652
13484	5	" Esias	15	"	12	"	"	1896	" "	13653
	6									
	7									
	8									
	9									
	10									
	11									
	12									
	13									
	14	No. 1 hereon dismissed under order of								
	15	the Commission to the Five Civilized								
	16	Tribes of March 31, 1905.								
	17									

ENROLLMENT
OF NOS. 2,3,4 & 5
APPROVED BY THE SECRETARY
OF INTERIOR Mar 19, 1903
HEREON

TRIBAL ENROLLMENT OF PARENTS

	Name of Father	Year	County	Name of Mother	Year	County
1	Wychehibbee	Dead	Bok Tuklo		Dead	Bok Tuklo
2	Willie Impson	"	Red River	No.1		
3	" "	"	" "	No.1		
4	" "	"	" "	No.1		
5	" "	"	" "	No.1		
6						
7						
8		No.1 died in Dec. 1899 proof of death filed Dec 2, 1902				
9		For child of No.2 see NB (March 3, 1905) #976				
10						
11		No.3 is duplicate of Surena Wright No.2 on Choctaw card No. 1087. Enroll-				
12		ment hereon cancelled under Departmental authority of June 25, 1906				
13		(I.T.D. 11182-1906) D.C. 27019-1906				
14					Date of Application for Enrollment.	
15					Nov 17/99	
16						
17						

132

RESIDENCE: Chickasaw Nation ~~COUNTY~~. **Choctaw Nation** Choctaw Roll CARD No.
POST OFFICE: Wayne, I.T. *(Not Including Freedmen)* FIELD No. 4933

Dawes' Roll No.	NAME	Relationship to Person First Named	AGE	SEX	BLOOD	TRIBAL ENROLLMENT		
						Year	County	No.
1	Seifried, William	Named	21	M	1/4			
2	" Eula Beatrice	Dau	1 week	F~~M~~	1/8			
3								
4								
5								
6								
7								
8								
9								
10								
11								
12								
13								
14								
15								
16								
17								

TRIBAL ENROLLMENT OF PARENTS

	Name of Father	Year	County	Name of Mother	Year	County
1	Wᵐ F Seifried	Dead	Non Citz	Julia Seifried	Dead	Choctaw Roll
2	No.1			Mary F Seifried		
3						
4						
5						
6						
7						
8						
9	On 1897 Chickasaw Roll, Page 62,					
10	Pontotoc Co. as Willie Seifried					
11	Transferred to Choctaw Roll by Dawes Commission					
12						
13	Wife Mary F Seifried on Card No D519					
14	No.1 admitted by Dawes Commission in 1896			On Chickasaw Card Sept 14 98		
15	as a Chickasaw by blood; Chickasaw case #270;			On this Card Nov 18/99		
16	no appeal. No.2 Enrolled April 20, 1901					
17	Correct name of No1 is William T Seifried. See letter of April 24, 1901 filed May 2-1901					

Date of Application for Enrollment.

133

Choctaw By Blood Enrollment Cards 1898-1914

RESIDENCE: Chickasaw Nation ~~COUNTY~~.
POST OFFICE: Wayne, I.T.

Choctaw Nation

Choctaw Roll *(Not Including Freedmen)*

CARD NO.
FIELD NO. 4934

Dawes' Roll No.	NAME	Relationship to Person First Named	AGE	SEX	BLOOD	TRIBAL ENROLLMENT		
						Year	County	No.
VOID.	1 Seifried, Minnie		23	F	1/4			
VOID.	2 " Henry	Bro	19	M	1/4			
VOID.	3 " Charley	"	17	"	1/4			
VOID.	4 " Mattie	Sister	14	F	1/4			
VOID.	5 " Mary	"	12	"	1/4			
VOID.	6 " Lucy	"	10	"	1/4			
	7							
	8							
	9							
	10							
	11							
	12							
	13							
	14							
	15							
	16							
	17							

TRIBAL ENROLLMENT OF PARENTS

	Name of Father		County	Name of Mother	Year	County
1	Wm F Seifried	Dead	Non Citz	Julia Seifried	Dead	Choctaw Roll
2	" " "	"	" "	" "	"	" " "
3	" " "	"	" "	" "	"	" " "
4	" " "	"	" "	" "	"	" " "
5	" " "	"	" "	" "	"	" " "
6	" " "	"	" "	" "	"	" " "
7						
8						
9						
10						
11	All on 1897 Chickasaw Roll, Page					
12	62, Pontotoc Co. Transferred to					
13	Choctaw Roll by Dawes Commission					
14	No6 on Chickasaw Roll as Lula			On Chickasaw Card Sept 1/99		
15	Seifried			On this Card Nov 18		
16	Nos 1,2,4,5 and 6 admitted by Dawes Commission in 1896 as					
17	Chickasaws by blood Chickasaw case #270; no appeal					

CANCELLED

134

Choctaw By Blood Enrollment Cards 1898-1914

RESIDENCE: Pontotoc COUNTY. **Choctaw Nation** **Choctaw Roll** CARD No.
POST OFFICE: Stonewall, Ind. Terr. (Not Including Freedmen) FIELD No. 4935

Dawes' Roll No.	NAME	Relationship to Person First Named	AGE	SEX	BLOOD	TRIBAL ENROLLMENT Year	County	No.
VOID. 1	Rowe, Leticia	Named	21	F	3/8	1897	Pontotoc	49
VOID. 2	" Rena	Dau	3mo	"	3/16			
VOID. 3	" Alaric	Son	1½ mo	M	3/16			
4								
5								
6								
7								
8								
9								
10								
11								
12								
13								
14								
15								
16								
17								

TRIBAL ENROLLMENT OF PARENTS

	Name of Father	Year	County	Name of Mother	Year	County
1	Wood Smith IW	1897	Pontotoc	Rena Smith	1897	Pontotoc
2	Clyde Rowe		white man	No 1		
3	" "		" "	No. 1		
4						
5						
6	On Chickasaw roll as Leticia Smith					
7						
8						
9	Transferred from Chickasaw card #201					
10	by order of the Commission this 29th Nov, 1899					
11						
12	For citizenship of mother see Choctaw					
13	card #307					
14	Correct way of spelling given name of No1 is "Letitia" See letter of her					
15	parents on file 4/27/01					
	No.3 Enrolled April 27, 1901					
16						
17						Date of Application for Enrollment 9/5/98

135

Choctaw By Blood Enrollment Cards 1898-1914

Dawes' Roll No.	NAME		Relationship to Person	AGE	SEX	BLOOD	TRIBAL ENROLLMENT		
							Year	County	No.
13485	1 Cassell, Serena	29	First Named	26	F	1/2	1896	Kiamitia	3796
13486	2 Everidge, Harvey	7	Son	4	M	1/2	1896	"	3797
13487	3 Cassell, Leathie	1	Dau	7mo	F	1/4			
	4								
	5								
	6								
	7								
	8								
	9	ENROLLMENT							
	10	OF NOS. 1,2 & 3 HEREON APPROVED BY THE SECRETARY							
	11	OF INTERIOR Mar 19, 1903							
	12								
	13								
	14								
	15								
	16								
	17								

TRIBAL ENROLLMENT OF PARENTS

	Name of Father	Year	County	Name of Mother	Year	County
1	C.C. Ervin		Kiamitia		Dead	Kiamitia
2	Will Everidge		"	No.1		
3	J. T. Cassell		non-citizen	No.1		
4						
5						
6						
7	No.1 on 1896 roll as Serena Ervin					
8	No.2 " 1896 " " Harry "					
9	No.3 Born Nov. 11, 1901. Enrolled June 10, 1902					
10	For child of No.1 see NB (Apr 26-06) Card #746					
11	" " " " " " (Mar 3 '05) " #1176					
12						
13						#1&2
14					Date of Application for Enrollment.	
15					Dec 4/99	
16						
17	P.O. Massey I.T. 4/21/05					

136

Choctaw By Blood Enrollment Cards 1898-1914

RESIDENCE: Gaines COUNTY.
POST OFFICE: Wilburton, I.T.

Choctaw Nation

Choctaw Roll
(Not Including Freedmen)

4937
CARD NO.
FIELD NO. 493'/

	NAME		Relationship to Person	AGE	SEX	BLOOD	TRIBAL ENROLLMENT		
							Year	County	No.
13488	1 Wade, Eli	23	First Named	20	M	Full	1896	Atoka	13979
	2								
	3								
	4								
	5								
	6								
	7								
	8								
	9								
	10								
	11								
	12								
	13								
	14								
	15								
	16								
	17								

ENROLLMENT
OF NOS. ~~~ 1 ~~~ HEREON
APPROVED BY THE SECRETARY
OF INTERIOR MAR 19 1903

TRIBAL ENROLLMENT OF PARENTS

	Name of Father	Year	County	Name of Mother	Year	County
1	Simeon Wade		Gaines	Amy Wade		Gaines
2						
3						
4						
5						
6						
7						
8						
9						
10						
11						
12						
13					Date of Application for Enrollment.	
14						
15					Dec 4/99	
16						
17						

137

Choctaw By Blood Enrollment Cards 1898-1914

RESIDENCE: Atoka COUNTY.
POST OFFICE: Atoka, I.T.

Choctaw Nation

Choctaw Roll
(Not Including Freedmen)

CARD NO.
FIELD NO. 4938

Dawes' Roll No.	NAME	Relationship to Person	AGE	SEX	BLOOD	TRIBAL ENROLLMENT		
						Year	County	No.
13489	1 Yarharmby, Sim 36	First Named	33	M	Full	1896	Atoka	14244
	2							
	3							
	4							
	5							
	6							
	7							
	8							
	9							
	10	ENROLLMENT						
	11	OF NOS. 1 HEREON APPROVED BY THE SECRETARY						
	12	OF INTERIOR MAR 19 1903						
	13							
	14							
	15							
	16							
	17							

TRIBAL ENROLLMENT OF PARENTS

	Name of Father	Year	County	Name of Mother	Year	County
1	Amos Yarharmby	Dead	Atoka	Daisy Yarharmby	Dead	Atoka
2						
3						
4						
5						
6						
7						
8	Sim Yarharmby on 1896 roll					
9						
10						
11						
12						
13					Date of Application for Enrollment.	
14						
15					Dec 4/99	
16						
17						

Choctaw By Blood Enrollment Cards 1898-1914

Dawes' Roll No.	NAME		Relationship to Person	AGE	SEX	BLOOD	TRIBAL ENROLLMENT		
							Year	County	No.
13490	1 Bacon, Daniel	40	First Named	37	M	Full	1896	Atoka	1780
13491	2 " Lizzie A	30	Wife	27	F	"	1896	"	1837
13492	3 " Elias	12	Son	9	M	"	1896	"	1838
13493	4 " Ed	1✓	Son	7mo	M	"			
15829	5 Frazier, Silly	3	Dau of No.2	3	F	"			
	6								
	7								
	8								
	9								
	10								
	11								
	12								
	13								
	14								
	15								
	16								
	17								

ENROLLMENT
OF NOS. 1 2 3 & 4   HEREON
APPROVED BY THE SECRETARY
OF INTERIOR   Mar. 19, 1903

ENROLLMENT
OF NOS. 5   HEREON
APPROVED BY THE SECRETARY
OF INTERIOR   Jun 12 1905

now living with Epsey Duke 9-D-228

TRIBAL ENROLLMENT OF PARENTS

	Name of Father	Year	County	Name of Mother	Year	County
1			Choctaw			Choctaw
2			"			"
3	No.1			No.2		
4	No.1			No.2		
5	Lewis Frazier		Choctaw	No.2		
6						
7	No.2 on 1896 roll as Lizzie Ann Bacon					
8	No.3 " 1896 " " Eli Bacon					
9	No.4 born May 1, 1902; enrolled Nov 22, 1902					
10	Nos 1&2 have separated					
11	No 5 was born Jan 6, 1900; application received March 4, 1905 under Act of Congress approved March 3, 1905.					
12	For children of Nos 1&2 see NB (March 3, 1905) #1388					
	" " " No.1 " " " " " #1435					
13						
14						Date of Application for Enrollment.
15	P.O. Cairo I.T. 4/17/05					Dec 4/99
16	P.O. Coalgate, I.T.					
17	P.O. Blanco 1/10/05					

139

Choctaw By Blood Enrollment Cards 1898-1914

RESIDENCE: Atoka   COUNTY. **Choctaw Nation**   **Choctaw Roll** *(Not Including Freedmen)*   CARD NO.

POST OFFICE: Atoka,   FIELD NO. 4940

Dawes' Roll No.	NAME		Relationship to Person	AGE	SEX	BLOOD	TRIBAL ENROLLMENT		
							Year	County	No.
13494	1 Jones, Frank	40	First Named	37	M	3/8	1896	Atoka	7286
	2								
	3								
	4								
	5								
	6								
	7								
	8								
	9								
	10								
	11								
	12								
	13								
	14								
	15								
	16								
	17								

ENROLLMENT
OF NOS. ~~1~~ HEREON
APPROVED BY THE SECRETARY
OF INTERIOR **MAR 19 1903**

TRIBAL ENROLLMENT OF PARENTS

	Name of Father	Year	County	Name of Mother	Year	County
1	Noel Jones		Atoka			Cherokee
2						
3						
4						
5						
6						
7			See testimony in enrollment of			
8			Noel Jones #4080			
9						
10			Nº1 in penitentiary at Columbus, Ohio Dec. 1902			
11						
12						
13						
14				Date of Application for Enrollment.	Dec 4/99	
15						
16						
17						

Choctaw By Blood Enrollment Cards 1898-1914

RESIDENCE: Atoka   COUNTY. **Choctaw Nation**   **Choctaw Roll** CARD NO.
POST OFFICE: Guertie, I.T.   *(Not Including Freedmen)* FIELD NO. 4941

Dawes' Roll No.	NAME	Relationship to Person First Named	AGE	SEX	BLOOD	TRIBAL ENROLLMENT		
						Year	County	No.
DEAD.	1 Lewis, John DEAD		63	M	Full	1896	Atoka	8343
	2							
	3							
	4							
	5							
	6							
	7							
	8 No. 1 HEREON DISMISSED UNDER							
	9 ORDER OF THE COMMISSION TO THE FIVE							
	10 CIVILIZED TRIBES OF MARCH 31, 1905.							
	11							
	12							
	13							
	14							
	15							
	16							
	17							

TRIBAL ENROLLMENT OF PARENTS

	Name of Father	Year	County	Name of Mother	Year	County
1		Dead	Choctaw		Dead	Choctaw
2						
3						
4						
5						
6	Nº1 is husband of Jullecher Lewis on Creek card #3415 and father of Nºˢ 2-3-4&5 thereon					
7	Nº1 is father of Thompson and Dickson Lewis on Chickasaw card #337					
8	No.1 died May 8, 1902: Proof of death filed July 7, 1902					
9						
10						
11						
12						
13					Date of Application for Enrollment.	
14						
15					Dec 4/99	
16						
17						

141

Choctaw By Blood Enrollment Cards 1898-1914

RESIDENCE:	Atoka	COUNTY.								
POST OFFICE:	Atoka, I.T.									

Choctaw Nation

Choctaw Roll *(Not Including Freedmen)*

CARD NO.

FIELD NO. **4942**

Dawes' Roll No.	NAME	Relationship to Person	AGE	SEX	BLOOD	TRIBAL ENROLLMENT		
						Year	County	No.
13495	1 McGahey, George F 31	First Named	28	M	1/16	1896	Atoka	9432
I.W. 1141	2 Allen, Martha 50	Mother	50	F	I.W.			
	3							
	4							
	5							
	6							
	7							
	8							
	9							
	10							
	11							
	12							
	13							
	14							
	15							
	16							
	17							

ENROLLMENT
OF NOS. 1 HEREON
APPROVED BY THE SECRETARY
OF INTERIOR Mar 19, 1903

ENROLLMENT
OF NOS. 2 HEREON
APPROVED BY THE SECRETARY
OF INTERIOR Nov 16 1904

TRIBAL ENROLLMENT OF PARENTS

Name of Father	Year	County	Name of Mother	Year	County
1 Alex McGahey	Dead	Choctaw			non citz
2 William Hunt	"	noncitizen	Mary Jackson	dead	" "
3					
4					
5					
6					
7					
8					
9	Admitted by Act of Council of Nov. 5,				
10					
11	On 1896 roll as G. F. McGahey				
	No 1 is son of Martha Allen on Choctaw card D 837				
12	No 1 was husband of Henrietta Horton on. Choctaw Card D #838				
13	No.2 transferred from Choctaw card #D-837, Oct 31, 1904: see decision of Oct. 15, 1904				
14				Date of Application for Enrollment.	
15				Dec 4/99	
16					
17	No.2 P.O. Cliff, I.T.				

Choctaw By Blood Enrollment Cards 1898-1914

RESIDENCE: Creek Nation	COUNTY.							CARD NO.	
POST OFFICE: Muskogee, I.T.	**Choctaw Nation**					**Choctaw Roll** *(Not Including Freedmen)*		FIELD NO. **4943**	

Dawes' Roll No.	NAME	Relationship to Person First Named	AGE	SEX	BLOOD	TRIBAL ENROLLMENT		
						Year	County	No.
1	~~Nevins, Julia~~	~~Named~~	~~43~~	~~F~~	~~1/2~~	~~1896~~	~~Atoka~~	~~9849~~
2								
3	~~Apr. 19 1906~~							
4	Decision Rendered							
5	~~Refused~~							
6								
7	Copy of Decision forwarded							
8	Attorneys for Choctaw and ~~Chickasaw Nations~~ ~~Apr 19 1906~~							
9								
10	Copy of Decision Forwarded							
11	Applicant Apr 19 1906							
12								
13	Record Forwarded Department							
14	Apr 19 1906							
15								
16								
17								

TRIBAL ENROLLMENT OF PARENTS

	Name of Father	Year	County	Name of Mother	Year	County
1	~~Lowes G Garland~~	~~Dead~~	~~Choctaw~~	~~Aurilla Garland~~	~~Dead~~	~~Choctaw~~
2						
3						
4				Action Approved by		
5				Secretary of Interior		
6				Oct 16 1906		
7	Feby 6th 1901 Julia Nevins on this date elects to be enrolled as			Notice of Departmental action		
8	a Cherokee and relinquishes all her right title and interest			forwarded attorney for Choctaw		
9	in and to the property and tribal funds of the Choctaw Nation.			and Chickasaw Nations Oct 26 1906		
10	Son on Card No D 533			~~Notice of Departmental~~		
11	No.1 Enrolled Aug 29, 1900 on Cherokee card #2206			action mailed applicant		
12	Elects to be ennrolled[sic] as a Cherokee; see testimony filed in Cherokee #2206			Oct 26 1906		
13	Has resided in Cherokee Nation ever since 1867			Date of Application for Enrollment.		
14	Never enrolled in Choctaw Nation until 1896		Claims			
15	to be on Cherokee roll of 1880 Has been ~~recognized as Cherokee citizen since 1867~~			Dec 4/99		
16	(By direction of A S McK) Intermarried with a Cherokee					
17						

143

Choctaw By Blood Enrollment Cards 1898-1914

Dawes' Roll No.	NAME		Relationship to Person	AGE	SEX	BLOOD	TRIBAL ENROLLMENT		
							Year	County	No.
13496	1 Gore, John	45	First Named	42	M	1/2	1893	Atoka	372
13497	2 " Minnie L	13	Dau	10	F	1/4	1893	"	373
	3								
	4								
	5								
	6								
	7								
	8								
	9 ENROLLMENT								
	10 OF NOS. 1 & 2 HEREON APPROVED BY THE SECRETARY								
	11 OF INTERIOR MAR 19 1903								
	12								
	13								
	14								
	15								
	16								
	17								

TRIBAL ENROLLMENT OF PARENTS

	Name of Father	Year	County	Name of Mother	Year	County
1	William Gore	Dead	Non Citz	Jane Gore	Dead	Kiamitia
2	No 1				"	Non Citz
3						
4						
5						
6			No1 on 1893 Pay Roll, Page 36, No 372, Atoka Co, as John Goore			
7			No2 " 1893 " " " 36 " 373 " " " Minnie Lee "			
8						
9			As to marriage of parents of No2, see testimony of			
10			William H Harrison			
11						
12						
13						Date of Application for Enrollment.
14						
15						Dec 5/99
16						
17	No.2 Hugo Okla					

144

RESIDENCE:	Towson	COUNTY.								

Choctaw Nation
(Not Including Freedmen)

Choctaw Roll

CARD NO.

FIELD NO. 494

Dawes' Roll No.	NAME	Relationship to Person First Named	AGE	SEX	BLOOD	TRIBAL ENROLLMENT		
						Year	County	No.
1	Aaron, Sillin	51	48	F	Full	1896	Towson	218
2								
3								
4								
5								
6								
7								
8								
9								
10								
11								
12								
13								
14								
15								
16								
17								

DEC 16 1902

CANCELLED

Duplicate of No. 2; Sealy Aaron, on Choctaw card #1355

TRIBAL ENROLLMENT OF PARENTS

	Name of Father	Year	County	Name of Mother	Year	County
1						
2						
3						
4						
5						
6						
7						
8	No other information could be					
9	obtained.					
10						
11						
12						
13						
14				Date of Application for Enrollment.		
15				Dec 5/99		
16						
17						

Choctaw By Blood Enrollment Cards 1898-1914

RESIDENCE:	Towson	COUNTY.	**Choctaw Nation**		**Choctaw Roll** *(Not Including Freedmen)*	CARD NO.
POST OFFICE:						FIELD NO. 4946

Dawes' Roll No.	NAME	Relationship to Person First Named	AGE	SEX	BLOOD	TRIBAL ENROLLMENT		
						Year	County	No.
DP	1 James, Labard 16		13	M	Full	1896	Towson	6787
	2							
	3							
	4							
	5							
	6							
	7							
	8							
	9							
	10							
	11							
	12							
	13							
	14							
	15							
	16							
	17							

DISMISSED
JAN 30 19__

TRIBAL ENROLLMENT OF PARENTS

	Name of Father	Year	County	Name of Mother	Year	County
1						
2						
3						
4						
5						
6						
7						
8	No other information could be					
9	obtained.					
10						
11						
12						
13					Date of Application for Enrollment.	
14						
15					Dec 5/99	
16						
17						

Choctaw By Blood Enrollment Cards 1898-1914

RESIDENCE: Atoka COUNTY. **Choctaw Nation** **Choctaw Roll** CARD NO.
POST OFFICE: Kiowa, I.T. *(Not Including Freedmen)* FIELD NO. 4947

Dawes' Roll No.	NAME	Relationship to Person	AGE	SEX	BLOOD	TRIBAL ENROLLMENT		
						Year	County	No.
13499	1 Holmes, Aaron 57	First Named	54	M	Full	1893	Tobucksy	404
13500	2 " Mary 63	Wife	60	F	"	1893	"	405
	3							
	4							
	5							
	6							
	7							
	8	ENROLLMENT						
	9	OF NOS. 1 & 2 ~ HEREON APPROVED BY THE SECRETARY						
	10	OF INTERIOR MAR 9 1903						
	11							
	12							
	13							
	14							
	15							
	16							
	17							

TRIBAL ENROLLMENT OF PARENTS

	Name of Father	Year	County	Name of Mother	Year	County
1	Ta-ih-cha	Dead	Gaines	Knih-ta-ie	Dead	Tobucksy
2	Na-chi-huttubbi	"	Choctaw	Ik-bo-hona	"	Atoka
3						
4						
5						
6						
7		No1 on 1893 Pay Roll, Page 44, No 404				
8		Tobucksy Co, as Aaron Holmes.				
9		No2 on 1893 Pay Roll, Page 44, No 405				
10		Tobucksy Co, as Mary Homes				
11						
12						
13						
14						
15				Date of Application for Enrollment.	Dec 5/99	
16						
17						

147

Choctaw By Blood Enrollment Cards 1898-1914

RESIDENCE: Atoka COUNTY.
POST OFFICE: Stringtown, I.T.

Choctaw Nation

Choctaw Roll
(Not Including Freedmen)

CARD NO.
FIELD NO. **4948**

Dawes' Roll No.	NAME	Relationship to Person First Named	AGE	SEX	BLOOD	TRIBAL ENROLLMENT Year	County	No.
13501	1 Hall, William 57	First Named	54	M	Full	1896	Atoka	6006
13502	2 " Caroline 27	Wife	24	F	1/4	1896	"	6007
	3							
	4							
	5							
	6							
	7	ENROLLMENT						
	8	OF NOS. 1&2 HEREON APPROVED BY THE SECRETARY						
	9	OF INTERIOR Mar 19 1903						
	10							
	11							
	12							
	13							
	14							
	15							
	16							
	17							

TRIBAL ENROLLMENT OF PARENTS

Name of Father	Year	County	Name of Mother	Year	County
1 Jim Hall	Dead	Choctaw		Dead	Choctaw
2 Lee Tiner	"	"	Jennie Hogewood		Choctaw
3					
4					
5					
6					
7					
8		As to citizenship of No2, see testimony			
9		Julius C Folsom, taken this day			
10					
11		Nos 1&2 have separated			
12		For child of No2 see NB (Apr 26-06) card #352			
13				Date of Application for Enrollment.	
14					
15				Dec 5/99	
16		Marriage Certificate P.300 Atoka Co Choctaw Nation			
17					

148

Choctaw By Blood Enrollment Cards 1898-1914

RESIDENCE: Chickasaw Nation COUNTY. **Choctaw Nation** **Choctaw Roll** CARD No.
POST OFFICE: Tishomingo, I.T. (Not Including Freedmen) FIELD No. 4949

Dawes' Roll No.	NAME		Relationship to Person	AGE	SEX	BLOOD	TRIBAL ENROLLMENT		
							Year	County	No.
13503	1 Folsom, John	36	First Named	33	M	1/2	1896	Chick Dist	4561
	2								
	3								
	4								
	5								
	6								
	7								
	8								
	9								
	10								
	11								
	12								
	13								
	14								
	15								
	16								
	17								

ENROLLMENT
OF NOS. ~~~ 1 ~~~ HEREON
APPROVED BY THE SECRETARY
OF INTERIOR   MAR 19 1903

TRIBAL ENROLLMENT OF PARENTS

	Name of Father	Year	County	Name of Mother	Year	County
1	Loring Folsom		Blue	Rhoda Morris		Choctaw
2						
3						
4						
5						
6						
7						
8	On 1896 roll as John Fulsom					
9						
10						
11						
12						
13						Date of Application
14						for Enrollment.
15						Dec 5/99
16						
17						

Choctaw By Blood Enrollment Cards 1898-1914

RESIDENCE: **Chickasaw Nation** COUNTY. **Choctaw**  **Roll** CARD No.
POST OFFICE: **Homer, I.T.** (Not Including Freedmen) FIELD No. **4950**

Dawes' Roll No.	NAME		Relationship to Person First Named	AGE	SEX	BLOOD	TRIBAL ENROLLMENT		
							Year	County	No.
13504	1 Morris, Rhoda S	60	First Named	57	F	1/4	1896	Chick Dist	8943
	2								
	3								
	4								
	5								
	6								
	7								
	8								
	9	ENROLLMENT							
	10	OF NOS. 1 HEREON APPROVED BY THE SECRETARY							
	11	OF INTERIOR MAR 19 1903							
	12								
	13								
	14								
	15								
	16								
	17								

TRIBAL ENROLLMENT OF PARENTS

	Name of Father	Year	County	Name of Mother	Year	County
1	Emziah Robinson	Dead	Non Citz	Emily Folsom	Dead	Eagle
2						
3						
4						
5						
6						
7						
8						
9						
10						
11						
12						
13					Date of Application for Enrollment.	
14						
15					Dec 5/99	
16						
17						

150

Choctaw By Blood Enrollment Cards 1898-1914

RESIDENCE: Chickasaw Nation COUNTY. **Choctaw Nation**
POST OFFICE: Connorville[sic], I.T.

Choctaw Roll   CARD No
FIELD No. 3951

Dawes' Roll No.	NAME	Relationship to Person First Named	AGE	SEX	BLOOD	TRIBAL ENROLLMENT		
						Year	County	No.
1	Anderson, Martha		24	F	Full			
2	Perry, Isaac	Son	4	M	1/2			
3								
4								
5								
6								
7								
8								
9								
10								
11								
12								
13								
14								
15								
16								
17								

TRIBAL ENROLLMENT OF PARENTS

	Name of Father	Year	County	Name of Mother	Year	County
1	McKee King	Dead	Blue		Dead	Choctaw
2	Houston Perry	"	Chickasaw	No1		
3						
4						
5						
6						
7						
8						
9		No1 wife of Rogers Anderson- Chickasaw				
10						
11		No1 on 1897 Chickasaw Roll, Page 54, Pontotoc Co				
12		No2 " 1897 " " " 54, " "				
13		Transferred to Choctaw Roll by Dawes Com			Date of Application for Enrollment	
14						
15					Dec 8/99	
16						
17						

Choctaw By Blood Enrollment Cards 1898-1914

Choctaw Nation

Choctaw Roll
(Not Including Freedmen)

CARD NO. FIELD NO. 4952

Dawes' Roll No.	NAME	Relationship to Person First Named	AGE	SEX	BLOOD	TRIBAL ENROLLMENT		
						Year	County	No.
14912	1 Christie, Ellis ⁴⁰	First Named	37	M	Full	1893	Atoka	171
	2							
	3							
	4							
	5							
	6							
	7							
	8							
	9							
	10							
	11							
	12							
	13							
	14							
	15							
	16							
	17							

ENROLLMENT
OF NOS. 1 HEREON
APPROVED BY THE SECRETARY
OF INTERIOR MAY 21 1903

TRIBAL ENROLLMENT OF PARENTS

	Name of Father	Year	County	Name of Mother	Year	County
1		Dead	Choctaw		Dead	Choctaw
2						
3						
4						
5						
6						
7						
8	On 1893 Pay Roll, Page 16, No 171,					
9	Atoka Co, as Ellis Christy					
10						
11						
12						
13						
14				Date of Application for Enrollment.		
15				Dec 8/99		
16						
17						

Choctaw By Blood Enrollment Cards 1898-1914

Dawes' Roll No.	NAME		Relationship to Person	AGE	SEX	BLOOD	TRIBAL ENROLLMENT		
							Year	County	No.
13506	1 King, Charles	28	First Named	25	M	Full	1896	Sans Bois	7437
13507	2 " Calvin	4	Son	1	"	7/8			
	3								
	4								
	5								
	6								
	7								
	8								
	9								
	10		ENROLLMENT						
	11		OF NOS. 1&2 HEREON APPROVED BY THE SECRETARY						
	12		OF INTERIOR Mar. 19, 1903						
	13								
	14								
	15								
	16								
	17								

TRIBAL ENROLLMENT OF PARENTS

	Name of Father	Year	County	Name of Mother	Year	County
1	Davis King	Dead	Skullyville	Louisa King	Dead	Sans Bois
2	No1			Levenia King		
3						
4						
5						
6						
7	No2 affidavit requested Received and filed Dec. 24, 1902					
8						
9	No. 1 is husband of Levenia King on Choctaw Card #5606					
10						
11						
12						
13						
14						
15				Date of Application for Enrollment.	Dec 14/99	
16						
17						

Choctaw By Blood Enrollment Cards 1898-1914

RESIDENCE: Chickasaw Nation ~~COUNTY.~~
POST OFFICE: Bradley, I.T.

Choctaw Nation

Choctaw Roll
(Not Including Freedmen)

CARD NO.
FIELD NO. **4954**

Dawes' Roll No.	NAME	Relationship to Person First Named	AGE	SEX	BLOOD	TRIBAL ENROLLMENT		
						Year	County	No.
1	Dunn, Mattie ✱	First Named	46	F	1/8		D	
2	" Hope	Son	8	M	1/16		D	
3	" John	"	6	"	1/16		D	
4	Smith, Ella ✱	Dau	17	F	1/16		D	
DP 5	Dunn, Jim	Son	3	M	1/16			
DP 6	Nix, John Henry	Son of No4	5mo	M	1/32			
7								
8								
Nos 9								
5&6 10	DISMISSED							
11								
12								
13								
14								
15	Nos 1,2,3&4 DENIED CITIZENSHIP BY THE CHOCTAW AND							
16	CHICKASAW CITIZENSHIP COURT Case #90T 6/29/04							
17								

TRIBAL ENROLLMENT OF PARENTS

	Name of Father	Year	County	Name of Mother	Year	County
1	William Shields	Dead	Non Citz	Sarah Shields		Choctaw
2	W.C. Dunn		" "	No1		
3	" " "		" "	No1		
4	John Smith		" "	No1		
5	W.C. Dunn		" "	No1		
6	Hal Nix		" "	No4		
7	Nos 1 to 4 inclusive, denied by Com in 1896, Case 776					
8	All admitted by U.S. Court Southern					
9	Dist. Dec 16/99. As to residence see					
10	testimony of W^m C Dunn					
11	No5 transferred from Choctaw R.393					
12	June 5th, 1900					
13	No.4 now the wife of Hal Nix Non Citizen: June 30th 1902 Evidence of marriage filed July 15th 1902					
14	No6 Born Feb 3rd-1902: Enrolled June 30th 1902					
15	Judgement[sic] of U.S. Ct admitting No1 to 4 incl vacated and set aside by Decree of Choctaw Chickasaw Ct^zen 12/7/02					
16	Nos 1 to 4 incl now in C.C.C.C. Case #90T					
17						

Date of Application for Enrollment.

154

Choctaw By Blood Enrollment Cards 1898-1914

RESIDENCE: Chickasaw Nation COUNTY. **Choctaw Nation** Choctaw Roll CARD NO.
POST OFFICE: Bradley I.T. (Not Including Freedmen) FIELD NO. **4955**

Dawes' Roll No.	NAME	Relationship to Person First Named	AGE	SEX	BLOOD	TRIBAL ENROLLMENT		
						Year	County	No.
1	Shields, Sarah ✳		78	F	1/4		D	
2								
3								
4								
5								
6								
7								
8								
9								
10								
11								
12								
13								
14								
15								
16								
17								

TRIBAL ENROLLMENT OF PARENTS

	Name of Father	Year	County	Name of Mother	Year	County
1			Choctaw			Non Citiz
2						
3						
4						
5						
6	No1 denied - 96 Case #776					
7	Admitted by U.S. Court Southern Dist, Case No. 118					
8	Dec 16/99. As to residence see testimony					
9	of Wᵐ C Dunn					
10	Judgement[sic] of U.S. Ct admitting No1 vacated and set aside by Decree of Choctaw Chickasaw Citizenship Court Dec 17'02					
11	No.1 now in C.C.C.C. Case #90T					
12						
13						
14					Date of Application for Enrollment.	
15					Dec 19/99	
16						
17						

Choctaw By Blood Enrollment Cards 1898-1914

RESIDENCE:	Chickasaw Natn	Choctaw **Nation**	Choctaw **Roll**		CARD NO.	**4956**
POST OFFICE:	Iona, I.T.				FIELD NO.	C 1

Dawes' Roll No.	NAME	Relationship to Person First Named	AGE	SEX	BLOOD	TRIBAL ENROLLMENT		
						Year	County	No.
1	Goodall, Charles		73	M	1/4		D	
2	" Mary	Wife	49	F			DIS	
3								
4								
5								
6								
7								
8								
9								
10								
11								
12								
13								
14								
15								
16								
17								

#2- DISMISSED
NOV 12 1904

No.1 DENIED CITIZENSHIP BY THE CHOCTAW AND CHICKASAW CITIZENSHIP COURT 521 Sept 1904

TRIBAL ENROLLMENT OF PARENTS

	Name of Father	Year	County	Name of Mother	Year	County
1	Wm Goodall	Dead	Non Citz	Betsy Goodall	Dead	Choctaw
2	John Brown	"	" "		"	Part Cherokee
3						
4						
5						
6						
7	No.1 denied by Commission in 1896 case No 258					
8	Nos 1&2 were admitted by the U.S. Court Southern Dist					
9	Case #103					
10						
11						
12						
13						
14	No2 Dismissed by C.C.C., 521 Sept 19'04. The Court not [illegible]					
15	No1 denied by C.C.C.C. as Charles Goodall or Chas Goodall					
16						
17					Date of Application for Enrollment.	9-6-98

156

RESIDENCE:	Chickasaw Natn							CARD NO.	**4957**
POST OFFICE:	Iona, I.T.	Choctaw **Nation**		Choctaw **Roll**				FIELD NO.	C 2

Dawes' Roll No.	NAME	Relationship to Person First Named	AGE	SEX	BLOOD	TRIBAL ENROLLMENT		
						Year	County	No.
1	Goodall, Richard	Named	47	M	1/8		Dis	
2	" Bettie	Wife	40	F			Dis	
3	" Andy	Son	16	M	1/16		Dis	
4	" Monroe	"	14	"	"		Dis	
5	" George	"	12	"	"			
6	" Mollie	Dau	8	F	"			
7								
8								
9								
10								
11	Nos 1 3 4 5 and 6, being void [illegible]							
12	[illegible]							
13	[illegible]							
#2-3-4 5-6								
16	NOV 18 1904							
17								

TRIBAL ENROLLMENT OF PARENTS

	Name of Father	Year	County	Name of Mother	Year	County
1	Chas Goodall			Mary Goodall	Dead	Non Citz
2	James Brown	Dead	Non Citz	Liddy Brown		
3	No1			No2		
4	No1			No2		
5	No1			No2		
6	No1			No2		
7	From 2 to 6 inclusive, void: Court at Ardmore having declared them improperly admitted.					
8	No.1 denied by Com in 1896 Case #258					
9	Nos 1 to 6 inclusive were admitted by the U.S. Court, Southern Dist, Ardmore I.T.					
10	Case No 103					
11	No5 is not found on roll of applicants admitted by U.S. Court Southern Dist					
12	[illegible]					
13	[illegible]					
14	DENIED CITIZENSHIP BY THE CHOCTAW AND					
15	CHICKASAW CITIZENSHIP COURT					1 28
16						
17				Date of Application for Enrollment	9/6/98	

157

Choctaw By Blood Enrollment Cards 1898-1914

RESIDENCE: Chickasaw Natn
POST OFFICE: Palmer, I.T.

Choctaw **Nation** Choctaw **Roll**

CARD NO. **4958**
FIELD NO. C 3

Dawes' Roll No.	NAME	Relationship to Person First Named	AGE	SEX	BLOOD	TRIBAL ENROLLMENT		
						Year	County	No.
1	Goodall, William	First Named	43	M	1/8		Dis	
2	" Elizabeth	Wife	39	F			Dis	
3	" Mary J	Dau	15	"	1/16		Dis	
4	" Dixie	Son	12	M	"		Dis	
5	" Rosa L	Dau	10	F	"		Dis	
6	" Maud F	"	7	"	"		Dis	
7	" Annie	"	5	"	"		Dis	
8	" Willie M	Son	3	M	"		Dis	
9	" Floy L	Dau	11mo	F	"			
10	" Effie	Dau	1 da	F	1/16			
11	Nos 2,3,4,5,6,7 and 8 dismissed by							
12	C.C. Case #521 Sept 1 1904 The Court							
13	having no jurisdiction							
14								
15								
16								
17								

#2-3-4-5
6-7-8-9-10 }

DISMISSED
NOV 18 1904

See P. C - 33

TRIBAL ENROLLMENT OF PARENTS

	Name of Father	Year	County	Name of Mother	Year	County
1	Chas Goodall			Mary Goodall	Dead	Non Citz
2	Edward Evans	Dead	Non Citz	Mary E Evans	"	"
3	No1			No2		
4	No1			No2		
5	No1			No2		
6	No1			No2		
7	No1			No2		
8	No1 No1			No2		
9	No1			Mary E Goodall		Non Citz
10	No1			"		"
11	From No.2 to No.8 inclusive, void; Court at Ardmore having declared them improperly admitted.					
12	No.1 denied by Com in 1896 Case #758			Southern Dist		
13	Nos 1 to 8 inclusive were admitted by the U.S. Court ^ Ardmore I.T.					
14	Case No 103			No9 enrolled Nov 23/99		
15	Judgement as to U.S. C. admitting No1 vacated and set aside by Decree of C.C.C. Dec 17 '02					
16	No. 10 born Dec 1 1901 Enrolled Dec. 7, 1901					1/28
17	No 9 also appears on Choctaw Card D-463					

Date of Application for Enrollment. 9/6/98

No1 to 8 incl now in C.C. C.C. Case #521

Choctaw By Blood Enrollment Cards 1898-1914

RESIDENCE: Chickasaw Natn   Choctaw **Nation**   Choctaw **Roll**   CARD NO. **4959**
POST OFFICE: Palmer, I.T.   FIELD NO.   C 4

Dawes' Roll No.	NAME	Relationship to Person First Named	AGE	SEX	BLOOD	TRIBAL ENROLLMENT Year	County	No.
1	Hill, Amanda		40	F	1/8		Dis	
2	" John W	Son	21	M	1/16		Dis	
3	" Sam	"	18	"	"		Dis	
4	" Ollie	Dau	17	F	1/16		Dis	
5	" Laura	"	15	"	"		Dis	
6	" Mollie	"	13	"	"		Dis	
7	" Bradley T	Son	9	M	"			
8	" Ada	Dau	7	F	"			
9	" Georgia H	Son	3	M	"			
10	" James R	"	1	"	"			
11	#2-3-4-5-6| 7-8-9-10]	DISMISSED						
12								
13	This family moved from							
14	Texas to the Chickasaw Natn about the middle of October, 1898							
15								
16								
17								

TRIBAL ENROLLMENT OF PARENTS

	Name of Father	Year	County	Name of Mother	Year	County
1	Chas Goodall			Mary Goodall	Dead	Non Citz
2	Geo. Hill		Non Citz	No 1		
3	" "		" "	No 1		
4	" "		" "	No 1		
5	" "		" "	No 1		
6	" "		" "	No 1		
7	" "		" "	No 1		
8	" "		" "	No 1		
9	" "		" "	No 1		
10	" "		" "	No 1		
11	No10 was born Nov					
12	No. 1 denied by Com in 1896, case #258					
13	Nos 1 to 9 inclusive were admitted by the U.S. Court					
14	Judgement[sic] of U.S. C admitting No1 vacated and set aside [remainder illegible]					
15	Southern Dist. Ardmore I.T. Case No 103					
16	No10 is not found on roll of applicants admitted by U.S. Court					
17	Nos 1 to 6 incl new in C.C.C.C. Case #521					

DENIED CITIZENSHIP BY THE CHOCTAW AND CHICKASAW CITIZENSHIP COURT

Choctaw By Blood Enrollment Cards 1898-1914

RESIDENCE: Chickasaw Natn
POST OFFICE: Iona, I.T.

Choctaw **Nation** Choctaw **Roll**

CARD NO. **4960**
FIELD NO. C

Dawes' Roll No.	NAME	Relationship to Person First Named	AGE	SEX	BLOOD	TRIBAL ENROLLMENT		
						Year	County	No.
1	Hill, Harriett	Named	35	F	1/8		Dis	
2	" Geo T	Son	16	M	1/16		Dis	
3	" James	"	14	"	"		Dis	
4	" Rosa	Dau	12	F	"		Dis	
5	" Silas	Son	9	M	"		Dis	
6	" John	"	8	"	"		Dis	
7	" Amos 9	"	5	"	"		Dis	
8	" Cora F 7	Dau	3	F	"		Dis	
9	" Jesse H 5	Son	1	M	"			
10	" Loyd Monroe 1	Son	1mo	M	"			
11								
12	This family moved from							
13	Texas to the Chickasaw Natn							
	about the middle of							
14	October, 1898							
	#2-3-4-5-							
	6-7-8-9-10	DISMISSED						
17		NOV 18 1904						

TRIBAL ENROLLMENT OF PARENTS

	Name of Father	Year	County	Name of Mother	Year	County
1	Chas Goodall			Mary Goodall	Dead	Non Citz
2	Sam Hill		Non Citz	No 1		
3	" "		" "	No 1		
4	" "		" "	No 1		
5	" "		" "	No 1		
6	" "		" "	No 1		
7	" "		" "	No 1		
8	" "			No 1		
9	" "					
10	" "		" "	No 1		

DENIED CITIZENSHIP BY THE CHOCTAW AND CHICKASAW CITIZENSHIP COURT

11   No1 denied by Com in 96 case #258 [illegible...]

12   Nos 1 to 8 inclusive were admitted by the U.S. Court Southern Dist, I.T.

13

14   No9 was born August 16th 1897   No10 Enrolled Aug 27, 1901

15

16   No9 is not found on roll of applicants admitted by U.S.Court Southern Dist.

17   Court case #103

Date of Application for Enrollment   9-6-98

160

Choctaw By Blood Enrollment Cards 1898-1914

RESIDENCE: Chickasaw Natn
POST OFFICE: Palmer, I.T.

Choctaw **Nation** Choctaw **Roll**

CARD NO. **4961**
FIELD NO. C

Dawes' Roll No.	NAME	Relationship to Person First Named	AGE	SEX	BLOOD	TRIBAL ENROLLMENT Year	TRIBAL ENROLLMENT County	TRIBAL ENROLLMENT No.
1	Arms, Nancy J	First Named	37	F	1/8			
2	" James A	Son	19	M	1/16		Dis	
3	" Oran J	"	16	"	"		Dis	
4	" Amos L	"	14	"	"		Dis	
5	" Charles	"	12	"	"		Dis	
6	" Nicholas	"	12	"	"		Dis	
7	" Lorin	"	8	"	"		Dis	
8	" Eunice	Dau	6	F	"		Dis	
9	" Laura T	"	5	"	"		Dis	
10								
11	Nos 2,3,4,5,6,7,8 and 9 dismissed by							
12	C.C.C.C. Case (illegible) Sept 1 1901							
13	The Court having no jurisdiction							
14	#2,3-4-5							
15	6,7-8-9							
16								
17								

#2,3-4-5 DISMISSED
6,7-8-9 NOV 13 1904

TRIBAL ENROLLMENT OF PARENTS

	Name of Father	Year	County	Name of Mother	Year	County
1	Chas Goodall			Mary Goodall	Dead	Non Citz
2	Thos Arms	Dead	Non Citz	No 1		
3	" "	"	" "	No 1		
4	" "	"	" "	No 1		
5	" "	"	" "	No 1		
6	" "	"	" "	No 1		
7	" "	"	" "	No 1		
8	" "	"	" "	No 1		
9	" "	"	" "	No 1		
10	No 1 denied by Com in 1896, Case No 258					
11	Nos 1 to 9 inclusive were admitted by the US Court, Southern Dist, Ardmore, I.T.					
12	Case No 103					
13	Nos 5&6 are twins					
14						
15						
16	No 1 denied by C.C.C.C. as Nancy J Ozbirn (nee Arms) or Nancy Arms					
17	For child of No 1 see NB 1011 (Act Apr 26-'06)					

DENIED CITIZENSHIP BY THE CHOCTAW AND CHICKASAW CITIZENSHIP COURT

Date of Application for Enrollment 9-6-99

161

Choctaw By Blood Enrollment Cards 1898-1914

RESIDENCE: Chickasaw Natn
POST OFFICE: Palmer, I.T.

Choctaw **Nation**   Choctaw **Roll**

CARD NO. **4962**
FIELD NO.

Dawes' Roll No.	NAME	Relationship to Person First Named	AGE	SEX	BLOOD	TRIBAL ENROLLMENT		
						Year	County	No.
1	Goodall, Cha[sic] ²⁵	Named	21	M	1/16		Dis	
2	" Sephrona ²¹	Wife	18	F			Dis	
3	" Alfred T ⁶	Son	2	M	1/32		Dis	
4	" Mary E ⁵	Dau	1	F	"		Dis	
5	" James Luther	Son		M	1/32			
6								
7								
8								
9	#1-2-3-4-5- DISMISSED							
10								
11								
12								
13								
14								
15								
16								
17								

TRIBAL ENROLLMENT OF PARENTS

	Name of Father	Year	County	Name of Mother	Year	County
1	Wm Goodall			Elizabeth Goodall		Non Citz
2	Hobbs		Non Citz	Rhoda Hobbs		" "
3	No 1			No 2		
4	No 1			No 2		
5	No 1					
6						
7						
8	zz Original recommendation for N⁵ was made July 30, 1900					
9	Not original applicants in 1896 in case #258					
10	Nos 1 to 4 inclusive were admitted by the U.S. Court Southern Dist. Ardmore, I.T.					
11	Case No 103					
12						
13						
14						
15						
16						
17						

162

Choctaw By Blood Enrollment Cards 1898-1914

RESIDENCE: Chickasaw Natn
POST OFFICE: Iona, I.T.

Choctaw **Nation**   Choctaw **Roll**

CARD NO. **4963**
FIELD NO. C

Dawes' Roll No.	NAME	Relationship to Person First Named	AGE	SEX	BLOOD	TRIBAL ENROLLMENT		
						Year	County	No.
1	Goodall, John	36	32	M	1/8		D	
2	" John H	10 Son	4	"	1/16		Dis	
3	" Charles B	5 "	1	"	"		Dis	
4	" Joseph Vester	Son	9mo	M	1/16			
5	No1 denied by Com in 1896 case #258							
6								
7								
8								
9	No 4 Rights of No 4							
10	disposed of in decision							
11	of Oct 5 1906-25-329							
12	Nos 2 and 3 dismissed by							
13	C. C. Case #521							
14	Sept 19 1913 The Court has no							
15	jurisdiction							
16	See memo No W-33							
17								

TRIBAL ENROLLMENT OF PARENTS

	Name of Father	Year	County	Name of Mother	Year	County
1	Chas Goodall			Mary Goodall	Dead	Non Citz
2	No1			Mary R Goodall		Chickasaw
3	No 1			" " "		"
4	No.1			" " "		Chickasaw
5						
6						
7						
8	~~No3 was born Feby 13 1897					
9	No 1 is the husband of Mary Goodall, claimant as an intermarried					
10	Chickasaw on Chickasaw					
11	Nos 1 to 3 inclusive were admitted by the U.S. Court, Southern Dist, Ardmore, I.T.					
12	Case No 103. Evidence of marriage of No 1 and Mary R Goodall filed Nov. 19 1901					
13						
14	No.4 born Feby 12, 1901; Enrolled Nov. 19 1901					
15						
16						
17						

Choctaw By Blood Enrollment Cards 1898-1914

RESIDENCE:	Chickasaw Natn			Choctaw **Nation**			Choctaw **Roll**	CARD NO. **4964**	
POST OFFICE:	Iona, I.T.							FIELD NO. C9	

Dawes' Roll No.	NAME	Relationship to Person First Named	AGE	SEX	BLOOD	TRIBAL ENROLLMENT		
						Year	County	No.
1	Goodall, Thomas 23	Named	19	M	1/16		Dis	
2	" Alice 22	Wife	18	F				
3	" Violet	Dau		F	1/32			
4								
5								
6								
7								
8								
9								
10	#1-2-3- DISMISSED							
11								
12								
13								
14								
15								
16								
17								

TRIBAL ENROLLMENT OF PARENTS

	Name of Father	Year	County	Name of Mother	Year	County
1	Richard Goodall			Bettie Goodall		Non Citz
2	Sid Stone		Non Citz	Mattie Stone		" "
3	N⁰ 1					
4						
5						
6						
7	No.1 not an original applicant in 1896 in case No 258					
8	No1 was admitted by the US Court, Southern Dist, Ardmore, I.T.					
9						
10	No2 was married to No1, June 30, 1898 under license issued by the					
11	Clerk of the U.S. Court					
12						
13	No2 is not found on roll of applicants admitted by U.S. Court, Southern Dist					
14						
15						
16						
17						

Choctaw By Blood Enrollment Cards 1898-1914

RESIDENCE: Atoka County, Choctaw Natn   Choctaw **Nation**   Choctaw **Roll**   CARD NO. **4965**

POST OFFICE: Coalgate, I.T.   FIELD NO.

Dawes' Roll No.	NAME	Relationship to Person First Named	AGE	SEX	BLOOD	TRIBAL ENROLLMENT		
						Year	County	No.
1	MᶜCarty, Mary L		18	F				
2								
3								
4								
5								
6								
7								
8								
9								
10								
11								
12								
13								
14								
15								
16								
17								

FEB -6 1902

CANCELLED

TRIBAL ENROLLMENT OF PARENTS

	Name of Father	Year	County	Name of Mother	Year	County
1	Elza R Poole		Non Citz	Georgia A Poole		Non Citz
2						
3						
4						
5						
6						
7						
8						
9						
10						
11						
12						
13						
14						
15						
16						
17						

Choctaw By Blood Enrollment Cards 1898-1914

RESIDENCE: Atoka County, Choctaw Natn
POST OFFICE: Coalgate, I.T.

Choctaw **Nation**   Choctaw **Roll**

CARD NO. **4966**
FIELD NO. C 11

Dawes' Roll No.	NAME	Relationship to Person First Named	AGE	SEX	BLOOD	TRIBAL ENROLLMENT Year	County	No.
1	Dillard, Robert [?]	First Named	26	M				
2								
3								
4								
5								
6								
7								
8								
9								
10								
11								
12								
13								
14								
15								
16								
17								

TRIBAL ENROLLMENT OF PARENTS

	Name of Father	Year	County	Name of Mother	Year	County
1	[Illegible]		Non Citz	Sarah A Dillard	Dead	Non Citz
2						
3						
4						
5						
6	No1 denied by the Dawes Com in 1896 [Illegible] Case #1085					
7	No1 was admitted by the U.S. Court, [Illegible], age 26o [illegible]					
8	No.1 is the husband of Dora Dillard on Ch[illegible] Card #4429					
9						
10	Son Valtensa[?] I. Dillard on Card C-366 Born Nov 30/91[?]					
11						
12						
13						
14						
15						
16						
17						

166

Choctaw By Blood Enrollment Cards 1898-1914

| RESIDENCE: | State of Texas | | Choctaw **Nation** | Choctaw **Roll** | | CARD NO. | **4967** |
| POST OFFICE: | Vineyard, Texas | | | | | FIELD NO. | C |

Dawes' Roll No.	NAME		Relationship to Person First Named	AGE	SEX	BLOOD	TRIBAL ENROLLMENT		
							Year	County	No.
DEAD.	1 Ross, Belle	DEAD.	Named	19	F				
*	2 " Elmore	6	Son	2	M				
	3 " Della May	4	Dau	10mo	F				
DEAD.	4 " Mary Belle	1	Dau	1mo	F				
5	DENIED CITIZENSHIP BY THE CHOCTAW AND								
6	CHICKASAW CITIZENSHIP COURT								
7									
8									
#3	9 DISMISSED								
10	DEC 12 1904								
11									
12	No. 1 and 4 HEREON DISMISSED UNDER								
13	ORDER OF THE COMMISSION TO THE FIVE CIVILIZED TRIBES OF MARCH 31, 1905.								
14									
15									
16	1901- Post office is now Elk, I.T.								
17	1901- " " " " Belton I.T.								

TRIBAL ENROLLMENT OF PARENTS

	Name of Father	Year	County	Name of Mother	Year	County
1	Edw L Dillard		Non Citz	Sarah A Dillard	Dead	Non Citz
2	James Ross		" "	No1		
3	" "			No1		
4	" "			No1		
5	No1 was denied by the Dawes Com in 1896, Choc Cit Case #654 No2 not in the application in 1896					
6						
7						
8						
9						
10						
11	No4 Enrolled May 20, 1901					
12	No2 was admitted as John E Ross. See letter Jos. P. Mullens filed in above Court Case #63 May 20, 1901					
13	No1 Died May 20, 1901; proof of death filed April 20, 1902					
14	No4 Died Nov 14, 1901; proof of death filed April 20, 1902					
15						
16						1/33
17						

Choctaw By Blood Enrollment Cards 1898-1914

RESIDENCE: Atoka County, Choctaw Natn
POST OFFICE: Coalgate, I.T.

Choctaw **Nation**   Choctaw **Roll**

CARD NO. **4968**
FIELD NO. C 13

Dawes' Roll No.	NAME	Relationship to Person First Named	AGE	SEX	BLOOD	TRIBAL ENROLLMENT		
						Year	County	No.
DP 1	Sanders, Sarah L 27	Named	27					
2	" Samuel M 12	Son	8					
3	" Arthur D 11	"	7					
4	" Carl H	"	5					
5	" Lessie R	Dau	3					
6	" William V 5	Son	1					
DP 7	" Fanny V	Dau	5mo					
DP 8	" Charles Edward 2	Son	2mo					
9								
10								
11								
12								
13	#1-7-8- DISMISSED							
14								
15								
16								
17								

TRIBAL ENROLLMENT OF PARENTS

	Name of Father	Year	County	Name of Mother	Year	County
1	Edw L Dillard		Non Citz	Sarah A Dillard	Dead	Non Citz
2	Chas B Sanders		" "	No1		
3	" " "		" "	No1		
4	" " "		" "	No1		
5	" " "		" "	No1		
6	" " "		" "	No1		
7	" " "		" "	No1		
8	" " "		" "	No.1		
9	Nos1 to 6 inclusive were admitted by the U.S. Court Central Dist Case No 63					
10	Nos1 to 6 inclusive denied by Dawes Com in 1896 Choc Cit Case #835					
11	No6 was born April 19, 1897					
12						
13						
14						
15				No.7 Enrolled May 24, 1900		
16		No.8 Born Feby 1, 1902: enrolled April 2, 1902				
17	[Illegible . . . . to light to read]					

DENIED CITIZENSHIP BY THE CHOCTAW AND CHICKASAW CITIZENSHIP COURT

Date of Application for Enrollment 4753
9-7-98

168

RESIDENCE:	Atoka County, Choctaw Natn							
POST OFFICE:	Coalgate, I.T.	Choctaw **Nation**		Choctaw **Roll**		CARD NO. **4969**		
						FIELD NO. C 14		

Dawes' Roll No.	NAME	Relationship to Person	AGE	SEX	BLOOD	TRIBAL ENROLLMENT		
						Year	County	No.
DEAD.	1 Poole, Georgia A	First Named	34	F				
*	2 " Chas U	Son	14	M				
*	3 " Thos F	"	13	"				
*	4 " Edward S	"	10	"				
*	5 " Myrtie M	Dau	8	F				
*	6 " Montie R	"	6	"				
131	7 " Elzy A	Son	2	M				
132	8 " Maggie May	Dau	8mo	F				
	9 " John Everett 2	Son	6wk	M				

Decision of U.S. Court Central District case set aside
aside by decree of Choctaw Chickasaw Citizenship Court
Dec' 17 1902. The Citizenship Court on Jan 20 1904 denied
the application for admission of Nos 1 to 6 inclusive as
citizens of the Choctaw Nation and the rights flowing
therefrom Case #43

No. 1 HEREON DISMISSED UNDER
ORDER OF THE COMMISSION TO THE FIVE
CIVILIZED TRIBES OF MARCH 31, 1905.

P.O. Address is now Elk, I.T. March 14, 1901

#8 and 9- DISMISSED NOV 17 1904   #7 DISMISSED JAN 26 1905

TRIBAL ENROLLMENT OF PARENTS

	Name of Father	Year	County	Name of Mother	Year	County
1	Edw L Dillard		Non Citz	Sarah A Dillard	Dead	Non Citz
2	Elzy R Poole		" "	No 1		
3	" " "		" "	No 1		
4	" " "		" "	No 1		
5	" " "		" "	No 1		
6	" " "		" "	No 1		
7	" " "		" "	No 1		
8	" " "		" "	No 1		
9	" " "		" "	No.1		
10						
11						
12						
13						
14						
15						
16						
17						

DENIED CITIZENSHIP BY THE CHOCTAW AND
CHICKASAW CITIZENSHIP COURT

Date of Application for Enrollment 1/33
9-7-98

Choctaw By Blood Enrollment Cards 1898-1914

RESIDENCE: Atoka County, Choctaw Natn
POST OFFICE: Coalgate, I.T.

Choctaw **Nation**   Choctaw **Roll**

CARD NO. **4970**
FIELD NO. C 15

Dawes' Roll No.	NAME	Relationship to Person First Named	AGE	SEX	BLOOD	TRIBAL ENROLLMENT Year	County	No.
✓ * 1	Sanders, Mary A	First Named	37	F				
✓ * 2	" Wm H	Son	11	M				
✓ * 3	" Dollie E	Dau	10	F				
✓ * 4	" Sarah P	"	8	"				
✓ 5	" Luther F	Son	5	M				
✓ * 6	" Emmett G	"	2	"				
✓ 7	" Archey L	"	6mo	"				
✓ 8	" Bessie May	Dau	1mo	F				
9								
10								
Nos 7 & 8 MAY 27 1904 DISMISSED								
12								
13								
14								
15								
16								
17 1900- Ardmore IT								

TRIBAL ENROLLMENT OF PARENTS

	Name of Father	Year	County	Name of Mother	Year	County
1	Edw L Dillard		Non Citz	Sarah A Dillard	Dead	Non Citz
2	J. A. Sanders		" "	No1		
3	" "		" "	No1		
4	" "		" "	No1		
5	DENIED CITIZENSHIP BY THE CHOCTAW AND		"	No1		
6	CHICKASAW CITIZENSHIP COURT		" "	No1		
7	" "		" "	No1		
8	" "		" "	No1		
9	Nos 1 to 6 inclusive denied by Dawes Commission in 1896 Choc Cit Case #789					
10	Nos 1 to 6 inclusive were admitted by the U.S. Court Central				63	
11						
12	No7 was born Feby 3rd					
13						
14	No 8 Enrolled June 23d 1900					
15	Husband of No1 and father of children on this card is on Choctaw Card #11436					
16	* Decision of U.S. Court Central District vacated and set aside by Decree of				Date of Application for Enrollment	1/33
17	Choctaw Chickasaw Cit Court Decr 17 '02 [remainder illegible]					9-7-98

170

Choctaw By Blood Enrollment Cards 1898-1914

RESIDENCE: Choctaw Natn Sans Bois County   Choctaw **Nation**   Choctaw **Roll**   CARD NO. **4971**
POST OFFICE: Enterprise, I.T.   FIELD NO.   C

Dawes' Roll No.	NAME	Relationship to Person First Named	AGE	SEX	BLOOD	TRIBAL ENROLLMENT		
						Year	County	No.
1	Martin Mary [R or B]	Named	32	F				
2	" Caid[illegible]	Dau	14	"				
3	" James H	Son	11	M				
4	" George W	"	10	"				
5	" Rosa C	Dau	3	F				
DP 6	" Alice F	"	6mo	"				
7	" Robt Lawrence	Son	5	M				
DP 8	" Mary Eveline	Dau	5mo	F				
9								
#6&8 10	DISMISSED DEC 12 1904							
11								
12								
13	For child of No1 see NB #1004 (Act Apr 26 '06)							
14								
15	DENIED CITIZENSHIP BY THE CHOCTAW AND							
1,2,3,4,5&7	CHICKASAW CITIZENSHIP COURT NOV 29 1904							
17								

TRIBAL ENROLLMENT OF PARENTS

	Name of Father	Year	County	Name of Mother	Year	County
1	[Illegible] H Cooper		Non Citz	Kizzie R Cooper		Non Citz
2	E. L. Martin		" "	No1		
3	" "		" "	No1		
4	" "		" "	No1		
5	" "		" "	No1		
6	" "		" "	No1		
7	" "		" "	No1		
8	" "		" "	No1		
9						
10	Nos1 to 6 inclusive were admitted by U S Court Southern Dist Case No 98					
11	[Illegible]					
12			No 3 by judgment of Dawes under illegible]			
13	No 5 was born Feby 7 1898					
14			No.8 Enrolled Sept 26th, 1900			
15						
16	Nos1,2,3,4,5&7 denied by Com in 1896 Case #1410			No7 enrolled Nov 21/98		
17						

Choctaw By Blood Enrollment Cards 1898-1914

RESIDENCE: **Atoka County,** Choctaw Nation

POST OFFICE: Globe,

Nation   **Roll**

CARD No. **4972**

FIELD No. C 17

Dawes' Roll No.	NAME		Relationship to Person First Named	AGE	SEX	BLOOD	TRIBAL ENROLLMENT		
							Year	County	No.
1	Long, Maudie	20		16	F				
2	" William		Brother	12	M				
3	" George		"	10	"				
4	" Sidney		"	8	"				
5									
6									
7									
8									
9									
10									
11									
12									
13									
14									
15									
16									
17									

TRIBAL ENROLLMENT OF PARENTS

	Name of Father	Year	County	Name of Mother	Year	County
1	T.T[?] Long		Non Citz	Nancy J Long	Dead	Non Citz
2	" "		" "	" " "	"	" "
3	" "		" "	" " "	"	" "
4	" "		" "	" " "	"	" "
5						
6						
7						
8	Nos 1 to 4 inclusive were denied by Com in 1896 case #1418					
9						
10						
11						
12						
13						
14						
15						
16						
17				Date of Application for Enrollment		9-7-98

172

Choctaw By Blood Enrollment Cards 1898-1914

RESIDENCE: Pontotoc County, Chick Nan
POST OFFICE: Hart, I.T.

Nation **Roll**

CARD NO. **4973**
FIELD NO. C 18

Dawes' Roll No.	NAME	Relationship to Person First Named	AGE	SEX	BLOOD	TRIBAL ENROLLMENT		
						Year	County	No.
1	Husbands, Frances E	Named	65	F				
2	Hale, Stephen A	G.Son	13	M				
3								
4								
5								
6								
7								
8								
9								
10								
11								
12								
13								
14								
15								
16								
17								

TRIBAL ENROLLMENT OF PARENTS

	Name of Father	Year	County	Name of Mother	Year	County
1	[Illegible] Benson	Dead	Non Citz	Susan Benson	Dead	Non Citz
2	John C Hale	"	" "	Melissa Hale	"	" " "
3						
4						
5						
6						
7						
8	No.1 denied by C.C.C.C. as Francis E Husbands or Francis Elizabeth Husbands					
9	No.1 was admitted by Com in 1896 case #1358					
10	No1 was admitted by the U.S. Com Central Dist #199					
11						
12	No 2 was admitted by the Dawes Commission. Case No 1358					
13	N°2 transferred to Choctaw card #D992 March 18, 1903					
14	No1 case in C.C.C.C Case #91					
15						
16						#1&2 1/36
17						

Choctaw By Blood Enrollment Cards 1898-1914

Dawes' Roll No.	NAME	Relationship to Person First Named	AGE	SEX	BLOOD	TRIBAL ENROLLMENT Year	County	No.
1	White, George L	First Named	33	M	1/16			
2	" Minnie L	Dau	10	F	1/32			
3	" Claud J	Son	8	M	1/32			
4	" Mertie E	Dau	6	F	1/32			
5	" George T	Son	4	M	1/32			
6	" Henry L	"	1	"	1/32			
7	" John Ransom	"	4mo	M	1/32			
8	" Jessica	Dau	6mo	F	1/32			
9								
10								
11	Nos6,7&8 DISMISSED							
12	MAY 27 1904							
13								
14								
15	Nos1 to 5 incl denied by C. [ ] Case #120							
16								
17								

TRIBAL ENROLLMENT OF PARENTS

	Name of Father	Year	County	Name of Mother	Year	County
1	Geo W White	Dead	non citizen	Cynthia A White	Dead	1/8 Choctaw
2	No 1			Martha J White		non citizen
3	No 1			" " "		" "
4	No 1			" " "		" "
5	No 1			" " "		" "
6	No 1			" " "		" "
7	No. 1			" " "		" "
8	N° 1			" " "		" "
9						

DENIED CITIZENSHIP BY THE CHOCTAW AND CHICKASAW CITIZENSHIP COURT

10 Nos1 to 5 inclusive denied by Com in 1896 case #545
11 No6 Henry L White born April 6, 1897, and not in decree
12 Lived in Choctaw Nation continuously for 9 years except 2 years when
13 away on business in Texas, and returned Aug 26, 1898

Judgement of U.S. C. admitting Nos1 to 5 incl vacated and set aside by Decree of C C.C. Dec 17 '02

14 Admitted at South M°Alester July 13, 1897 Court Case No.64
15 Nos1 to 5 incl now in C C C. Cases #120 and #125   Date of Application Nov 23/98
16 No.7 Enrolled May 24, 1900
17 No 8 Born Nov 7 1901, enrolled May 28, 1902

Choctaw By Blood Enrollment Cards 1898-1914

RESIDENCE:	Chickasaw Nation					CARD NO.	**4975**
POST OFFICE:	Ardmore, Ind. Ter.	Choctaw **Nation** Choctaw **Roll**				FIELD NO.	C 20

Dawes' Roll No.	NAME	Relationship to Person First Named	AGE	SEX	BLOOD	TRIBAL ENROLLMENT		
						Year	County	No.
1	Jones, Nannie	Named	24	F	I.W,			
2	" Martha	Dau	3	"	1/32			
DP 3	" Myra E	"	8mo	"	1/32			
4								
5								
6	#3 DISMISSED							
7								
8								
9								
10	Nos1&2 denied by Com in 1896 Case #18							
11								
12								
13								
14								
15								
16								
17								

TRIBAL ENROLLMENT OF PARENTS

	Name of Father	Year	County	Name of Mother	Year	County
1	Geo W Bolen	Dead	non citizen	Mary Bolen		non citizen
2	John L Jones		1/16 Choctaw	No. 1		
3	" " "		"	No 1		
4						
5						
6						
7						
8	Add above names to Card No 80					
9	No1 wife of John L Jones, married to him in Chickasaw Nation					
10	March 13, 1890. He was not there a recognized citizen of Choctaw					
11	Nation.					
12	Both admitted by U.S. Court, Southern District in case of Martha					
13	Jones et al. vs Choctaw Nation, Case No 88, Dec. 21, 1897					
14						
15	No3 enrolled Dec 18/99 Affidavit irregular					
16	and returned for correction.					
17	Returned corrected and filed Feby 20th, 1900					

Nov 22/98

Choctaw By Blood Enrollment Cards 1898-1914

RESIDENCE:	Chickasaw Natn		**Choctaw Nation**		Choctaw **Roll**	CARD NO. **4976**	
POST OFFICE:	Wallville, I.T.					FIELD NO. C 21	

Dawes' Roll No.	NAME	Relationship to Person First Named	AGE	SEX	BLOOD	TRIBAL ENROLLMENT		
						Year	County	No.
0 1	Wall, Thomas		33	M				
0 2	" Hiram T	Son	6	"				
0 3	" Bessie L	Dau	3	F				
4								
5								
6								
7								
8								
9								
10								
11								
12								
13								
14								
15								
16								
17								

TRIBAL ENROLLMENT OF PARENTS

	Name of Father	Year	County	Name of Mother	Year	County
1	Saml C Wall		Choc Citz	Rachel Wall	Dead	Non Citz
2	No 1			Mary E Wall	"	" "
3	No 1			" " "	"	" "
4						
5						
6	Nos 1-2-3 denied by Com in 1896 case #540					
7	Nos 1-2-3 were admitted by the U.S. Court, Southern Dist Jan 19 1898					
8	Court Case No 121					
9	Judgement of U.S. Ct admitting [remainder illegible]					
10	No2 was admitted as "Hiram Wall", No3 as "Bessie Wall"					
11						
12	For child of No1 see NB (Apr 26 '06) #1093					
13						
14	[Information illegible]					
15						
16					Date of Application for Enrollment.	1/91 9-14-98
17						

Choctaw By Blood Enrollment Cards 1898-1914

| RESIDENCE: | Chickasaw Natn | | | | | CARD NO. | **4977** |
| POST OFFICE: | Wallville, I.T. | Choctaw **Nation** | Choctaw **Roll** | | | FIELD NO. | C 22 |

Dawes' Roll No.	NAME	Relationship to Person First Named	AGE	SEX	BLOOD	TRIBAL ENROLLMENT		
						Year	County	No.
1	Hogg, Eunice Ellen	First Named	16	F				
2	" Effie	Dau	2mo	"				
3	" Ora Nellie	Dau	5mo	F				
4								
5								
6								
7								
8								
9								
10								
11								
12								
13								
14								
15								
16								
17								

#2-3 DISMISSED

No1 Denied by C.C.C.C [remainder illegible]

TRIBAL ENROLLMENT OF PARENTS

	Name of Father	Year	County	Name of Mother	Year	County
1	Sam'l C Wall		Choc Citz	Ellen Wall		Non Citz
2	Thos J Hogg		Non Citz	No1		
3	" " "		" "	No1		
4						
5						
6	No.1 denied by Com in 1896 case #540					
7	No1 was admitted by the U.S. Court Southern Dist, Jan 19, 1898 Court Case 126					
8	and was married to Thos J Hogg Oct 7 1897, under U.S. license					
9	Evidence of marriage filed June 3, 1901.					
10						
11	No2 was born July 16, 1898					
12						
13	No.3 Enrolled June 3, 1901.					
14						
15						
16						
17	For child of No1 see NB (Apr 26-06) #1274					

Choctaw By Blood Enrollment Cards 1898-1914

RESIDENCE: **Chickasaw Natn**
POST OFFICE: **Whitebead, I.T.**

Choctaw **Nation**   Choctaw **Roll**

CARD No. **4978**
FIELD No. **C 23**

Dawes' Roll No.	NAME	Relationship to Person First Named	AGE	SEX	BLOOD	TRIBAL ENROLLMENT		
						Year	County	No.
1	Harper, Daisy	First Named	18	F				
2	" Lawrence	Son	2	M				
3	" Gracie Ellen	Dau	3mo	F				
4	" James Custer	Son	5mo	M				
5								
6								
7								
8								
9								
10								
11								
12								
13								
14								
15								
16								
17								

#2-3-4 DISMISSED JAN 23 1905

TRIBAL ENROLLMENT OF PARENTS

	Name of Father	Year	County	Name of Mother	Year	County
1	Sam C Wall		Choctaw Citz	Ellen Wall		Non Citz
2	Jas N Harper		Non Citz	No 1		
3	" " "		" "	No. 1		
4	" " "		" "	Nº 1		
5	No.1 denied by Com in 1896 Case #540					
6	No1 was admitted by the U.S. Court Southern Dist. Jan 19, 1898					
7	Court Case No 126, and was married to Jas N Harper under					
8	license issued by Clerk of the Court Denton County Texas					
9	Dec. 31, 1894					
10						
11	No2 was born Oct 1, 1896					
12	No.3 Enrolled June 28ᵗʰ 1900					
13	Nº4 Born June 27, 1902, enrolled Nov. 1, 1902					
14	DENIED CITIZENSHIP BY THE CHOCTAW AND					
15	CHICKASAW CITIZENSHIP COURT					
16						
17	For child of No1 see NB (Apr 26'06) #1120					

Date of Application for Enrollment   9-14-98

Choctaw By Blood Enrollment Cards 1898-1914

Dawes' Roll No.	NAME	Relationship to Person First Named	AGE	SEX	BLOOD	TRIBAL ENROLLMENT		
						Year	County	No.
1	Wall, Samuel C	First Named	51	M				
2	" Ellen	Wife	54	F				
3	" Sam F [or T]	Son	13	M				
4								
5								
6								
7								
8								
9								
10								
11								
12								
13								
14								
15								
16								
17								

TRIBAL ENROLLMENT OF PARENTS

	Name of Father	Year	County	Name of Mother	Year	County
1	Noah Wall	Dead	Choctaw Citz	Eunic[sic] Wall	Dead	Non Citz
2	John Jackson	"	Non Citz	Ellen Jackson	"	" "
3	No 1			No 2		
4						
5						
6						
7						
8	Nos. 1-2-3 denied by Com in 1896, case #540					
9	Nos 1-2-3 were admitted by the U.S. Court Southern Dist, Jan 19, 1898					
10	Court Case No 126					
11						
12						
13						
14						
15						
16						
17						

Choctaw By Blood Enrollment Cards 1898-1914

RESIDENCE: **Chickasaw Natn**
POST OFFICE: **Johnsonville, I.T.**

Choctaw **Nation**   Choctaw **Roll**

CARD NO. **4980**
FIELD NO. **C 25**

Dawes' Roll No.	NAME	Relationship to Person First Named	AGE	SEX	BLOOD	TRIBAL ENROLLMENT		
						Year	County	No.
1	Hendrix, Sarilda	Named	18	F				
2	" Ozelia	Dau	8mo	"				
3	" Effie Florence	Dau	1mo	"				
4								
5								
6								
7								
8								
9								
10								
11								
12								
13								
14								
15								
16								
17								

Nos 2&3 DISMISSED SEP 15 1904

DENIED CITIZENSHIP BY THE CHOCTAW AND CHICKASAW CITIZENSHIP COURT

TRIBAL ENROLLMENT OF PARENTS

	Name of Father	Year	County	Name of Mother	Year	County
1	Eli T Nail		Non Citz	Mary E Nail		Non Citz
2	Chas Hendricks[sic]		" "	No 1		
3	" " "		" "	No.1		
4						
5						
6		No. 1 denied by Com in 1896 Case #1146				
7		No1 was admitted by the U.S. Court Southern District Dec 22, 1897				
8		Cou't Case No 116, as Sarilda Nail and was married to Thos. Hendrix				
9		Dec 24, 1896				
10		No2 was was[sic] Dec 28				
11		No3 born Sept 19th, 1901; Enrolled Oct 16th, 1901				
12						
13						
14						
15						
16						1/85
17					Date of Application for Enrollment	9-14-98

RESIDENCE: Michigan

POST OFFICE: Detroit, Mich

Choctaw **Nation**   Choctaw **Roll**

CARD No. **4981**

FIELD No. C 26

Dawes' Roll No.	NAME	Relationship to Person First Named	AGE	SEX	BLOOD	TRIBAL ENROLLMENT		
						Year	County	No.
1	Thomas, John	40	36	M				
2								
3								
4								
5								
6								
7								
8								
9								
10								
11								
12								
13								
14								
15								
16								
17								

CANCELLED

TRIBAL ENROLLMENT OF PARENTS

	Name of Father	Year	County	Name of Mother	Year	County
1	Wm Thomas	Dead	Non Citz	Mary E Thomas	Dead	Non Citz
2						
3						
4						
5	No1 denied by Com in 1896 case #1386					
6	Was admitted by U.S. Court Southern Dist. Dec 22, 1897					
7	Court Case No					
8	No1 is dead. See testimony of Amanda Tyra M.C.R. #5435 - April 30, 1902					
9						
10						
11						
12	No. ~ 1 ~ HEREON DISMISSED UNDER ORDER OF THE COMMISSION TO THE FIVE CIVILIZED TRIBES OF MARCH 31, 1905.					
13						
14						
15						
16						
17						

Choctaw By Blood Enrollment Cards 1898-1914

RESIDENCE: Chickasaw Natn
POST OFFICE: Johnsonville, I.T.

Choctaw **Nation**   Choctaw **Roll**

CARD NO. **4982**
FIELD NO. C 27

Dawes' Roll No.	NAME	Relationship to Person First Named	AGE	SEX	BLOOD	TRIBAL ENROLLMENT		
						Year	County	No.
1	Nail, Mary E		38	F	1/8			
2	" James M	Son	16	M	1/16			
3	" Charles C	"	14	"	1/16			
4	" Eli T	"	9	"	1/16			
5	" Maudie A	Dau	7	F	1/16			
6	" Myrtle F	"	4	"	1/16			
7	" Young H	Son	2mo	M	1/16			
8								
9								
10	No 7 DISMISSED							
11	SEP 15 1904							
12								
13								
14	DENIED CITIZENSHIP BY THE CHOCTAW AND							
15	CHICKASAW CITIZENSHIP COURT							
16								
17								

TRIBAL ENROLLMENT OF PARENTS

	Name of Father	Year	County	Name of Mother	Year	County
1	Wm Thomas	Dead	Non Citz	Mary E Thomas	Dead	Non Citz
2	Eli Thomas Nail	"	" "	No 1		
3	" " "	"	" "	No 1		
4	" " "	"	" "	No 1		
5	" " "	"	" "	No 1		
6	" " "	"	" "	No 1		
7	" " "	"	" "	No 1		
8						
9	Nos 1 to 6 inclusive denied by Com in 1896 case #					
10	Nos 1 to 6 inclusive were admitted by U.S. Court, Southern Dist.					
11	Dec 22, 1896, Court Case No [illegible]					
12						
13	No.2 was admitted as "James A", No.4 as "Thomas Eli"					
14						
15						
16					Date of Application 1 82	
17					for Enrollment 1-98	

Choctaw By Blood Enrollment Cards 1898-1914

Dawes' Roll No.	NAME	Relationship to Person First Named	AGE	SEX	BLOOD	TRIBAL ENROLLMENT Year	County	No.
✓ * 1	Sessions, A. B.	Named	34	M				
✓ * 2	" George A	Son	3	"				
✓ 3	" Joseph W	"	7/mo	"				
✓ 4	" Gracie E	Dau	3mo	F				
✓ 5	" Charles M	Son	3wks	M				
6								
7								
8								
9								
10								
11								
12								
Nos 13	DISMISSED MAY 27 1904							
14								
15								
16								
17								

TRIBAL ENROLLMENT OF PARENTS

	Name of Father	Year	County	Name of Mother	Year	County
1	Wm Sessions	Dead	Non Citz	Mary M Sessions	Dead	Non Citz
2	No 1			Mamie Sessions	" "	
3	No 1			" "	" "	
4	No 1			" "	" "	
5	N" 1			" "	" "	
6						
7	Nos 1&2 denied by Com in 1896 case #452					
8	Nos 1&2 were admitted by the U.S. Court Central Dist, Jan 20,1898, Court Case No 10					
9						
10						
11	No.3 was born Jan 27, 1898					
12						
13						
14						
15						
16						
17						

DENIED CITIZENSHIP BY THE CHOCTAW AND CHICKASAW CITIZENSHIP COURT

Choctaw By Blood Enrollment Cards 1898-1914

RESIDENCE: Chickasaw Natn
POST OFFICE: Wynnewood, I.T.

Choctaw **Nation** Choctaw **Roll**

CARD NO. **4984**
FIELD NO. C 29

Dawes' Roll No.	NAME	Relationship to Person First Named	AGE	SEX	BLOOD	TRIBAL ENROLLMENT		
						Year	County	No.
✻ 1	Harrison, Mary E	First Named	47	F				
✻ 2	" Walter A	Son	24	M				
✻ 3	" Eva May	Dau	18	F				
✻ 4	" O Edgar	Son	14	M				
✻ 5	" Ruth Hazel	Gr.Dau	3 wks	F				
6								
7								⟩
8								
9								
10								
11								
12								
13								
No. 5 14	DISMISSED MAY 27 1904							
15								
16								
17								

TRIBAL ENROLLMENT OF PARENTS

	Name of Father	Year	County	Name of Mother	Year	County
1	Wm Sessions	Dead	Non Citz	Mary M Sessions	Dead	Non Citz
2	F.M. Harrison		" "			No 1
3	" "		" "			No 1
4	" "		" "			No 1
5	Nº2		" "	Ida Harrison		non citz
6	Nos 1 to 4 inclusive were denied by Com in 1896 case #452					
7	Nos 1 to 4 inclusive were admitted by the U.S. Court Central Dist Jan 20, 1898					
8	Court Case No 10					
9						
10	No2 was admitted as "W.A." No3 as "Eva" and "O. Edgar" as "Eddie"					
11	Nº2 is now the husband of Ida Harrison non citizen. Evidence of marriage filed Sept 29,1902					
12	Nº5 Born Sept 7, 1901. Enrolled Set 29, 1902					
13						
14						
15						
16						
17	For child of No3 see NB (Apr 26'06) Card #905			Date of Application for Enrollment.		9-14-98

DENIED CITIZENSHIP BY THE CHOCTAW AND CHICKASAW CITIZENSHIP COURT

184

Choctaw By Blood Enrollment Cards 1898-1914

RESIDENCE:	Chickasaw Natn							CARD NO.	**4985**
POST OFFICE:	Wynnewood, I.T.	Choctaw **Nation**		Choctaw **Roll**				FIELD NO.	C 30

Dawes' Roll No.	NAME	Relationship to Person First Named	AGE	SEX	BLOOD	TRIBAL ENROLLMENT		
						Year	County	No.
1	Fleming, Martha	Named	38	F				
2	" Newton	Son	16	M				
3	" Joseph	"	13	"				
4	" William	"	11	"				
5	" Jessie Lee	Dau	8	F				
6	" Mamie G	"	1	"				
7	" Lizzie V	"	4mo	"				
8								
9								
10								
11								
12								
Nos6&13	MAY 27 1904 DISMISSED							
14								
15								
16								
17								

TRIBAL ENROLLMENT OF PARENTS

	Name of Father	Year	County	Name of Mother	Year	County
1	Wm Sessions	Dead	Non Citz	Mary M Sessions	Dead	Non Citz
2	John Fleming	" "	Nol			
3	" "	" "	Nol			
4	" "	" "	Nol			
5	" "	" "	Nol			
6	" "	" "	Nol			
7	" "	" "	Nol			
8	Nos1 to 5 inclusive were denied by Com in 1896 case #452					
9	Nos1 to 5 inclusive were admitted [by] U.S. Court Central Dist Jan 20,1898					
10	Court Case No 10					
11						
12	No5 was admitted as Jessie Fleming					
13	No6 was born Dec 10/89					
14						
15					No7 enrolled Dec 14/99	
16	For child of No2 see NB #1071 (Act Apr 26'06)					
17						

DENIED CITIZENSHIP BY THE CHOCTAW AND
CHICKASAW CITIZENSHIP COURT

Choctaw By Blood Enrollment Cards 1898-1914

RESIDENCE: Chickasaw			Choctaw **Nation**		Choctaw **Roll**	CARD NO. **4986**	
POST OFFICE: Wynnewood, I.T.						FIELD NO. C 31	

Dawes' Roll No.	NAME	Relationship to Person	AGE	SEX	BLOOD	TRIBAL ENROLLMENT		
						Year	County	No.
✓ * 1	Fleming, Laura	First Named	38	F				
✓ * 2	" Bessie	Dau	11	"				
✓ * 3	" Frank	Son	9	M				
✓ * 4	" Ada	Dau	6	F				
✓ * 5	Earl	Son	2	M				
✓ 6	" Jewel	"	6mo	"				
7								
8								
9								
10								
11								
12								
13								
No.6 14	MAY 27 1904 DISMISSED							
15								
16								
17								

TRIBAL ENROLLMENT OF PARENTS

	Name of Father	Year	County	Name of Mother	Year	County
1	Louis Hays	Dead	Non Citz	Mary Hays	Dead	Non Citz
2	Henry Fleming	" "		No1		
3	" "	" "		No1		
4	" "	" "		No1		
5	" "	" "		No1		
6	" "	" "		No1		
7	Nos 1to5 were admitted by U.S. Court, Central Dist Aug 26, 1897					
8	Court Case No 40					
9	Nos1to5 inclusive were denied by Dawes Com in '96 Choc Cit Case #433					
10						
11	No6 was born March 3, 1898					
12						
13						
14						
15						
16						
17						

DENIED CITIZENSHIP BY THE CHOCTAW AND CHICKASAW CITIZENSHIP COURT

APPLICANT

Date of Application for Enrollment 9-14-98

186

| RESIDENCE: | Chickasaw Nation | | Choctaw **Nation** | | Choctaw **Roll** | | CARD No. **4987** |
| POST OFFICE: | Center, I.T. | | | | | | FIELD No. C 32 |

Dawes' Roll No.	NAME	Relationship to Person First Named	AGE	SEX	BLOOD	TRIBAL ENROLLMENT		
						Year	County	No.
1	Olive, Roberta	Named	24	F	1/16			
2	" Jesse Lee	Son	5	M	1/32			
3	" Hettie	Dau	10mo	F	1/32			
4								
5								
6	#3							
7								
8								
9								
10								
11								
12								
13								
14								
15								
16								
17								

TRIBAL ENROLLMENT OF PARENTS

	Name of Father	Year	County	Name of Mother	Year	County
1	S. F. Rhoades		Non Citz	Cleopatra Rhoades	Dead	Non Citz
2	Thos G Olive		" "	No. 1		
3	" " "		" "	No 1		
4						
5						
6						
7						
8	Nos 1&2 were denied by Com in 1896 Case No 59					
9	Were admitted by the U.S. Court, Southern Dist. Mrs. Roberta Oliver and					
10	Jesse Lee Oliver Dec 22nd 1897, Court Case No. 128					
11						
12						
13	No1 denied by C.C.C.C. as Roberta Olive or Roberta Oliver					
14	No2 " " " " Jesse Lee " " Jesse Lee "					
15						1/73
16						9-14-98
17						

187

Choctaw By Blood Enrollment Cards 1898-1914

RESIDENCE:	Chickasaw Natn		Choctaw **Nation**			Choctaw **Roll**		CARD NO. **4988**	
POST OFFICE:	Center, I.T.							FIELD NO. C 33	

Dawes' Roll No.	NAME	Relationship to Person First Named	AGE	SEX	BLOOD	TRIBAL ENROLLMENT		
						Year	County	No.
1	Rigsby, Ellen N	First Named	18	F				
2	" Cora Patsy	Dau	1	"				
3	" Beatrice	Dau	6wks	F				
4								
5								
6								
7	NOV 12 1904							
8								
9								
10								
11								
12								
13								
14								
15								
16								
17								

#2-3- DISM

TRIBAL ENROLLMENT OF PARENTS

	Name of Father	Year	County	Name of Mother	Year	County
1	L.F. Rhoades		Non Citz	Cleopatra Rhoades	Dead	Non Citz
2	T.J. Rigsby		" "	No 1		
3	" "		" "	No.1		
4						
5						
6	No.1 was denied by Com in 1896, case #59					
7	Was admitted by the U.S. Court, Southern Dist as Ella N Rhoades					
8	Dec 22, 1897, Court Case No 128 and married to T. J. Rigsby					
9	the first Sunday in October 1897, under license issued by					
10	Clerk of the U.S. Court at Pauls Valley					
11	No3 Enrolled December 27, 1900					
12						
13						
14	No1 denied by C.C.C.C. as Ella N Rhoades					
15	For child of No1 see NB (Apr 26'06) #1277			No2 enrolled 2/14/99		
16						1/72
17						

DENIED CITIZENSHIP BY THE CHOCTAW AND CHICKASAW CITIZENSHIP COURT

188

Choctaw By Blood Enrollment Cards 1898-1914

RESIDENCE: Chickasaw Natn
POST OFFICE: Center, I.T.

Choctaw **Nation**   Choctaw **Roll**

CARD NO. **4989**
FIELD NO. C 34

Dawes' Roll No.	NAME	Relationship to Person First Named	AGE	SEX	BLOOD	TRIBAL ENROLLMENT		
						Year	County	No.
1	Rhoades Emmet L	Named	22	M				
2								
3								
4								
5								
6								
7								
8								
9								
10								
11								
12								
13								
14								
15								
16								
17								

TRIBAL ENROLLMENT OF PARENTS

	Name of Father	Year	County	Name of Mother	Year	County
1	L.F. Rhoades		Non Citz	Cleopatra Rhoades	Dead	Non Citz
2						
3						
4						
5						
6						
7		Denied by Com in 1896 case #59				
8		Was admitted by the U.S. Court Southern Dist Court Case No 128				
9		Dec 22, 1897				
10						
11						
12						
13		For child of No 1 see NB (Apr 26 '06) #1278				
14						
15						
16						
17						

Choctaw By Blood Enrollment Cards 1898-1914

| | RESIDENCE: | Chickasaw Natn | | | | | | | | CARD NO. 4990 |
| POST OFFICE: | Center, I.T. | | | | | | | | | FIELD NO. C 35 |

Choctaw **Nation** Choctaw **Roll**

Dawes' Roll No.	NAME	Relationship to Person First Named	AGE	SEX	BLOOD	TRIBAL ENROLLMENT		
						Year	County	No.
1	Rhoades, Andrew O		25	M				
2	" Lessie L	Son	7mo	"				
3	" Roy Cecil	Son	3mo	M				
4	" Floyd	son	2wk	M				
5								
6								
7								
8								
9								
10								
11								
12								
13								
14								
15								
16								
17								

#2-3-4 DISMISSED NOV 12 1902

TRIBAL ENROLLMENT OF PARENTS

	Name of Father	Year	County	Name of Mother	Year	County
1	L.F. Rhoades		Non Citz	Cleopatra Rhoades	Dead	Non Citz
2	No1			Ada Rhoades		" "
3	No1			" "		" "
4	No1			" "		" "
5						
6						
7	No.1 denied by Com'n 1896 case #59					
8	No1 admitted by the U.S. Court Southern Dist Court Case No					
9						
10	No 2 Lessie L Rhoades was born Feb					
11						
12	No1 was married to Ada Rhoades May 31					
13						
14	No 4 born Jany 3d, 1902 Enrolled Jany 14, 1902					
15						
16	For child of No1 see NB (Apr 26'06) #1276				1/69	
17	No.3 Enrolled May 27			Date of Application for Enrollment	9-14-98	

DENIED CITIZENSHIP BY THE CHOCTAW AND CHICKASAW CITIZENSHIP COURT

190

Choctaw By Blood Enrollment Cards 1898-1914

Dawes' Roll No.	NAME	Relationship to Person First Named	AGE	SEX	BLOOD	TRIBAL ENROLLMENT		
						Year	County	No.
1	Puthuff, Alpha	Named	27	F				
2	" Osa Lee	Son	9	M				
3	" Carrie	Dau	7	F				
4	" Herman	Son	5	M				
5	" Nora	Dau	4mo	F				
6								
7								
8								
9								
10								
11								
12								
13								
14	DISMISSED MAY 27 1904							
15								
16								
17								

TRIBAL ENROLLMENT OF PARENTS

	Name of Father	Year	County	Name of Mother	Year	County
1	Thos Brown		Non Citz	Minerva Brown		Non Citz
2	Wm Puthuff		" "	No1		
3	" "		" "	No1		
4	" "		" "	No1		
5	" "		" "	No1		
6						
7	Nos1 to 5 inclusive denied by the Com in 1896 Choc Chic Cit Case #903					
8	Nos1 to 5 inclusive were admitted by the U.S. Court, Central Dist. Jan 19, 1898					
9	Case No 162					
10	Alpha Puthuff was admitted as Alpha Brown, her maiden name					
11	"Osa Lee" was admitted as "Osa"					
12						
13	No.5 was born April 5, 1898					
14						
15						
16						1/94
17					Date of Application for Enrollment.	9-14-98

DENIED CITIZENSHIP BY THE CHOCTAW AND CHICKASAW CITIZENSHIP COURT

Choctaw By Blood Enrollment Cards 1898-1914

RESIDENCE: Chickasaw Natn
POST OFFICE: Duncan, I.T.

Choctaw **Nation**   Choctaw **Roll**

CARD No. **4992**
FIELD No. C 37

Dawes' Roll No.	NAME	Relationship to Person First Named	AGE	SEX	BLOOD	TRIBAL ENROLLMENT Year	County	No.
✓ * 1	Brown, Thos P	First Named	56	M				
✓ * 2	" Cynthia M	Wife	51	F				
✓ * 3	Barnes, Mary E	Dau	22	"				
✓ * 4	Brown, Daniel P	Son	20	M				
✓ * 5	" Robert L	"	16	"				
✓ * 6	" Martha J	Dau	14	F				
✓ * 7	" Henry B	Son	11	M				
✓ 8	Barnes, Homer	G.Son	3mo	"				

9
Decision of U.S. Court C.D. of Jan 19, 1898 admitting
Nos1 to 7 inclusive vacated and set aside by decree of
Choctaw Citizenship Court Dec 17" 1902.
Denied by the Choctaw Chickasaw Citizenship
Court January 21 '04 Case #33

No 8 DISMISSED MAY 27 1904

TRIBAL ENROLLMENT OF PARENTS

	Name of Father	Year	County	Name of Mother	Year	County
1	Rolen Brown	Dead		Peggy Brown	Dead	
2	Wm Richardson		Non Citz	Mary Ann Richardson		Non Citz
3	No1			No2		
4	No1			No2		
5	No1			No2		
6	No1			No2		
7	No1			No2		
8	Charles Barnes		Non Citz			No3

DENIED CITIZENSHIP BY THE CHOCTAW AND
CHICKASAW CITIZENSHIP COURT

9 Nos1 to 7 inclusive denied by Com in 1896 Choc Cit Case #903
10 JNos 1 to 7 inclusive were admitted by the U.S. Court Southern Dist. Jan 19 1898
11 Court Case No 162
12
13 No1 was admitted as "Thomas" "Cynthia M" as "Minerva", "Mary E" as "Mary"
14 "Daniel P" as "Daniel", "Robert L" as "Robert", "Martha J" as "Martha" "Henry B" as
15 "Henry"
16
17 No8 enrolled Dec 14/99 See copy of letter attached

Date of Application
for Enrollment. 9-14-98

For child of No5 see NB #1040 (Act Apr 26 '06)
" children " " 3 " " #1041 " " " "
" child " " 4 " " #1042 " " " " 192

Choctaw By Blood Enrollment Cards 1898-1914

RESIDENCE:	Pickens					CARD No. **4993**
POST OFFICE:	Bailey, I.T.	Choctaw **Nation**	Choctaw **Roll**			FIELD No. C

Dawes' Roll No.	NAME	Relationship to Person First Named	AGE	SEX	BLOOD	TRIBAL ENROLLMENT		
						Year	County	No.
1	Brown, David T	First Named	24	M				
2	" Mary F	wife	18	f	IW			
3								
4								
5								
6								
7								
8								
9								
10								
11								
12								
13								
14	DISMISSED							
15	MAY 13 190?							
16								
17								

	TRIBAL ENROLLMENT OF PARENTS						
	Name of Father	Year	County	Name of Mother	Year	County
1	Thos P Brown		Non Citz	Cynthia M Brown		Non Citz
2	Robt Fry		" "	Florence Fry	dead	" "
3	DENIED CITIZENSHIP BY THE CHOCTAW AND					
4	CHICKASAW CITIZENSHIP COURT					
5						
6	No1 denied by the Comm. in 1896 Choc Cit Case #90?					
7	No1 was admitted by U.S.Court, Southern Dist Jan					
8						
9	Was admitted as David [Illegible]					
10						
11	Sept 12 - 99	Residing in Chickasaw Nation at time				
12		of the marriage. Marriage under license				
13		issued by Clerk of the U.S. Court at Ardmore				
14		See to this - See evidence of Thos				
15		P Brown				
16						1/96
17					Date of Application for Enrollment.	9-14-98

193

Choctaw By Blood Enrollment Cards 1898-1914

RESIDENCE: Pickens
POST OFFICE: Burt, I.T.

Choctaw **Nation** Choctaw **Roll**

CARD NO. **4994**
FIELD NO.

Dawes' Roll No.	NAME	Relationship to Person First Named	AGE	SEX	BLOOD	TRIBAL ENROLLMENT Year	County	No.
1	Brown, William J	First Named	29	M				
2	" Bertha A	Dau	6	F				
3	" James P	Son	2	M				
4	" Edward L	"	1mo	"				
5	" Fannie	wife	22	IW				
6								
7								
8								
9								
10								
11								
12								
13								
14	MAY 27 1904 DISMISSED							
15								
16								
17								

TRIBAL ENROLLMENT OF PARENTS

	Name of Father	Year	County	Name of Mother	Year	County
1	Thos P Brown		Non Citz	Cynthia M Brown		Non Citz
2	No1			Fannie A Brown		" "
3	No1			" " "		" "
4	No1			" " "		" "
5	Z R Warren		Non Citizen	Emily Warren	Dead	" "

DENIED CITIZENSHIP BY THE CHOCTAW AND CHICKASAW CITIZENSHIP COURT

6 Nos 1, 2, 3 and 5 denied by the Comm in 1896 Chw. Cit Case #903

7 Nos 1 to 3 inclusive were admitted by the U.S. Court Central Dist. Jan 19, 1898

8 Court Case No. 162

9 No 5 Original judgment reformed and Fannie A Brown included by nunc pro tunc entry of

10 March 31, 1899 U.S. Court Cent. Dist. Case #162

11 No4 was born August 20, 1898

12

13 No1 was admitted as "William", No2 as "Bertha", No3 as "James"

14

15 Sept 12-99 - As to residence see testimony

16 of Thos P Brown

17

Date of Application for Enrollment. 9-14-98

194

Choctaw By Blood Enrollment Cards 1898-1914

RESIDENCE: Blue County
POST OFFICE: Fulsom, I.T.

Choctaw **Nation**   Choctaw **Roll**

CARD NO. **4995**
FIELD NO. C

Dawes' Roll No.	NAME	Relationship to Person First Named	AGE	SEX	BLOOD	TRIBAL ENROLLMENT		
						Year	County	No.
1	Mainard, Usley	Named	62	F				
2	Ivey, Elisha W	Son	32	M				
3	" Bertie L	G. Dau	9	F				
4								
5								
6								
7								
8								
9								
10								
11								
12								
13								
14								
15								
16								
17								

TRIBAL ENROLLMENT OF PARENTS

	Name of Father	Year	County	Name of Mother	Year	County
1	Benj Hill	Dead	Non Citz	[Illegible] Hill	Dead	Non Citz
2	[Illegible] L Ivey	"	" "	No1		
3	No2			Sedema L Ivey		Non Citz
4						
5						
6						
7	Nos 1,2 and 3 [admitted] by Com in 1896 case #8					
8	Nos 1, 2 [and 3 admitted] by the U.S. Court Atoka Dist Oct 22, 1897					
9	Court Case No. [illegible]					
10						
11						
12						
13						
14						
15						
16						
17				Date of Application		9-14-98

195

Choctaw By Blood Enrollment Cards 1898-1914

RESIDENCE: Blue County
POST OFFICE: Fulsom, I.T.

Choctaw **Nation** Choctaw **Roll**

CARD No. **4996**
FIELD No. C 41

Dawes' Roll No.	NAME	Relationship to Person First Named	AGE	SEX	BLOOD	TRIBAL ENROLLMENT Year	County	No.
1	Steppick, Nancy Ann	Named	42	F				
2	Gregory, John H[?]	Son	23	M				
3	Steppick, Chas F	"	11	"				
4	" Thos J	"	9	"				
5	" Geo W	"	8	"				
6	" Wm O	"	6	"				
7	" Bessie L	Dau	3	F				
DP 8	" James C	Son	1	M				
DP 9	Gregory, Sabra Ivegean	Gr Dau	6mo	F				
10								
#8-9- 11	DISMISSED JAN 1908							
12								
13								
14								
15								
16								
17								

TRIBAL ENROLLMENT OF PARENTS

	Name of Father	Year	County	Name of Mother	Year	County
1	[Illegible] Ivey	Dead	Non Citz	[Illegible]		Non Citz
2	John Gregory	"	"	No1		
3	Joe Steppick	"	"	No1		
4	" "	"	"	No1		
5	" "	"	"	No1		
6	" "	"	"	No1		
7	" "	"	"	No1		
8	N°2			Eva Gregory		noncitizen
9	Nos1 to 7 inclusive were denied by Com in 1896 Case #8					
10	Nos1 to 7 inclusive were admitted by the U.S. Court Ardmore, I.T.					
11	Dec 22, 1897, Court Case No [?]					
12	Nos 1-3-4-5-6-7 were admitted as Steppick					
13						
14	No8 was born June 27, 1897					
15	Birth affidavit of No8 received and filed Feby 27th 1900					
16	N°2 is husband of Eva Gregory Certificate of marriage filed March 26, 1903					
17	N°9 Application received Nov 20,1902 returned for evidence of marriage Received and filed March 26,1903					

For child of No2 see NB 997 (Act Apr 26-06)

196

Choctaw By Blood Enrollment Cards 1898-1914

RESIDENCE: Creek Natn

POST OFFICE: Eufaula, I.T.

Choctaw **Nation**   Choctaw **Roll**

CARD NO. **4997**

FIELD NO. C 42

Dawes' Roll No.	NAME	Relationship to Person First Named	AGE	SEX	BLOOD	TRIBAL ENROLLMENT		
						Year	County	No.
1	Ivey, Thomas L	Named	34	M				
2	" Willie L	Son	2mo	"				
3	" Walter Taylor	Son	1W	M				
4								
5								
6								
#2-3- 7	DISMISSED							
8	JAN 25 1905							
9								
10								
11								
12								
13								
14								
15								
16								
17								

TRIBAL ENROLLMENT OF PARENTS

	Name of Father	Year	County	Name of Mother	Year	County
1	Marcus L Ivey	Dead	Non Citz	Usley Mainard		Non Citz
2	No 1			Lue H Ivey		" "
3	No 1			" " "		" "
4	Not denied by Com in 1896 case #8					
5	Admitted by U.S. Court, Atoka, I.T. Dec. 22, 1897, Com. Case No. 115					
6						
7						
8	No2 enrolled Oct 30/99 subject to receipt of evidence of marriage of parents					
9	Letter requesting same this day. Rec'd & filed Jan 11, 1900					
10	No 3 Enrolled February 6, 1901					
11	DENIED CITIZENSHIP BY THE CHOCTAW AND					
12	CHICKASAW CITIZENSHIP COURT					
13						
14	For child of No1 See NB 987 (Act Apr 26-06)					
15						
16						1/111
17					Date of Application for Enrollment.	9-14-98

RESIDENCE:	Blue County			CARD NO. **4998**
POST OFFICE:	Fulsom, I.T.	Choctaw **Nation** Choctaw **Roll**		FIELD NO. C 43

Dawes' Roll No.	NAME	Relationship to Person First Named	AGE	SEX	BLOOD	TRIBAL ENROLLMENT Year	County	No.
1	Ivey, Marcus L	Named	38	M				
2	" James L	Son	12	M				
3	" William J	"	10	"				
4	" Thos F	"	8	"				
5	" Nora E	Dau	6	F				
6	" Louis A	Son	4	M				
DP 7	" Elizabeth U	Dau	2	F				
DP 8	" Marcus A	Son	6mo	M				
9								
10								
11	#7-8- DISMISSED							
12	JAN 23 1905							
13								
14								
15	#2 DISMISSED							
16	JAN 24 1905							
17								

TRIBAL ENROLLMENT OF PARENTS

	Name of Father	Year	County	Name of Mother	Year	County
1	Marcus L Ivey		Non Citz	Usley Mainard		Non Citz
2	No 1			Mary E Ivey		" "
3	No 1			" " "		" "
4	No 1			" " "		" "
5	No 1			" " "		" "
6	No 1			" " "		" "
7	No 1			" " "		" "
8	No 1			" " "		" "
9	Nos1 to 6 inclusive were denied by Com in 1896 Case 8					
10	Nos1 to 6 were admitted by U.S. Court, Ardmore I.T. Dec 22, 1897					
11	Court Case No 115					
12						
13	No7 was born Aug 26, 1896 Received and filed July 19, 1901					
14	No8 " " Feb 22, 1898 Received and filed July 15, 1901					
15						
16	For child of No1 see NB #993 - (Act Apr 26'06)					
17				Date of Application for Enrollment		9-14-98

DENIED CITIZENSHIP BY THE CHOCTAW AND CHICKASAW CITIZENSHIP COURT

Choctaw By Blood Enrollment Cards 1898-1914

						TRIBAL ENROLLMENT		
Dawes' Roll No.	NAME	Relationship to Person First Named	AGE	SEX	BLOOD	Year	County	No.
1	Segroves, Thos W	First Named	52	M				
2	" Elizabeth	Wife	50	F				
3	" James B	Son	27	M				
4	" Charley W	"	21	"				
5	" Geo Franklin	"	18	"				
6	" Doc Thomas	"	16	"				
7	" William C	"	11	"				
8	" Zachariah	"	9	"				
9	" Paralee	Dau	6	F				
10	" Louie	Dau in law	21	F	IW			
11	" Ethel L	G.Dau	4mo	"				
12	" Dorothy May	Dau of No3	1mo	F				
13								
14	#10-11-12 DISMISSED							
15	Nos 1 to 9 inclusive were admitted by U.S. Court, Ardmore, I.T., Dec 22, 1898							
16	Court Case No 115		No.12 Born June 17-1901 Enrolled July 18" 1902					
17	No3 now the husband of Georgie Ghouley non citizen Evidence of marriage filed July 18th 1902							

RESIDENCE: Chickasaw Natn
POST OFFICE: Woolsey, I.T.
Choctaw **Nation**   Choctaw **Roll**
CARD NO. 4999
FIELD NO. C 44

TRIBAL ENROLLMENT OF PARENTS

	Name of Father	Year	County	Name of Mother	Year	County
1	Wm Segroves	Dead	Non Citz	Jane Segroves	Dead	Non Citz
2	Zach Bottoms	" "	Elizabeth Bottom	"	" "
3	No1			No2		
4	No1			No2		
5	No1			No2		
6	No1			No2		
7	No1			No2		
8	No1			No2		
9	No1			No2		
10	Wm Spear		Non Citz	Eliza Spear		Non Citz
11	No4			No10		
12	No3			Georgie Segroves		
13	No10 is the wife of No4 Charley W Segroves License issued by Simon Wolf County Judge of Pontotoc County					
14	Chickasaw Nation to C W Segroves, as a Chickasaw to marry Miss Louie Spear a U.S. Citizen					
15	Oct 3,1898. Married Oct 4, 1898. License and certificate exhibited					
16	No11 enrolled Dec 14/99					
17	Nos1 to 9 inclusive were denied by Com in 1896 Case #8					

DENIED CITIZENSHIP BY THE CHOCTAW AND CHICKASAW CITIZENSHIP COURT

Date of Application for Enrollment.

For child of No6 see NB #1034 (Act Apr 26'06)
   "   "   " No3 "   " #1035 "   "

199

Choctaw By Blood Enrollment Cards 1898-1914

RESIDENCE: Blue County			Choctaw **Nation** Choctaw **Roll**			CARD No. **5000**	
POST OFFICE: Fulsom, I.T.						FIELD No. C 45	

Dawes' Roll No.	NAME	Relationship to Person First Named	AGE	SEX	BLOOD	TRIBAL ENROLLMENT		
						Year	County	No.
1	Montgomery, Emmett	Named	16	M				
2								
3								
4								
5								
6								
7								
8								
9								
10								
11								
12								
13								
14								
15								
16								
17								

TRIBAL ENROLLMENT OF PARENTS

	Name of Father	Year	County	Name of Mother	Year	County
1	Sam Montgomery	Dead	Non Citz	Lucinda Montgomery	Dead	Non Citz
2						
3						
4						
5						
6	No.1 denied by Com. in 1896 case #8					
7	Admitted by U.S. Court, Ardmore, I.T. Dec 22, 1898, Court Case No 115					
8						
9						
10						
11						
12						
13						
14						
15						
16						
17					Date of Application for Enrollment.	9-14-98

DENIED CITIZENSHIP BY THE CHOCTAW AND CHICKASAW CITIZENSHIP COURT

200

Choctaw By Blood Enrollment Cards 1898-1914

RESIDENCE:	Chickasaw Natn									

RESIDENCE: Chickasaw Natn
POST OFFICE: Paoli, I.T.

Choctaw **Nation**   Choctaw **Roll**

CARD No. **5001**
FIELD No. C 46

Dawes' Roll No.	NAME	Relationship to Person First Named	AGE	SEX	BLOOD	TRIBAL ENROLLMENT		
						Year	County	No.
1	Atwood, Thos		37	M				
2								
3								
4								
5								
6								
7								
8								
9								
10								
11								
12								
13								
14								
15								
16								
17								

TRIBAL ENROLLMENT OF PARENTS

	Name of Father	Year	County	Name of Mother	Year	County
1	Isaac Atwood	Dead	Non Citz	Annie Atwood	Dead	Non Citz
2						
3						
4						
5						
6	No1 denied by Com in 1896, case #8					
7	Admitted by U.S. Court, Ardmore, I.T. Dec 22, 1897, Court Case No 115					
8						
9	No1 is not very bright					
10						
11						
12						
13						
14						
15						
16						
17						

Date of Application for Enrollment.   9-14-98

1/114

Choctaw By Blood Enrollment Cards 1898-1914

RESIDENCE: Chickasaw Natn
POST OFFICE: Woolsey, I.T.

Choctaw **Nation**   Choctaw **Roll**

CARD NO. **5002**
FIELD NO. C 47

Dawes' Roll No.	NAME	Relationship to Person First Named	AGE	SEX	BLOOD	TRIBAL ENROLLMENT		
						Year	County	No.
1	Segroves, Sam M	Named	26	M				
2	" , Rosa Lee	Dau	21mo	F				
3	" , Buler May	Dau	9mo	F				
4	" William Edgar	Son	9mo	M				
5								
6								
7	#2-3-4 DISMISSED							
8								
9								
10	No1 Samuel Montgomery Segroves [illegible]							
11								
12								
13								
14								
15								
16								
17								

TRIBAL ENROLLMENT OF PARENTS

	Name of Father	Year	County	Name of Mother	Year	County
1	Thos W Segroves		Non Citz	Elizabeth Segroves		Non Citz
2	No1			Elsie Segroves		" "
3	No.1			" "		" "
4	Nº1			" "		" "
5						
6	No 1 denied by Com in 1896 case #8					
7	Was admitted by U.S. Court, Ardmore, I.T. Dec. 22, 1897, Court Case No 115					
8						
9	DENIED CITIZENSHIP BY THE CHOCTAW AND					
10	CHICKASAW CITIZENSHIP COURT					
11						
12						
13	No.3 Enrolled June 26, 1900					
14	Nº4 Born Oct. 7, 1901 enrolled July 23, 1902					
15						
16	For child of No1 see NB #1028 (Act Apr 26 '06)					
17						

202

Choctaw By Blood Enrollment Cards 1898-1914

RESIDENCE: Chickasaw Natn
POST OFFICE: Heard, I.T.

Choctaw **Nation**   Choctaw **Roll**

CARD NO. **5003**
FIELD NO. C 48

Dawes' Roll No.	NAME	Relationship to Person First Named	AGE	SEX	BLOOD	TRIBAL ENROLLMENT		
						Year	County	No.
1	Bottoms, W^m I	Named	10	M				
2	" Claudia[sic] M	Brother	6	"				
3	" Bettie J	Sister	3	F				
4								
5								
6								
7								
8								
9								
10								
11								
12								
13								
14								
15								
16								
17								

TRIBAL ENROLLMENT OF PARENTS

	Name of Father	Year	County	Name of Mother	Year	County
1	N.W. Bottoms	Dead	Non Citz	Marie L Bottoms		Non Citz
2	" "	" "	" "	" "	" "
3	" "	" "	" "	" "	" "
4						
5						
6						
7	Nos 1-2-3 were denied by Com in 1896 Case #8					
8	Nos 1-2-3 were admitted by the U.S. Court Ardmore, I.T. Dec 22, 1897					
9	Court Case No 115					
10						
11						
12						
13						
14						
15						
16						
17						

Choctaw By Blood Enrollment Cards 1898-1914

<table>
<tr><td>RESIDENCE: Chickasaw Natn</td><td rowspan="2">Choctaw **Nation**   Choctaw **Roll**</td><td>CARD NO. **5004**</td></tr>
<tr><td>POST OFFICE: Chickasha, I.T.</td><td>FIELD NO. C 49</td></tr>
</table>

Dawes' Roll No.	NAME	Relationship to Person First Named	AGE	SEX	BLOOD	TRIBAL ENROLLMENT		
						Year	County	No.
1	Kirkland, Inez	Named	18	F				
2	" Roxie A	Sister	14	"				
3	" Sallie	"	10	"				
4								
5								
6								
7								
8								
9								
10								
11								
12								
13								
14								
15								
16								
17								

TRIBAL ENROLLMENT OF PARENTS

	Name of Father	Year	County	Name of Mother	Year	County
1	Wm Kirkland		Non Citz	Sarah Kirkland		Non Citz
2	" "		" "	" "		" "
3	" "		" "	" "		" "
4						
5						
6						
7	Nos 1-2-3 were denied by Com in 1896 Case #8					
8	No* 1-2-3 were admitted by the U.S. Court, Ardmore, I.T. Dec 22 1897					
9	Court Case No 115					
10						
11	No2 was admitted under name of Roxie					
12						
13						
14						
15						
16						
17			Date of Application for Enrollment			9-14-98

Choctaw By Blood Enrollment Cards 1898-1914

| RESIDENCE: | Chickasaw Natn | | | | | | CARD NO. | **5005** |
| POST OFFICE: | Elmore, I.T. | Choctaw **Nation** | | Choctaw **Roll** | | | FIELD NO. | C |

Dawes' Roll No.	NAME	Relationship to Person First Named	AGE	SEX	BLOOD	TRIBAL ENROLLMENT		
---	---	---	---	---	---	Year	County	No.
1	Crawford, Kate	Named	24	F				
2	" Nora Lee	Dau	3	"				
3	" William J.B.	Son	9mo	M				
4								
5								
6								
7								
8								
9								
10								
11								
12								
13								
14								
15								
16								
17								

#3 DISMISSED JAN 23 1905

TRIBAL ENROLLMENT OF PARENTS

	Name of Father	Year	County	Name of Mother	Year	County
1	Jim Reagen	Dead	Non Citz	Jane Reagen	Dead	Non Citz
2	William Crawford		" "	No 1		
3	" "		" "	No 1		
4						
5	Nos 1-2 were denied by Com in 1896 Case # 8					
6	Nos 1-2 were admitted by the U.S. Court. Ardmore. I.T. Dec 22, 1897					
7	Court Case No 115					
8						
9	No3 was born Dec 11, 1898					
10						
11	DENIED CITIZENSHIP BY THE CHOCTAW AND					
12	CHICKASAW CITIZENSHIP COURT					
13						
14						
15						
16						
17						

205

Choctaw By Blood Enrollment Cards 1898-1914

RESIDENCE:	Chickasaw Natn						CARD NO.	**5006**
POST OFFICE:	Ada, I.T.		Choctaw **Nation**		Choctaw **Roll**		FIELD NO.	C 51

Dawes' Roll No.	NAME	Relationship to Person First Named	AGE	SEX	BLOOD	TRIBAL ENROLLMENT		
						Year	County	No.
1	Hatcher, Lutitia		15	F				
2	" John A	Son	6wks	M				
3	" Ollie Everet[sic]	Son	2mo	M				
4	" Ben Noble	Son	1mo	M				
5								
6								
#2-3-4 7	DISMISSED							
8	JAN 23 1905							
9								
10								
11								
12								
13								
14	DENIED CITIZENSHIP BY THE CHOCTAW AND							
15	CHICKASAW CITIZENSHIP COURT							
16								
17								

TRIBAL ENROLLMENT OF PARENTS

	Name of Father	Year	County	Name of Mother	Year	County
1	John W Morrow		Non Citz	Rebecca Morrow		Non Citz
2	E.M. Hatcher		" "	No1		
3	" " "		" "	No.1		
4	" " "		" "	N⁰1		
5	No.1 was denied by Com in 1896, case #8					
6	Was admitted under the name of Letitia Morrow, by the U.S. Court,					
7	Ardmore, I.T. Dec. 22, 1897, Court Case No 115. Was married to					
8	Martin Hatcher, July 25, 1898, under license issued by Clerk of					
9	Court at Ada, I.T					
10						
11	Parents of No1 are enrolled on Choctaw card #5023					
12	No.3 Enrolled June 8th, 1901					
13	N⁰4 Born July 18, 1902; enrolled Aug 14, 1902					
14						
15				No2 enrolled Dec 16/99		
16						1/122
17				Date of Application for Enrollment		9-14-98

Choctaw By Blood Enrollment Cards 1898-1914

RESIDENCE: Chickasaw Natn   Choctaw **Nation**   Choctaw **Roll**   CARD NO. **5007**
POST OFFICE: Purcell, I.T.   FIELD NO. C 52

Dawes' Roll No.	NAME	Relationship to Person First Named	AGE	SEX	BLOOD	TRIBAL ENROLLMENT		
						Year	County	No.
1	Jones, Martha J		58	F				
2								
3								
4								
5								
6	Not denied by C. C. C. as Martha Jones							
7								
8								
9								
10								
11								
12								
13								
14								
15								
16								
17								

TRIBAL ENROLLMENT OF PARENTS

	Name of Father	Year	County	Name of Mother	Year	County
1	Thos Boone	Dead	Non Citz	Louisa Boone	Dead	Non Citz
2						
3						
4						
5		No. 1 was denied by Com in 1896, case No 18				
6		Was admitted by the U. S. Court, Ardmore, I.T. Dec 21, 1897				
7		Court case No 88				
8						
9		Was admitted as Martha Jones				
10						
11						
12						
13						
14						
15						
16						1/126
17						9-14-98

Choctaw By Blood Enrollment Cards 1898-1914

| RESIDENCE: | State of Texas | | | | | | | | CARD NO. | 5008 |
| POST OFFICE: | Bryson, Texas | | Choctaw **Nation** | | | Choctaw **Roll** | | | FIELD NO. | C 53 |

Dawes' Roll No.	NAME	Relationship to Person First Named	AGE	SEX	BLOOD	TRIBAL ENROLLMENT		
						Year	County	No.
1	Bottoms, Wm F	Named	63	M				
2								
3								
4								
5								
6								
7								
8								
9								
10								
11								
12								
13								
14								
15								
16								
17								

TRIBAL ENROLLMENT OF PARENTS

	Name of Father	Year	County	Name of Mother	Year	County
1	Nelson Bottoms	Dead	Non Citz	Sally A Bottoms	Dead	Non Citz
2						
3						
4						
5						
6						
7						
8		No 1 denied in 96 Case #8				
9		Was admitted by the U.S. Court, Ardmore, I.T. Dec 22, 1898				
10		Court Case No 115				
11						
12						
13						
14						
15						
16						1/128
17					Date of Application for Enrollment.	9-14-98

DENIED CITIZENSHIP BY THE CHOCTAW AND CHICKASAW CITIZENSHIP COURT

Choctaw By Blood Enrollment Cards 1898-1914

RESIDENCE: Chickasaw Natn   Choctaw **Nation**   Choctaw **Roll**   CARD No. **5009**
POST OFFICE: Roberson, I.T.   FIELD No. C 54

Dawes' Roll No.	NAME	Relationship to Person	AGE	SEX	BLOOD	TRIBAL ENROLLMENT		
						Year	County	No.
DP	1 Winter, Charles	First Named	63	M	IW	1896	Chick Dist	15205
	2							
	3							
	4							
	5							
	6							
	7							
	8							
	9							
	10							
	11							
	12							
	13							
	14							
	15							
	16							
	17							

DISMISSED

TRIBAL ENROLLMENT OF PARENTS

	Name of Father	Year	County	Name of Mother	Year	County
1	Henry Winter	Dead	Non Citz	Margaret Winter	Dead	Non Citz
2						
3						
4						
5						
6						
7	No1 was denied in 96 Case #519					
8	Was admitted by the U.S. Court, Ardmore, I.T. Nov 15, 1897					
9	Court Case No 116					
10						
11						
12	On 1896 roll as Chas. Winters					
13						
14						
15						
16						1/130
17						

Choctaw By Blood Enrollment Cards 1898-1914

RESIDENCE: Chickasaw Natn
POST OFFICE: Foster, I.T.

CARD NO. **5010**
FIELD NO. C 55

Dawes' Roll No.	NAME	Relationship to Person First Named	AGE	SEX	BLOOD	TRIBAL ENROLLMENT Year	TRIBAL ENROLLMENT County	TRIBAL ENROLLMENT No.
1	Pyburn, Licuella[sic]	First Named	30	F				
2	" M. H.	Son	12	M				
3	" Benj. H	"	10	"				
4	" James B	"	8	"				
5	" Mary L	Dau	6	F				
6	" John F	Son	8mo	M				
7	" Willie Ann	Dau	4mo	F				
8								
9	DISMISSED MAY 7 1904							
10								
11								
12								
13								
14	For child of No1 see NB #1017 (Act Apr 26 '06)							
15								
16								
17								

TRIBAL ENROLLMENT OF PARENTS

	Name of Father	Year	County	Name of Mother	Year	County
1	John Mitchell		Non Citz	Mary Mitchell		Non Citz
2	John W Pyburn		" "	No 1		
3	" "		" "	No 1		
4	" "		" "	No 1		
5	" "		" "	No 1		
6	" "		" "	No 1		
7	" "		" "	No 1		
8						
9	Nos 1 to 5 inclusive were denied by Com in 1896 case #					
10	Nos 1 to 5 were admitted by the U.S. Court, Central Dist Aug 25, 1897					
11	Court No 116					
12						
13						
14	No6 was born Jan 1, 1898					
15		No.7 Enrolled July 20, 1900				
16						
17				Date of Application for Enrollment	9-14-98	

DENIED CITIZENSHIP BY THE CHOCTAW AND CHICKASAW CITIZENSHIP COURT

Choctaw By Blood Enrollment Cards 1898-1914

| RESIDENCE: | Chickasaw Natn | P.O. Wynnewood I.T. | | | | | CARD No. | **5011** |
| POST OFFICE: | Elmore, I.T. | | | | | | FIELD No. | C |

Dawes' Roll No.	NAME	Relationship to Person First Named	AGE	SEX	BLOOD	TRIBAL ENROLLMENT		
						Year	County	No.
1	Welch, Emma	Named	28	F				
2	" Adella B	Dau	12	"				
3	" John N	Son	10	M				
4	" Christina P	Dau	8	F				
5	" William M	Son	5	M				
6	" Docia A	Dau	3	F				
7	" Rosa M	"	8mo	"				
8	" Joe Ella	"	2mo	"				
9								
10								
11	Nos7&8 MAY 27 1904 DISMISSED							
12								
13								
14								
15	DISMISSED							
16	JAN 23 1905							
17								

	TRIBAL ENROLLMENT OF PARENTS						
	Name of Father	Year	County	Name of Mother	Year	County
1	John Mitchell		Non Citz	Mary Mitchell		Non Citz
2	Tom Welch		" "	No 1		
3	" "		" "	No 1		
4	" "		" "	No 1		
5	" "		" "	No 1		
6	" "		" "	No 1		
7	" "		" "	No 1		
8	" "		" "	No 1		

DENIED CITIZENSHIP BY THE CHOCTAW AND CHICKASAW CITIZENSHIP COURT

9 Nos 1 to 6 inclusive were denied by Com in 1896 case #29
10 Nos 1 to 6 inclusive were admitted by the U.S. Court, Central Dist
11 Aug 25, 1897
12 No2 admitted as "Odella B", No3 as "John M", No5 as "Melton"
13 These people were admitted under the name of Welsh
14
15 For child of No2 see (Act Apr 26'06) NB #1050
1079
16 No7 was born Jan 16, 1898
17 No8 born Oct. 28, 1901: Enrolled Dec 13 1901

Date of Application for Enrollment 9-14-98

Choctaw By Blood Enrollment Cards 1898-1914

| RESIDENCE: | Chickasaw Natn | | | | | | CARD NO. | **5012** |
| POST OFFICE: | Wallville, I.T. | | Choctaw **Nation** | | Choctaw **Roll** | | FIELD NO. | C 57 |

Dawes' Roll No.	NAME	Relationship to Person	AGE	SEX	BLOOD	TRIBAL ENROLLMENT		
						Year	County	No.
1	Randolph, Dick	First Named	40	M				
2	" Myrtie	Wife	33	F				
3	" Minnie	Dau	15	"				
4	" DeCose	Son	8	M				
5	" Herman	"	6	"				
6	" Hughie	"	3	"				
7	" Lena R	Dau	11mo	F				
8	Myers, Lelia Blanche	Gran. dau	4mo	F	#7-8-9-10	DISMISSED		
9	Randolph, Vivian	Dau	2yrs	F		JAN 2 - 190		
10	Myers, John Boyd	Grand son	1mo	M				
11								

Nos 1 to 6 inclusive were denied
by Com in 1896 case # 1182

No2 denied by C.C.C.C. as "Myrtie Randolph"
"   "   "   or "Myrtle Randolph"
No3 "   "   "   as "Minnie Randolph"

TRIBAL ENROLLMENT OF PARENTS

	Name of Father	Year	County	Name of Mother	Year	County
1	Geo Randolph	Dead	Non Citz	Mary Randolph	Dead	Non Citz
2	Giles Thompson	"	Choc Citz	Ellen Thompson		Choc Citz
3	No1			No2		
4	No1			No2		
5	No1			No2		
6	No1			No2		
7	No1			No2		
8	William Myers		Intermarried	No3		
9	No1			No2		
10	William Myers on Choctaw Card #D535					
11	Nos1 to 6 inclusive were admitted by the U.S. Court, Ardmore, I.T. Jan 19, 1898					
12	Court Case No 125					
13	No10 Born May 10th 1902: Enrolled June 28th 1902					
14	No7 was born Oct 8, 1897					
15	No.3 is the wife of William Myers on Choctaw					
16	Evidence of marriage filed with #D535					1/138
17	No.8 Enrolled Feby 9th, 1901				Date of Application for Enrollment.	9-14-98

DENIED CITIZENSHIP BY THE CHOCTAW AND
CHICKASAW CITIZENSHIP COURT

No.9 Born Oct. 18, 1899: Enrolled Nov. 26, 1901
Nos1 to 6 incl now in C.C.C.C. Case No 271

Choctaw By Blood Enrollment Cards 1898-1914

RESIDENCE: Chickasaw Natn
POST OFFICE: Whitebead, I.T.

Choctaw **Nation**   Choctaw **Roll**

CARD NO. **5013**
FIELD NO. C 58

Dawes' Roll No.	NAME	Relationship to Person First Named	AGE	SEX	BLOOD	TRIBAL ENROLLMENT Year	County	No.
1	Thompson, DeCosa	Named	27	M				
2	" Ellen	Dau	8	F				
3								
4								
5								
6								
7								
8								
9								
10								
11								
12								
13								
14								
15								
16								
17								

#4-3- DISMISSED MAY 27 190_

TRIBAL ENROLLMENT OF PARENTS

	Name of Father	Year	County	Name of Mother	Year	County
1	Giles Thompson	Dead	Choc Citz	Ellen Thompson		Choc Citz
2	No1			Mary Thompson		Non Citz
3						
4						
5						
6	Nos 1&2 were denied by Com in 1896 Case #1182					
7	Nos 1&2 were admitted by the U.S. Court, Ardmore, I.T. Jan 19 1898					
8	Court Case No 125					
9						
10	No1 is of unsound mind					
11						
12	No.2 is same person as Ella Thompson on Choctaw card #5076					
13						
14						
15						
16						
17	See C 11					

Date of Application for Enrollment.

213

Choctaw By Blood Enrollment Cards 1898-1914

RESIDENCE: Atoka County
POST OFFICE: Jeffs[sic], I.T.

Choctaw **Nation**   Choctaw **Roll**

CARD No. **5014**
FIELD No. C 59

Dawes' Roll No.	NAME	Relationship to Person First Named	AGE	SEX	BLOOD	TRIBAL ENROLLMENT Year	County	No.
1	Mitchell, John	Named	60	M				
2	" William	Son	17	"				
3	" Robert H	"	15	"				
4	" Docia A	Dau	13	F				
5	" Myrtle L	"	11	"				
6	" Jessie Lee	GrandDau	3½ mo	F				
7	" Roy Addus	Gr Son	1 mo	M				
8	" Mattie	Gr Dau	1 mo	F				
9								
10	DISMISSED MAY 27 1904							
11	No.4 is the wife of William Sulliven[sic],							
12	A U.S. Citizen: Oct. 10, 1902							
13	For children of No2 see NB #1005 (Act Apr 26'06)							
14	" " " No4 " " #1082 " " "							
15								
16	Nos 1 to 5 inclusive were admitted by the U.S. Court, Central Dist							
17	Aug 26, 1897, Court Case No 116							

TRIBAL ENROLLMENT OF PARENTS

	Name of Father	Year	County	Name of Mother	Year	County
1	David Mitchell	Dead	Non Citz	Rebecca Mitchell	Dead	Non Citz
2	No1			Mary F Mitchell		" "
3	No1			" " "		" "
4	No1			" " "		" "
5	No1			" " "		" "
6	No2			Maud E Mitchell		" "
7	Nº3			Nancy M Mitchell		" "
8	Nº2			Maud E Mitchell		" "
9	Mary Mitchell, wife of No.1 and mother of above children					
10	on Choctaw card D.416					
11	No6 Enrolled April 11, 1901					
12	The correct name of No2 is William J Mitchell. See affidavit of John Mitchell filed April 11, 1901					
13	Nº3 is now the husband of Nancy M Mitchell, non-citizen. Evidence of marriage filed April 28, 1902					
14	Nº7 Born March 20, 1902: enrolled April 28, 1902					
15	Nº2 is now the husband of Maude E Mitchell, non-citizen. Evidence of marriage filed Sept 18, 1902					
16	Nº8 Born Aug 21, 1902: enrolled Sept 18, 1902					
17	Nos 1 to 8 incl now in C.CC.C. Case #1013 Nos 1 to 5 denied by Com in 1896,					

DENIED CITIZENSHIP BY THE CHOCTAW AND CHICKASAW CITIZENSHIP COURT

case #29

Date of Application for Enrollment.

9-14-98

214

Choctaw By Blood Enrollment Cards 1898-1914

RESIDENCE: Atoka County
POST OFFICE: Jeffs[sic], I.T.

Choctaw **Nation**   Choctaw **Roll**

CARD NO. **5015**
FIELD NO. C 60

Dawes' Roll No.	NAME	Relationship to Person First Named	AGE	SEX	BLOOD	TRIBAL ENROLLMENT		
						Year	County	No.
✓	1 Mitchell, John W	Named	23	M				
	2							
	3							
	4							
	5							
	6							
	7							
	8							
	9							
	10							
	11							
	12							
	13							
	14							
	15							
	16							
	17							

TRIBAL ENROLLMENT OF PARENTS

Name of Father	Year	County	Name of Mother	Year	County
1 John Mitchell		Non Citz	Mary F Mitchell		Non Citz
2					
3					
4					
5					
6					
7					
8					
9					
10					
11					
12					
13					
14					
15					
16					
17					

Choctaw By Blood Enrollment Cards 1898-1914

| RESIDENCE: | Atoka County | | | | | | CARD No. **5016** |
| POST OFFICE: | Jeffs[sic], I.T. | Choctaw **Nation** | Choctaw **Roll** | | | | FIELD No. C 61 |

Dawes' Roll No.	NAME	Relationship to Person First Named	AGE	SEX	BLOOD	TRIBAL ENROLLMENT		
						Year	County	No.
✓ 1	Mitchell, Andrew J	Named	54	M				
2								
3								
4								
5								
6								
7								
8								
9								
10								
11								
12								
13								
14								
15								
16								
17								

DENIED CITIZENSHIP BY THE CHOCTAW AND CHICKASAW CITIZENSHIP COURT

TRIBAL ENROLLMENT OF PARENTS

	Name of Father	Year	County	Name of Mother	Year	County
1	David Mitchell	Dead	Non Citz	Rebecca J Mitchell	Dead	Non Citz
2						
3						
4						
5						
6						
7	No1 was denied by Com in 1896, case #19					
8	Was admitted by the U.S. Court, Central Dist. Aug 25, 1897					
9	Court Case No					
10						
11	No1 is [illegible]					
12						
13						
14						
15						
16						I 140
17					Date of Application for Enrollment	9-14-98

216

Choctaw By Blood Enrollment Cards 1898-1914

RESIDENCE:	Chickasaw Natn		Choctaw **Nation** Choctaw **Roll**	CARD No. **5017**	
POST OFFICE:	Chickasha, I.T.			FIELD No. C 62	

Dawes' Roll No.	NAME	Relationship to Person First Named	AGE	SEX	BLOOD	TRIBAL ENROLLMENT		
						Year	County	No.
1	Kirkland, Joseph	Named	26	M				
2	" Beulah	Dau	3	F				
3	" Emily	"	1	"				
4	" Lora Pruda	"	3mo	F				
5	" Laura M	"	1mo	F				
6								
7	#3-4-5- DISMISSED	JAN						
8								
9								
10								
11								
12								
13								
14								
15								
16								
17								

TRIBAL ENROLLMENT OF PARENTS

	Name of Father	Year	County	Name of Mother	Year	County
1	Wm Kirkland	Dead	Non Citz	Sarah Kirkland		Non Citz
2	No 1			Ermine Kirkland		" "
3	No 1			" "		" "
4	No. 1			" "		" "
5	N⁰ 1			" "		" "
6	Nos 1&2 were denied by Com in 1896 Case #8					
7	Nos 1-2 were admitted by the U.S. Court, Ardmore, I.T. Dec 22, 1897					
8	Court Case No 115					
9						
10	No.3 was born Oct 25, 1897					
11	N⁰5 Born April 15, 1902: Enrolled May 23, 1902					
12						
13	DENIED CITIZENSHIP BY THE CHOCTAW AND					
14	CHICKASAW CITIZENSHIP COURT					
15						
16						
17					Date of Application for Enrollment.	9-15-98

Choctaw By Blood Enrollment Cards 1898-1914

RESIDENCE:	Chickasaw Natn						CARD NO. **5018**
POST OFFICE:	Chickasha, I.T.	Choctaw **Nation** Choctaw **Roll**					FIELD NO. C 63

Dawes' Roll No.	NAME	Relationship to Person First Named	AGE	SEX	BLOOD	TRIBAL ENROLLMENT		
						Year	County	No.
1	Kirkland, William		24	M				
2	" Monte	Son	4	"				
3	" Lee	"	2	"				
4	" Myrtle	Dau	5mo	F				
5								
6								
7								
8								
9								
10								
11								
12								
13								
14								
15								
16								
17								

#4 DISMISSED JAN 2

DP

TRIBAL ENROLLMENT OF PARENTS

	Name of Father	Year	County	Name of Mother	Year	County
1	Wm Kirkland	Dead	Non Citz	Sara Kirkland		Non Citz
2	No 1			Inez Kirkland		" "
3	No 1			" "		" "
4	No 1			" "		" "
5						
6						
7	Nos 1-2-3 were denied by Com in 1896 Case #8					
8	Nos 1-2-3 were admitted by the U.S. Court. Ardmore. I.T. Dec 22, 1897					
9	Court Case No 115					
10						
11						
12						
13	No4 was born May 13. 1898					
14						
15						
16						
17						

DENIED CITIZENSHIP BY THE CHOCTAW AND CHICKASAW CITIZENSHIP COURT

Date of Application for Enrollment 9-15-98

218

Choctaw By Blood Enrollment Cards 1898-1914

RESIDENCE: Chickasaw Natn
POST OFFICE: Paoli, I.T.

Choctaw **Nation** Choctaw **Roll**

CARD NO. **5019**
FIELD NO. C 64

Dawes' Roll No.	NAME	Relationship to Person First Named	AGE	SEX	BLOOD	Year	County	No.
1	Kirkland, Eldredge	Named	45	M				
2	" Jesse E	Son	16	"				
3	" Mary P	Dau	14	F				
4	" Wm W	Son	11	M				
5	" Sallie G	Dau	2	F				
6	" Charley Adnew	Son	2mo	M				
7								
8								
9								
10								
11								
12								
13								
14								
15								
16	For child of No3 see NB 994 - (Act Apr 26-06)							
17	" " " No1 " " 1075 " " "							

TRIBAL ENROLLMENT OF PARENTS

	Name of Father	Year	County	Name of Mother	Year	County
1	Wm H Kirkland	Dead	Non Citz	Prudie Kirkland	Dead	Non Citz
2	No1			Ephelia Kirkland		" "
3	No1			" "		" "
4	No1			" "		" "
5	No1			" "		" "
6	No1			" "		" "
7						
8	Nos 1 to 4 inclusive, denied by Com in 1896 case #8					
9	Nos 1 to 5 inclusive, were admitted by the U.S. Court, Ardmore, I.T.					
10	Dec 22, 1897 Court Case No 115					
11						
12	No5 was born Nov 18, 1897					
13						
14	No6 Enrolled July 29, 1901					
15						
16						
17	No.5 Enrolled March 21st, 1900					

Choctaw By Blood Enrollment Cards 1898-1914

RESIDENCE: Chickasaw Nation
POST OFFICE: Ada, Ind. Ter.

Choctaw **Nation**   Choctaw **Roll**

CARD NO. **5020**
FIELD NO. C 65

Dawes' Roll No.	NAME	Relationship to Person First Named	AGE	SEX	BLOOD	TRIBAL ENROLLMENT		
						Year	County	No.
1	Putnam, Pearl	Named	27					
2	" Hattie J	dau	8					
3	" Frankie L	"	5					
DP 4	" Lena	"	9mo					
5								
6								
7	#4 DISMISSED							
8		905						
9								
10								
11								
12								
13								
14								
15								
16								
17								

TRIBAL ENROLLMENT OF PARENTS

	Name of Father	Year	County	Name of Mother	Year	County
1	William F Bottoms		Non Citizen	Jane Bottoms		Non Citizen
2	Ezekiel M Putnam		" "	No 1		
3	" " "		" "	No 1		
4	" " "		" "	No 1		
5						
6						
7	Nos 1-2-3 denied in 1896 case #2					
8	All admitted by United States Court at Ardmore, Dec 22nd 1897 Case 115					
9	except Lena, born January 21st 1898					
10						
11						
12						
13						
14	DENIED CITIZENSHIP BY THE CHOCTAW AND					
15	CHICKASAW CITIZENSHIP COURT					
16						1/150
17						

Choctaw By Blood Enrollment Cards 1898-1914

RESIDENCE: Jack County Texas

POST OFFICE: Bryson Texas

Choctaw **Nation** Choctaw **Roll**

CARD NO. **5021**

FIELD NO. C 66

Dawes' Roll No.	NAME	Relationship to Person First Named	AGE	SEX	BLOOD	TRIBAL ENROLLMENT		
						Year	County	No.
1	Bennett, Pauline E 26	First Named	22	F				
2	" William F 6	Son	2	M				
3	" Boyd S 4	"	2mo	"				
4								
5	#2883 DISMISSED							
6								
7								
8								
9								
10								
11								
12								
13								
14								
15								
16								
17								

TRIBAL ENROLLMENT OF PARENTS

	Name of Father	Year	County	Name of Mother	Year	County
1	William F Bottoms		Non Citizen	Jane Bottoms		Non Citizen
2	Orion Bennett		" "	No1		
3	" "		" "	No1		
4						
5						
6	No1 denied by Com in 1896 case #8					
7	No1 admitted by United States Court at Ardmore Dec 22nd 1897 Case 115					
8	No2 born September 30th 1896					
9	No3 " July 15th 1898					
10						
11						
12						
13	DENIED CITIZENSHIP BY THE CHOCTAW AND					
14	CHICKASAW CITIZENSHIP COURT					
15						
16						
17						

221

						TRIBAL ENROLLMENT		
Dawes' Roll No.	NAME	Relationship to Person First Named	AGE	SEX	BLOOD	Year	County	No.
1	Bottoms, William H	Named	42	M				
2	" Rosa B	dau	20	F				
3	" William E	son	14	M				
DP 4	Riddle, Donia Myrtle	Grand Dau	3 mo	F				
DP 5	" Hattie Pearl	Grand Dau	1 mo	F				
6								
7								
8	#4-5- DISMISSED							
9	Jan							
10								
11								
12								
13								
14								
15								
16								
17								

RESIDENCE: Choctaw Nation
POST OFFICE: Allen, Ind Ter

Choctaw Nation   Choctaw Roll

CARD NO. 5022
FIELD NO. C 67

TRIBAL ENROLLMENT OF PARENTS

	Name of Father	Year	County	Name of Mother	Year	County
1	William F Bottoms		Non Citizen	Jane Bottoms		Non Citizen
2	No 1			Dona "		
3	No 1			" "		
4	G A Riddle		" "	No 2		
5	" " "			No 2		
6	Nos 1-2-3 were denied by Com in 1896 Case #8					
7	Admitted by United States Court at Ardmore Dec 22nd 1897 Case 115					
8						
9						
10	No.2 is now the wife of G.A. Riddle					
11			Mar 27th, 1900			
12	No5 born Oct 12th 1901: Enrolled Nov. 15th 1901					
13	DENIED CITIZENSHIP BY THE CHOCTAW AND					
14	1,2&3 CHICKASAW CITIZENSHIP COURT					
15	For child of No3 see (Act Apr 26'06) NB #1052					
16	" " " " 2 " " " " 1080					1/146
17	Oct 12 1901 PO Pauh H			No 4 Enrolled May 2		

Choctaw By Blood Enrollment Cards 1898-1914

RESIDENCE:	Chickasaw Nation					CARD NO.	5023
POST OFFICE:	Ada, Ind. Ter.	Choctaw **Nation**	Choctaw **Roll**			FIELD NO.	C 68

Dawes' Roll No.	NAME	Relationship to Person First Named	AGE	SEX	BLOOD	TRIBAL ENROLLMENT		
						Year	County	No.
1	Morrow, Rebecca	Named	40	F				
2	"　William F	son	19	M				
3	"　Walter J	"	17	"				
4	"　Mary J	dau	11	F				
5	"　Beulah	"	9	"				
6	"　Minnie	"	5	"				
7	"　Winnie	"	5	"				
8	"　Martin F	Son	5mo	M				
9	"　Boyd	"	1mo	"				
10								
11	Nos 1 to 7 inclusive denied							
12	by Com in 1896, case #8							
13								
14								
15	#8-9- DISMISSED							
16	JAN 190							
17								

TRIBAL ENROLLMENT OF PARENTS

	Name of Father	Year	County	Name of Mother	Year	County
1	William F Bottoms		Non Citizen	Jane Bottoms		Non Citizen
2	John Morrow		"　"	No 1		
3	"　"			No 1		
4	"　"			No 1		
5	"　"			No 1		
6	"　"			No 1		
7	"　"			No 1		
8	"　"			No 1		
9	"　"			No 1		

DENIED CITIZENSHIP BY THE CHOCTAW AND CHICKASAW CITIZENSHIP COURT

10　Admitted by United States Court at Ardmore Dec 22nd 1897 Case 115
11　Judgment of U.S. Ct admitting Nos 1 to 7 vacated (remainder illegible)
12　No3 admitted as Walter Morrow
13　No4　"　"　Jewell　"
14
15　No1 is mother of No1 on Choctaw card #5006
16　No2 is now the husband of Emma P Morrow on Choctaw card #D796 - a non citizen
17　No9 Born Sept 25, 1902 Proof filed Oct 24, 1902
For child of No2 see NB #1029 (Act Apr 26'06)

Choctaw By Blood Enrollment Cards 1898-1914

RESIDENCE: Chickasaw Natn
POST OFFICE: Paoli, I.T.

Choctaw **Nation**　Choctaw **Roll**

CARD NO. **5024**
FIELD NO. C 69

Dawes' Roll No.	NAME	Relationship to Person First Named	AGE	SEX	BLOOD	TRIBAL ENROLLMENT Year	County	No.
1	Bottoms, Zachriah[sic] T	Named	39	M				
2	" William L 23	Son	19	"				
3	" Frances C 20	Dau	16	F				
4	" James Z 18	Son	14	M				
5	" Joseph S 16	"	12	"				
6	" Bertha M 14	Dau	10	F				
7	" Septemer 9	"	5	"				
8	" Easier E 7	"	3	"				
9	" Gracie 4	"	7mo	"				
10	" Thomas B 2	son	3mo	M				
11	Moore, Lonnie 1	G Dau[sic]	2mo	M				
12	DISMISSED							
13	JAN 24 1905	No2 is now husband of Hattie Lee Bottoms on Choc Card #D788						
14		Nos 1 to 8 inclusive were denied by Com in '96 Case #8						
15		No10 Enrolled May 24, 1900						
16	DISMISSED	JAN 24 1905						
17								

#11 (row 12), #9-1 (row 16)

TRIBAL ENROLLMENT OF PARENTS

	Name of Father	Year	County	Name of Mother	Year	County
1	Smith Bottoms	Dead	Non Citz	Nancy Bottoms	Dead	Non Citz
2	No1			Winnie E Bottoms		" "
3	No1			" "		" "
4	No1			" "		" "
5	No1					
6	No1					" "
7	No1					" "
8	No1			" "		" "
9	No1			" "		" "
10	No1			" "		" "
11	Leonidas L Moore		noncitizen	No.3		
12	Nos1 to 8 inclusive were admitted by the U.S. Court, Ardmore, I.T.					
13	Dec 22, 1897 Court Case No 115					
14				No3 is now the wife of Leonidas L Moore a noncitizen. Evidence		
15	No9 was born Jan 17, 1898			of marriage requested July 31,1901. Filed Aug 19, 1901		
16				For child of No2 see (Apr 26-06) NB #1045　1/158		
17	No.11 Enrolled July 31, 1901			Date of Application for Enrollment.　9-15-98		

Choctaw By Blood Enrollment Cards 1898-1914

| RESIDENCE: | Chickasaw Natn | | | | | | CARD NO. **5025** | | |
| POST OFFICE: | Foster, I.T. | Choctaw **Nation** | | Choctaw **Roll** | | | FIELD NO. C 70 | | |

Dawes' Roll No.	NAME	Relationship to Person First Named	AGE	SEX	BLOOD	TRIBAL ENROLLMENT Year	County	No.
1	Hunter, John M		52	M				
2	"	ENROLLMENT CASE OF Z. T. BOTTOMS, ET AL.						
3	"	Transmitted to Dept. 3-21-16 for						
4	"	temporary use. To be returned.						
5		Zachariah T Bottoms, et al.						
6		#9-10-11						
7		5024						
8								
9		Court No. 115 Dawes No. 8						
10		Z.T. Bottoms, et al, vs Choctaw Nation At Ardmore 5						
11								
12		Choctaw No, 8 1896						
13		Z. T. Bottoms vs Louis Hill 75-T						
14								
15		#75 Z.T. Bottoms vs Nations						
16								
17		No. 75						

	Name of F							County
	Z. T. Bottoms, et al, vs Choctaw-Chickasaw Nations (1)							
1	Jno F Hunter	Dead	Non Citz	Mary Hunter	Dead	Non Citz		
2	P V Doss	"	"	"	Sina Doss	"	"	"
3	No1			No2				
4	No1			No2				
6	Nos1 to 4 inclusive were denied by Com in 1896 Case # 1334							
7	Nos1 to 4 inclusive were admitted by the U.S. Court, Ardmore, I.T. Jan 17 1898 #73							

225

| RESIDENCE: Chickasaw Natn | | | | | Choctaw **Nation** Choctaw **Roll** | | CARD No. **5026** | | |
| POST OFFICE: Wallville, I.T. | | | | | | | FIELD No. C 71 | | |

Dawes' Roll No.	NAME	Relationship to Person First Named	AGE	SEX	BLOOD	TRIBAL ENROLLMENT		
						Year	County	No.
1	Thompson, Walidemir[?]	Named	25	M	1/8			
2	" Dollie	Dau	10mo	F	1/16			
DP 3	" Myrtle	"	7mo	"	1/16			
DP 4	" Claudia Ellen	Dau	4mo	F	1/16			
DP 5	" Giles Clide	Son		M	1/16			
6								
# 7								
3-4-5 8	DISMISSED							
9								
10								
11								
12								
13								
14								
15	DENIED CITIZENSHIP BY THE CHOCTAW AND							
16	CHICKASAW CITIZENSHIP COURT							
17								

TRIBAL ENROLLMENT OF PARENTS

	Name of Father	Year	County	Name of Mother	Year	County
1	Giles Thompson	Dead	Choc Citz	Ellen Thompson		Choc Citz
2	No1			Mary Thompson		Non Citz
3	No1			" "		" "
4	No1			" "		" "
5	No1			" "		" "
6	Nos1&2 were denied by Com in 1896 Case #1182					
7	Nos1&2 were admitted by the U.S. Court, Ardmore, I.T. Dec 22, 1897					
8	Case No 125					
9						
10	No3 enrolled Oct 30/99 subject to receipt of evidence of marriage of parents					
11	Letter, requesting same, this day Rec'd and filed Nov [illegible]					
12						
13	No.4 born April 29, 1901. Enrolled Nov 30, 1901					
14	No5 born August 11, 1902. Enrolled December 4, 1902					
15						
16						1/163
17				Date of Application for Enrollment	9-15-98	

Choctaw By Blood Enrollment Cards 1898-1914

RESIDENCE: Chickasaw Natn
POST OFFICE: Ardmore, I.T.

Choctaw **Nation**   Choctaw **Roll**

CARD NO. **5027**
FIELD NO. C

Dawes' Roll No.	NAME	Relationship to Person First Named	AGE	SEX	BLOOD	TRIBAL ENROLLMENT		
						Year	County	No.
1	Brown, S. A.	Named	37	M				
2	" Mattie C	Wife	22	F				
3	" Harry A	Son	7	M				
4	" Andrew C	"	18mo	"				
5								
#4 DISMISSED								
7	JAN							
8								
9								
10								
11								
12								
13								
14								
15								
16								
17								

	TRIBAL ENROLLMENT OF PARENTS					
Name of Father	Year	County	Name of Mother	Year	County	
1 A. R. Brown		Non Citz	Jennie Brown		Non Citz	
2 Woody Jones	Dead		Martha J Jones		" "	
3 No 1			No 2			
4 No 1			No 2			
5						
6						
7						
8						
9						
10						
11						
12						
13						
14						
15						
16						
17						

Date of Application for Enrollment

Choctaw By Blood Enrollment Cards 1898-1914

RESIDENCE: Chickasaw Natn
POST OFFICE: Purcell, I.T.

Choctaw **Nation**   Choctaw **Roll**

CARD NO. **5028**
FIELD NO. C

Dawes' Roll No.	NAME	Relationship to Person First Named	AGE	SEX	BLOOD	TRIBAL ENROLLMENT		
						Year	County	No.
1	Young, D. A.	First Named	50	M				
2	" Maude L	Dau	14	F				
3	" James P	Son	8	M				
4	" Martha A	Dau	7	F				
5								
6	Maud							
7	" 3	" Pate						
8	" 4							
9								
10	No1 DECISION RENDERED							
11	REFUSED							
12								
13	COPY OF DECISION FORWARDED ATTORNEYS FOR CHOCTAW AND							
14	CHICKASAW NATIONS							
15	COPY OF DECISION FORWARDED							
16	APPLICANT							
17	RECORD FORWARDED DEPARTMENT.							

TRIBAL ENROLLMENT OF PARENTS

	Name of Father	Year	County	Name of Mother	Year	County
1	James Young	Dead	Non Citz	Alice Young	Dead	Non Citz
2	No1			Miley A Young	"	" "
3	No1			" "	"	" "
4	No1			" "	"	" "
5	Nos 2 3 4 denied by Com in 1896 case #18					
6	Nos 1 to 4 inclusive were admitted by the U.S. Court, Ardmore, I.T.					
7	Dec 21, 1897 Court Case No 88					
8						
9	No2 admitted as "Maude" No3 as "Pate" and No4 as "Allie"					
10						
11						
12						
13						
14						
15						
16						
17						

Date of Application for Enrollment 9-15-98

Choctaw By Blood Enrollment Cards 1898-1914

Dawes' Roll No.	NAME	Relationship to Person First Named	AGE	SEX	BLOOD	TRIBAL ENROLLMENT Year	County	No.
1	Clemens, Mary S	Named	27	F				
2	" John F	Son	8	M				
3	" Nettie P	Dau	6	F				
4	" James W	Son	3	M				
5	" Joseph E	"	4mo	"				
6								
7								
8								
9								
10								
11								
12								
13								
14								
15								
16								
17								

No.5 DISMISSED SEP 15 1904

TRIBAL ENROLLMENT OF PARENTS

	Name of Father	Year	County	Name of Mother	Year	County
1	John M Hunter		Non Citz	Martha Hunter		Non Citz
2	W.A. Clemens		" "	No 1		
3	" "		" "	No 1		
4	" "		" "	No 1		
5	" "		" "	No 1		
6	Nos 1 to 4 inclusive were denied by Com in 1896 Case # 1334					
7						
8	Nos 1 to 4 inclusive were admitted by the U.S. Court, Ardmore, I.T.					
9	Jan 17, 1898					
10						
11	No5 was born May 18,					
12						
13	No1 admitted as "Mary W Hunter now Mrs W A Clements"					
14	No3 " " "Pearl Clements"					
15	No4 " " "William Clements"					
16						
17					Date of Application for Enrollment	9-15-98

DENIED CITIZENSHIP BY THE CHOCTAW AND CHICKASAW CITIZENSHIP COURT

229

RESIDENCE:	Chickasaw Natn							CARD NO.	5030
POST OFFICE:	Woodford, I.T.		Choctaw **Nation**		Choctaw **Roll**			FIELD NO.	C 75

Dawes' Roll No.	NAME	Relationship to Person	AGE	SEX	BLOOD	TRIBAL ENROLLMENT		
						Year	County	No.
1	Ross, Alice E	First Named	25	F				
2	" William F	Son	7	M				
3	" James S	"	5	"				
4	" John R	"	1	"				
5	" Thomas Stark	"	4mo	"				
6	" Looue[sic] Ann	Dau	2mo	F				
7								
8								
9								
10								
11								
12								
13								
14								
15								
16								
17								

Nos 4-5020 DISMISSED Sept 15 1914

TRIBAL ENROLLMENT OF PARENTS

	Name of Father	Year	County	Name of Mother	Year	County
1	Jno M Hunter		Non Citz	Martha Hunter		Non Cit
2	Thos S Ross			No 1		
3	" " "			No 1		
4	" " "			No 1		
5	" " "			No 1		
6	" " "			No 1		
7	Nos 1-2-3 were denied by Com in 1896 Case #1334					
8	Nos 1-2-3 were admitted by the U.S. Court, Ardmore, I.T. Jan 17, 1898					
9						
10	No4 was born Oct 29, 1896					
11						
12	No1 admitted as "Alice E Hunter now Mrs. Thos T. Ross"					
13	No2 " " "William Ross"					
14	No3 " " "James " "					
15	No6 Enrolled Sept 23 1901			No3 enrolled Nov 1/99		
16						
17						9-15-98

DENIED CITIZENSHIP BY THE CHOCTAW AND CHICKASAW CITIZENSHIP COURT

Choctaw By Blood Enrollment Cards 1898-1914

RESIDENCE: Chickasaw Natn
POST OFFICE: Purdy, Ind. Ter.

Choctaw **Nation**   Choctaw **Roll**

CARD NO. **5031**
FIELD NO. C 76

Dawes' Roll No.	NAME	Relationship to Person First Named	AGE	SEX	BLOOD	TRIBAL ENROLLMENT Year	County	No.
	1 Thompson Mary A	Named	40	F	IW		Choctaw residing in Chickasaw District	
VOID	2 Freeney Benjamin A	son	11	M	1/8		"	CCR#0 48
VOID	3 " Martha E	dau	9	F	1/8		"	CCR#2 195
VOID	4 " Mary A	"	6	"	1/8		"	
	5 Thompson Winnie E	"	1mo	"				
	6 Thompson, Lee Wesley	Son	6wks	M				
	7							
	8 Nos 2,3 and 4 are duplicates of Nos 1,2 and 3 on Choctaw card #158							
	9							
	10							
	11							
	12							
	13							
	14							
	15							
	16							
	17							

	TRIBAL ENROLLMENT OF PARENTS					
	Name of Father	Year	County	Name of Mother	Year	County
1	Henry Meyers	dead	Non citzn	Elizabeth E Meyers		Non citzn
2	A.G. Freeney	dead	Choctaw Citizen	No.1		
3	" "	"	" "	No.1		
4	" "	"	" "	No.1		
5	Hiram Thompson		Non Citz	No.1		
6	Hiram Thompson		white man	N°1		
7	Husband of No.1 is No1 on Choctaw rejected card #R301					
8	Admitted by United States at South McAlester August 25th 1898 Case 227					
9	except No.5 born September 1st 1898					
10						
11	Benjamin A Freeney admitted as "Benjiman[sic] Andrew Thompson"					
12	Martha E " " " "Martha Elizabeth Thompson"					
13	No1 admitted by Com in 1896 case #2711					
14	Aug 9/99. See Choctaw Card No 158					
15	Nos 2-3-4 are duplicated thereon					
16	No5 white child by No1, white woman, Father Hiram Thompson a white man					
17	N°6 Born July 29 1902 name placed on this card Sept 9,1902				9/8/99	

N°6 is the child of white parents No6 cancelled and transferred to 7R 301

231

Choctaw By Blood Enrollment Cards 1898-1914

RESIDENCE: Chickasaw Nation
POST OFFICE: Pauls Valley, Ind Ter

Chickasaw Nation Choctaw Roll

CARD NO. **5032**
FIELD NO. C 77

Dawes' Roll No.	NAME	Relationship to Person First Named	AGE	SEX	BLOOD	TRIBAL ENROLLMENT		
						Year	County	No.
1	Paul Sammie		7	M				
2								
3								
4								
5								
6								
7								
8								
9								
10								
11								
12								
13								
14								
15								
16								
17								

TRIBAL ENROLLMENT OF PARENTS

	Name of Father	Year	County	Name of Mother	Year	County
1	Sam Paul	dead	Chickasaw Citzn	Altha Paul		non-citizen
2						
3						
4						
5						
6						
7	Admitted by United States Court at Ardmore March 19th 1898					
8						
9						
10						
11						
12						
13						
14						
15						
16						
17						

Choctaw By Blood Enrollment Cards 1898-1914

RESIDENCE: Chickasaw Nation
POST OFFICE: Purcell, Ind. Ter.

Choctaw **Nation** Choctaw **Roll**

CARD NO. **5033**
FIELD NO. C 78

Dawes' Roll No.	NAME	Relationship to Person First Named	AGE	SEX	BLOOD	TRIBAL ENROLLMENT		
						Year	County	No.
1	Patterson A D	First Named	32	M				
2	" Dora	wife	24	F				
3	" Mary Lou	Dau	1mo	F				
4								
5								
6								
7								
8								
9								
10								
11								
12								
13								
14								
15								
16								
17								

#3 TSMISSED

JAN 1905

TRIBAL ENROLLMENT OF PARENTS

	Name of Father	Year	County	Name of Mother	Year	County
1	James Patterson	dead	Non Citzn	Mary Patterson	dead	Non Citzn
2	William Boone	"	" "	Mary Ann Boone	"	" "
3	No 1			No 2		
4						
5						
6						
7						
8	Nos 1&2 denied by Com in 1896 case #18					
9	Admitted by United States Court at Ardmore Dec 21st 1897 Case 88					
10						
11						
12						
13						
14						
15						
16						
17						

233

Choctaw By Blood Enrollment Cards 1898-1914

RESIDENCE:	Chickasaw Natn		Choctaw **Nation**	Choctaw **Roll**	CARD NO.	**5034**
POST OFFICE:	Foster, I.T.				FIELD NO.	C 79

Dawes' Roll No.	NAME	Relationship to Person First Named	AGE	SEX	BLOOD	TRIBAL ENROLLMENT Year	TRIBAL ENROLLMENT County	TRIBAL ENROLLMENT No.
✓	1 Hunter, Marvin S	Named	29	M				
DP	2 " Walter Wright	Son	3mo	"				
DP	3 " Roy Ransom	Son	3mo					
	4							
	5							
	6							
	7							
	8							
	9 #2&3 DISMISSED							
	10 SEP 15 1904							
	11							
	12							
	13							
	14							
	15							
	16							
	17							

TRIBAL ENROLLMENT OF PARENTS

	Name of Father	Year	County	Name of Mother	Year	County
1	John M Hunter		Non Citz	Marth[sic] Hunter		Non Citz
2	No 1			Mattie L Hunter		" "
3	No. 1		"	"		" "
4						
5	No. 1					
6						
7	No.1 denied by Com in 1896 case #1334					
8	Was admitted by the U.S. Court, Ardmore, I.T. Jan 17, 1898					
9	Marriage License and Certificate dated February 13, 1898 received					
10	and filed December 14, 1900					
11	No 3 Enrolled Dec. 14, 1900					
12						
13						
14						
15						
16						
17					Date of Application for Enrollment	9-15-98

DENIED CITIZENSHIP BY THE CHOCTAW AND CHICKASAW CITIZENSHIP COURT

Choctaw By Blood Enrollment Cards 1898-1914

RESIDENCE:	Chickasaw Natn					CARD NO.	**5035**
POST OFFICE:	Ardmore, I.T.	Choctaw **Nation**	Choctaw **Roll**			FIELD NO.	C 80

Dawes' Roll No.	NAME	Relationship to Person First Named	AGE	SEX	BLOOD	TRIBAL ENROLLMENT		
						Year	County	No.
1	Jones, John L	Named	31	M				
2	" Maudie Lee	Dau	6	F				
3	" John P	Son	3	M				
4								
5								
6								
7	Not Enrolled by C C C as "John Jones"							
8	No2 " " "Maud Jones"							
9								
10								
11								
12								
13								
14								
15								
16								
17								

TRIBAL ENROLLMENT OF PARENTS

	Name of Father	Year	County	Name of Mother	Year	County
1	Woody Jones	Dead	Non Citz	Martha J Jones		Non Citz
2	No 1			Nannie Jones		" "
3	No 1			" "		" "
4						
5						
6						
7	Nos 1,2 & 3 denied by Com in 1896 case #18					
8						
9	Nos 1-2-3 were admitted by the U.S. Court, Ardmore, I.T. Dec 21, 1897 Court Case No 88					
10						
11	No.1 was admitted as "John Jones"					
12	No2 " " "Maud " "					
13						
14	Wife of No1 and mother of Nos 2 and 3 is Non Choctaw card					
15						
16						2/6
17						9-15-98

Choctaw By Blood Enrollment Cards 1898-1914

RESIDENCE: Chickasaw Natn   P.O. Foster I.T.
POST OFFICE: Roberson, I.T.

Choctaw **Nation**   Choctaw **Roll**

CARD NO. **5036**
FIELD NO. C 81

Dawes' Roll No.	NAME	Relationship to Person First Named	AGE	SEX	BLOOD	TRIBAL ENROLLMENT Year	TRIBAL ENROLLMENT County	TRIBAL ENROLLMENT No.
1	Womack, James H	Named	60	M				
2	" Amanda J	Wife	50	F				
3	" James P	Son	26	M				
4	" William L	"	19	"				
5	" Robert H	"	18	"				
6	" John B	"	15	"				
7	" Margaret E	Dau	9	F				
8	" Jesse	Son	6	M				
9	" William F	Gr Son	6mo	M				
10	" Willie	Gr Dau	6mo	F				
11								
12	Nos 1 to 8 incl: denied by							
13	Judgement[sic] of C.C.C.C Feb 29 '04							
14	9 & 10 DISMISSED							
15	MAY 27 1904							
16	Nos 1 to 8 inclusive now in C.C.C. Case # [illegible]							
	Nos 1 to 8 inclusive denied by Com in 1896 case #498.							

TRIBAL ENROLLMENT OF PARENTS

	Name of Father	Year	County	Name of Mother	Year	County
1	James Womack	Dead	Non Citz	Polly Womack	Dead	Non Citz
2	James Forsythe	"	" "	Dorcas Forsythe	"	" " "
3	No 1			No 2		
4	No 1			No 2		
5	No 1			No 2		
6	No 1			No 2		
7	No 1			No 2		
8	No 1			No 2		
9	No 4			Lillie Womack		non-citz
10	No 3			Fannie Womack		" "

DENIED CITIZENSHIP BY THE CHOCTAW AND CHICKASAW CITIZENSHIP COURT

11 Nos 1 to 8 inclusive were admitted by the U.S. Court, South McAlester, I.T.
12 Jan 18, 1898 Court Case No 131 } No 3 & 6 now the husband of Fannie Womack noncitizen.
13   Evidence of marriage filed Oct. 2, 1902
14 No 1 admitted as "James Womack" No 10 Born March 12, 1902. Enrolled Oct 2, 1902
15 No 2 " " "Amanda " "
16 No 4 is now the husband of Lillie Womack-non-citizen. Evidence of marriage filed Sept 23,1902   2/7
17   No 9 Born March 21, 1902, enrolled Sept 23,1902   for Enrollment.   9-15-98

Choctaw By Blood Enrollment Cards 1898-1914

RESIDENCE: Chickasaw Natn				Choctaw **Nation**	Choctaw **Roll**		CARD NO. **5037**	
POST OFFICE: Naples, I.T.							FIELD NO. C 82	

Dawes' Roll No.	NAME	Relationship to Person First Named	AGE	SEX	BLOOD	TRIBAL ENROLLMENT		
						Year	County	No.
0 1	Wheat, William E	Named	50	M				
0 2	" Jesse G	Son	13	"				
0 3	" Myrtie E	Dau	7	F				
4								
5								
6								
7								
8								
9								
10								
11								
12								
13								
14								
15								
16								
17								

TRIBAL ENROLLMENT OF PARENTS

	Name of Father	Year	County	Name of Mother	Year	County
1	R.S. Wheat		Non Citz	Elizabeth Wheat	Dead	Non Citz
2	No 1			Minnie Wheat	"	Choc Citz
3	No 1			" "	"	" "
4				ACTION APPROVED BY		
5				SECRETARY OF INTERIOR.		
6	Nos 1,2 & 3 denied by Com in 1896 case # 1182					
7	Nos 1-2-3 were admitted by the U.S. Court, Ardmore, I.T.					
8	Jan 19, 1898 Court Case No 125					
9						
10						
11						
12	No2 was admitted as "Jessie Wheat"					
13	No3 " " " "Myrtie " "					
14	No1 " " " "William " "					
15						
16						
17						

Choctaw By Blood Enrollment Cards 1898-1914

| RESIDENCE: | Chickasaw Natn | | | | | Choctaw **Nation** | Choctaw **Roll** | CARD NO. **5038** |
| POST OFFICE: | Whitebead, I.T. | | | | | | | FIELD NO. C 83 |

Dawes' Roll No.	NAME	Relationship to Person First Named	AGE	SEX	BLOOD	TRIBAL ENROLLMENT		
						Year	County	No.
1	Thompson, W^m J		22	M				
DP 2	" Winona	Dau	5mo	F				
3								
#2 DISMISSED 4								
5								
6								
7								
8								
9								
10								
11								
12	March 26, 1909 Dept refers letter of Kopple & Mirellat for report							
13	April 7, 1909 Report to Dept.							
14								
15								
16								
17								

TRIBAL ENROLLMENT OF PARENTS

	Name of Father	Year	County	Name of Mother	Year	County
1	Giles Thompson	Dead	Choc Citz	Ellen Thompson		Choc Citz
2	N^o1			Savannah Thompson		non-citz
3						
4	No.1 denied by Com in 1896 case # 1182					
5	Was admitted by the U.S. Court, Ardmore, I.T. Jan 19, 1898 Court Case No 125					
6						
7						
8	N^o1 is now the husband of Savannah Thompson a non-citizen					
9	of marriage received and filed Nov 14, 1902					
10	N^o2 Born June 22, 1902, enrolled Nov. 14, 1902					
11	DENIED CITIZENSHIP BY THE CHOCTAW AND					
12	CHICKASAW CITIZENSHIP COURT					
13						
14						
15						
16	May 2, 1904 Dept holds case is not illegible to Goldsby case and declines to take action					7/1
17	looking to enrollment of applicants					9-15-98

June 11, 1909 Parties notified.

Date of Application for Enrollment.

238

Choctaw By Blood Enrollment Cards 1898-1914

RESIDENCE: Chickasaw Natn
POST OFFICE: Homer, I.T.

Choctaw **Nation**   Choctaw **Roll**

CARD NO. **5039**
FIELD NO. C 84

Dawes' Roll No.	NAME	Relationship to Person First Named	AGE	SEX	BLOOD	TRIBAL ENROLLMENT Year	County	No.
1	Pickens, John T	First Named	33	M				
2	" Ernest	Son	9	"				
3	" Maud	Dau	7	F				
4	" James	Son	2	M				
5	" John Jr	"	2	"				
6	" Mary	Dau	1mo	F				
7								
8	#1-2-3- DISMP							
9	4-5-6-							
10								
11								
12								
13								
14								
15								
16								
17								

TRIBAL ENROLLMENT OF PARENTS

	Name of Father	Year	County	Name of Mother	Year	County
1	John Pickens		Non Citz	Mary Pickens		Non Citz
2	No 1			Mary R Pickens		" "
3	No 1			" "		" "
4	No 1			" "		" "
5	No 1			" "		" "
6	No 1			" "		" "
7						
8	Nos 1 to 3 inclusive denied by Com in 1896 case # 379					
9	Nos 1 to 3 inclusive were admitted by the U.S. Court, South McAlester, Aug 30, 1897					
10	Court Case #87					
11						
12			Not Enrolled June 23d, 1900			
13						
14						
15						
16						7/13
17						

239

Choctaw By Blood Enrollment Cards 1898-1914

| RESIDENCE: | Chickasaw Natn | | Choctaw **Nation** | | Choctaw **Roll** | | CARD NO. **5040** |
| POST OFFICE: | Brady, I.T. | | | | | | FIELD NO. C 85 |

Dawes' Roll No.	NAME	Relationship to Person First Named	AGE	SEX	BLOOD	TRIBAL ENROLLMENT		
						Year	County	No.
✓	1 Pickens, James W		44	M				
✓	2 " Walter	Son	18	"				
✓	3 " Annie	Dau	6	F				
✓	4 " James Jr	Son	4	M				
	5 " Andrew Jr	"	2	"				
	6 " Ethel	Dau	2mo	F				
	7							
	8							
#1-2-3-	9	DISMISSED						
4-5-6-	10							
	11							
	12							
	13							
	14							
	15							
	16							
	17							

TRIBAL ENROLLMENT OF PARENTS

	Name of Father	Year	County	Name of Mother	Year	County
1	John Pickens		Non Citz	Mary Pickens		Non Citz
2	No1			Dilla Pickens	Dead	" "
3	No1			Virginia Pickens		" "
4	No1			" "		" "
5	No1			" "		" "
6	No1			" "		" "
7						
8	Nos 1 to 4 inclusive denied by Com in 1896 case # 579					
9	Nos 1 to 4 inclusive were admitted by the U.S. Court, South McAlester, I.T.					
10	Aug 30, 1897 Court Case No 87					
11						
12	No5 was born Nov 5, 1896					
13	No6 " " July 1, 1898					
14	No1 was admitted as "James Pickens"					
15						
16						2/16
17					Date of Application for Enrollment	9-15-98

| RESIDENCE: | Chickasaw Natn | | | | | CARD NO. | **5041** |
| POST OFFICE: | , I.T. | | | | | FIELD NO. | C 86 |

Choctaw **Nation**   Choctaw **Roll**

Dawes' Roll No.	NAME	Relationship to Person First Named	AGE	SEX	BLOOD	TRIBAL ENROLLMENT		
						Year	County	No.
✓ ✓	1 Pickens, Geo W		42	M				
✓	2 " Geo L	Son	7	"				
✓	3 " Mary Myrtle	Dau	4	F				
✓	4 " Jessie Lee	"	3	"				
	5 " Girtie May	"	3½ mo	"				
	6 " Albert	Son	1 mo	M				
	7							

#1-2-3- DISMISSED
4-5-6- DEC

	10							
	11							
	12							
	13							
	14							
	15							
	16							
	17							

TRIBAL ENROLLMENT OF PARENTS

	Name of Father	Year	County	Name of Mother	Year	County
1	John Pickens		Non Citz	Mary Pickens		Non Citz
2	No 1			Nety Pickens		" "
3	No 1			" "		" "
4	No 1			" "		" "
5	No 1			" "		" "
6	No 1			" "		" "
7						
8	Above named persons were admitted by the U.S. Court, South McAlester, I.T.					
9	Aug 30, 1897 Court Case No					
10						
11	Nos 1 to 4 inclusive denied by Com in 1896 case # 579					
12						
13	No1 admitted as "Geo Pickens"					
14	No2 " " "G. L. " "					
15	No3 " " "Josie " '					
16	No5 Enrolled January 2 1901				²/18	
17	Nº6 Born Sept 5, 1902, enrolled Oct 6, 1902			Date of Application 9-		

241

| RESIDENCE: | Chickasaw Natn | | | | | | CARD NO. 5042 |
| POST OFFICE: | Elmore, I.T. | Choctaw **Nation** | | Choctaw **Roll** | | | FIELD NO. C 87 |

Dawes' Roll No.	NAME	Relationship to Person First Named	AGE	SEX	BLOOD	TRIBAL ENROLLMENT		
						Year	County	No.
✓✓	1 Pickens, Andrew	Named	40	M				
✓✓	2 " Flounce	Dau	16	F				
✓✓	3 " Virgie	"	14	"				
✓✓	4 " Fulton	Son	12	M				
✓	5 " Tolbert	"	9	"				
✓	6 " Carlton	"	6	"				
	7 " Bessie	Dau	2	F				
	8 Gaines, Carl Edmond	Gr Son	6wks	M				
	9							
#1-2-3- 4- 5-6-7-8-		DISMISSED DEC 3						
	12							
	13							
	14							
	15							
	16 For child of No4 see NB #1014 (Act Apr 26 '06)							
	17							

TRIBAL ENROLLMENT OF PARENTS

	Name of Father	Year	County	Name of Mother	Year	County
1	John Pickens		Non Citz	Mary Pickens		Non Citz
2	No 1			Mollie Pickens		" "
3	No 1			" "		" "
4	No 1			" "		" "
5	No 1			" "		" "
6	No 1			" "		" "
7	No 1			" "		" "
8	N.P. Gaines		non-citizen	N°2		
9	Nos 1 to 6 inclusive, denied by Com in 1896 case #579					
10	Nos 1 to 6 inclusive were admitted by the U.S. Court, Ardmore, I.T.					
11	Aug 30, 1897 Court Case No 87					
12						
13	No7 was born Oct 8, 1896					
14	No6 was admitted as "Carrolton Pickens"					
15	N°2 is now the wife of N.P. Gaines a non-citizen. Evidence of marriage filed Sept 4, 1902					
16	N°8 Born July 25, 1902, enrolled Sept. 4, 1902				2/20	
17				Date of Application for Enrollment.	9-15-98	

Choctaw By Blood Enrollment Cards 1898-1914

RESIDENCE: Chickasaw Natn
POST OFFICE: Elmore, I.T.

Choctaw **Nation**   Choctaw **Roll**

CARD NO. **5043**
FIELD NO. C 88

Dawes' Roll No.	NAME	Relationship to Person First Named	AGE	SEX	BLOOD	TRIBAL ENROLLMENT Year	County	No.
1	Pickens, Frank	Named	29	M				
2	" Jonia	Dau	2	F				
3	" Frankie	Son	4mo	M				
4	" William Edear	Son	6wks	M				
5								
6								
7								
8								
9								
10								
11								
12								
13								
14								
15								
16								
17								

#1-2-3-4

TRIBAL ENROLLMENT OF PARENTS

	Name of Father	Year	County	Name of Mother	Year	County
1	John Pickens		Non Citz	Mary Pickens		Non Citz
2	No 1			Mary Pickens		" "
3	No 1			" "		" "
4	No 1			" "		" "
5						
6						
7	No.1 denied by Com in 1896 case # 579					
8	Nos 1--[sic] Was admitted by the U.S. Court, South McAlester, Aug 30, 1897					
9	Case No 87					
10						
11	No3 was born May 18 1898					
12	Evidence of marriage of No 1 to Mary C Pickens filed December 21. 1900					
13	No4 Enrolled December 21, 1900					
14						
15						
16						
17						

Date of application for Enrollment. 9-15-99

Choctaw By Blood Enrollment Cards 1898-1914

RESIDENCE: Chickasaw Natn
POST OFFICE: Mill Creek, I.T.

Choctaw **Nation**   Choctaw **Roll**

CARD NO. **5044**
FIELD NO. C 89

Dawes' Roll No.	NAME		Relationship to Person First Named	AGE	SEX	BLOOD	TRIBAL ENROLLMENT Year	County	No.
✓	1 Short, Mary P	31	First Named	27	F				
✓	2 " Samuel E	12	Son	8	M				
✓	3 " Thos Z	11	"	7	"				
✓	4 " Jonathan	9	"	5	"				
✓	5 " Pearl	8	Dau	4	F				
✓	6 " Henry	7	Son	3	M				
	7 " Maggie	5	Dau	1	F				
#1-2-3-4-5-6-7 DISMISSED Dec 3, 1904	8								
	9								
	10								
	11								
	12								
	13								
	14								
	15								
	16								
	17								

TRIBAL ENROLLMENT OF PARENTS

	Name of Father	Year	County	Name of Mother	Year	County
1	John Pickens		Non Citz	Mary Pickens		Non Citz
2	N.J. Short		" "	No 1		
3	" "		" "	No 1		
4	" "		" "	No 1		
5	" "		" "	No 1		
6	" "		" "	No 1		
7	" "		" "	No 1		
8	Nos1 to 6 inclusive denied by Com in 1896 case # 579					
9	Nos1 to 6 inclusive were admitted by the U.S. Court, South McAlester,					
10	Aug 30, 1897 Court Case No 87					
11						
12						
13	No7 was born July 30, 1897					
14						
15						
16						
17				Date of Application for Enrollment.	9-15-98	

²/24

Choctaw By Blood Enrollment Cards 1898-1914

RESIDENCE: Chickasaw Natn	CARD No. **5045**
POST OFFICE: Brady, I.T.	FIELD No. C 90

Choctaw **Nation**   Choctaw **Roll**

Dawes' Roll No.	NAME	Relationship to Person First Named	AGE	SEX	BLOOD	TRIBAL ENROLLMENT Year	County	No.
✓	1 McDonald, Lula	First Named	20	F				
	2 " Nellie	Dau	2	"				
	3 " Lucy Ella	"	9mo	"				
	4 " William Elmer	Son	5mo	M				
	5							
	6							
#1-2-3-4- DISMI___L___	8							
DEPT 1904	9							
	10							
	11							
	12							
	13							
	14							
	15							
	16							
	17							

TRIBAL ENROLLMENT OF PARENTS

	Name of Father	Year	County	Name of Mother	Year	County
1	James W Pickens		Non Citz	Mary Pickens	Dead	Non Citz
2	J.W. McDonald		" "	No1		
3	" "		" "	No1		
4	" "		" "	No1		
5						
6	No1 Denied by Commission in 1896 Case #379					
7						
8	No1 Was admitted by the U.S. Court, South McAlester Aug 30, 1897 Court Case No 87					
9						
10	No1 was admitted as "Lula Pickens"					
11	No2 was born Nov 27, 1896					
12						
13	No4 Enrolled June 27, 1901					
14	Full name of No 1 is Lula Canzada See letter of					
15	J.M. McDonald filed July 13, 1901			No3 enrolled Aug 10/99		
16						
17				Date of Application for Enrollment		

Choctaw By Blood Enrollment Cards 1898-1914

RESIDENCE:	Chickasaw Nation						CARD No.	5046
POST OFFICE:	Purcell Ind Ter	Choctaw **Nation**		Choctaw **Roll**			FIELD No.	C 91

Dawes' Roll No.	NAME	Relationship to Person First Named	AGE	SEX	BLOOD	TRIBAL ENROLLMENT		
						Year	County	No.
1	Jennings, A.P.	Named	39	M	IW			
2								
3								
4	DIS							
5								
6								
7								
8								
9								
10								
11								
12								
13								
14								
15								
16								
17								

TRIBAL ENROLLMENT OF PARENTS

	Name of Father	Year	County	Name of Mother	Year	County
1	Arlburn Jennings		non citizen	Sarah Jennings		non citizen
2						
3						
4						
5						
6	No. 1 denied by Com in 1896 case # 1041					
7	Admitted by U.S. Court Southern District Case No 142 Decree of					
8	Dec 22, 1897					
9						
10	Married in 1880 in Texas under Texas law [illegible]cord to Indian					
11	Territory in 1881 and wife. Afterward enrolled as Choctaw					
12						
13	Wife and children of No. 1 on Choctaw card #181					
14						
15				Date of Application		Nov 21/98
16						
17						

| RESIDENCE: | Atoka County | | | | | | CARD No. | **5047** | |
| POST OFFICE: | Jeffs[sic], I.T. | Choctaw **Nation** | | Choctaw **Roll** | | | FIELD No. | C 92 | |

Dawes' Roll No.	NAME	Relationship to Person First Named	AGE	SEX	BLOOD	TRIBAL ENROLLMENT		
						Year	County	No.
✓ ✓	1 Mitchell, Alfred H 29		25	M				
✓ ✓	2 " Ollie 7	Dau	3	F				
✓	3 " Stella May 4	"	3mo	"				
✓	4 " Grace 4	Dau	3mo	F				
	5							
3&4	6							
	7	DISMISSED						
	8	MAY 27 1904						
	9							
	10							
	11							
	12							
	13							
	14							
	15							
	16							
	17							

TRIBAL ENROLLMENT OF PARENTS

	Name of Father	Year	County	Name of Mother	Year	County
1	John Mitchell		Non Citz	Mary F Mitchell		Non Citz
2	No1			Cynthia Mitchell		" "
3	No1		" "	" "		" "
4	No.1		" "	" "		" "
5	Nos 1 & 2 denied by Com in 1896 case # 29					
6	Nos 1-2 were admitted by the U.S. Court, South McAlester, I.T.					
7	Aug 25, 1897 Court Case No 116					
8						
9						
10	No3 was born May 26, 1898					
11	Evidence of marriage between No1 and Cynthia M Mitchell filed Feby 21, 1902					
12	No4 Born Nov. 2, 1901; enrolled Feby 21, 1902					
13						
14	DENIED CITIZENSHIP BY THE CHOCTAW AND					
15	CHICKASAW CITIZENSHIP COURT					
16						
17	Purdy I.T. 2/21/02				Date of Application for Enrollment.	9-15-99

Choctaw By Blood Enrollment Cards 1898-1914

RESIDENCE: Atoka County
POST OFFICE: Kiowa, Ind Ter

Choctaw **Nation**   Choctaw **Roll**

CARD NO. **5048**
FIELD NO. C 93

Dawes' Roll No.	NAME	Relationship to Person First Named	AGE	SEX	BLOOD	TRIBAL ENROLLMENT		
						Year	County	No.
1	Marlow, Jasper 43		39	M	1/8			
2	" Robert C 16	Son	12	"	1/16			
3	" Haley Margaret	Dau	10	F	1/16			
4	" Earnest J 12	Son	8	M	1/16			
5	" Roy 8	"	4	"	1/16			
6								
7								
8								
9								
10								
11								
12								
13								
14								
15								
16								
17								

TRIBAL ENROLLMENT OF PARENTS

	Name of Father	Year	County	Name of Mother	Year	County
1	Reuben Marlow	Dead	non citizen	Margaret Marlow		non citizen
2	No 1			Eva Marlow		" "
3	No 1			" "		" "
4	No 1			" "		" "
5	No 1			" "		" "
6						
7						
8						
9						
10	Admitted at South McAlester July 13, 1897, Court Case No. 64					
11	Have resided in Choctaw Nation continuously for 13 years					
12						
13						
14						
15						
16					Date of	Nov 23 98
17						

248

Choctaw By Blood Enrollment Cards 1898-1914

RESIDENCE: Chickasaw Nation
POST OFFICE: Ryan, Ind. Ter.

Choctaw **Nation**   Choctaw **Roll**

CARD NO. **5049**
FIELD NO. C

Dawes' Roll No.	NAME	Relationship to Person First Named	AGE	SEX	BLOOD	TRIBAL ENROLLMENT		
						Year	County	No.
	1 Williams, Nancy J 48		42	F				
	2 " Maggie * 22	dau	18	"				
	3 " Edna E * 20	"	16	"				
	4 Lewis, Bayless Earle	G.Son	3 wks	M				
	5							
	6							
	7							
No4	8 DISMISSED							
	9 SEP 15 1904							
	10							
	11							
#1	12 DISMISSED							
	13							
	14 JAN 2 190							
	15							
	16							
	17							

TRIBAL ENROLLMENT OF PARENTS

	Name of Father	Year	County	Name of Mother	Year	County
1	William Hill	dead	Non Citzn	Jane Hill	dead	Non Citzn
2	Lucusqus Williams		" "	No1		
3	" "		" "	No1		
4	Wade H Lewis		" "	No2		
5	DENIED CITIZENSHIP BY THE CHOCTAW AND					
6	CHICKASAW CITIZENSHIP COURT					
7						
8	Nos1,2,&3 denied by Com in 1896 case # 415					
9	Admitted by United States Court at Ardmore Dec 22nd 1897 Case 104					
10	No4 Enrolled January 2, 1901					
11	No2 is now the wife of Wade H Lewis a noncitizen. Evidence of marriage					
12	filed January 30, 1901					
13						
14						
15						
16						
17						

249

| RESIDENCE: | Chickasaw Nation |
| POST OFFICE: | Ryan, Ind. Ter. |

Choctaw **Nation**   Choctaw **Roll**

CARD NO. **5050**
FIELD NO. C 95

Dawes' Roll No.	NAME	Relationship to Person First Named	AGE	SEX	BLOOD	TRIBAL ENROLLMENT		
						Year	County	No.
1	Williams, Thomas W ²⁷	First Named	23	M				
2	" Reeno M	dau	1	F				
3	" Thos William	Son	2mo	M				
4	" James Simon	Son	3wks	M				
5								
6								
7								
8	Nos. 2-3 & 4 DISMISSED SEP 15 1903							
10								
11								
12	DENIED CITIZENSHIP BY THE CHOCTAW AND							
13	CHICKASAW CITIZENSHIP COURT							
14								
15								
16	No.3 Enrolled June 23d. 1900							
17								

TRIBAL ENROLLMENT OF PARENTS

	Name of Father	Year	County	Name of Mother	Year	County
1	Lucusqus Williams	dead	Non Citzn	Nancy J Williams		Non Citzn
2	No 1			Stella C "		" "
3	No. 1			" " "		" "
4	N⁰ 1			" " "		" "
5						
6	No.1 denied by Com in 1896 case # 415					
7						
8	Admitted by United States Court at Ardmore Dec 22ⁿᵈ 1897 Case 115					
9						
10	No.1 married to Stella C Clark under State law					
11	No2 born September 12ᵗ 1897					
12	N⁰4 Born April 5, 1902; enrolled April 29,1902					
13	The Commission at the time of the enrollment					
14	of Thomas W Williams were satisfied as to his					
15	marriage to Stella C Williams.					
16	A S McKennon					
17	Commissioner May 24, 1900					

DATE OF APPLICATION FOR ENROLLMENT   2/44

Choctaw By Blood Enrollment Cards 1898-1914

RESIDENCE: Chickasaw Nation
POST OFFICE: Ryan, Ind. Ter.

Choctaw **Nation**   Choctaw **Roll**

CARD NO. **5051**
FIELD NO. C

Dawes' Roll No.	NAME	Relationship to Person First Named	AGE	SEX	BLOOD	TRIBAL ENROLLMENT Year	TRIBAL ENROLLMENT County	TRIBAL ENROLLMENT No.
1	Williams Robert B	Named	23	M				
2	" Kittie	wife	21	F				
3	" Nannie R	dau	3	"				
4	" Lucusqus H	son	11mo	M				
5	" Robert Maines	Son	4mo	M				
6	" Paul Aubrey	Son	3wks	M				
7								
8								
9	DISMISSED							
10	SEP 15 1904							
11								
12								
13								
14								
15								
16								
17								

TRIBAL ENROLLMENT OF PARENTS

	Name of Father	Year	County	Name of Mother	Year	County
1	Lucusqus Williams	dead	Non Citzn	Nancy J Williams		Non Citzn
2	David Baker	" "	Rachel A Smith		" "
3	No 1			No 2		
4	No 1			No 2		
5	No. 1			No. 2		
6	No 1			No 2		
7						
8	Denied by Com in 1896 case # 465					
9	Admitted by United States Court at Ardmore Dec 22nd 1897 Case 104					
10						
11	No4 born October 23^d 1897					
12	No.6 Born March 22, 1902: Enrolled April 9, 1902					
13						
14	DENIED CITIZENSHIP BY THE CHOCTAW AND					
15	CHICKASAW CITIZENSHIP COURT					
16						²742
17				No.5 Enrolled May 24, 1900		

Choctaw By Blood Enrollment Cards 1898-1914

RESIDENCE: Choctaw Nation
POST OFFICE: Sans Bois, Ind. Ter

Choctaw **Nation**   Choctaw **Roll**

CARD No. **5052**
FIELD No. C 97

Dawes' Roll No.	NAME	Relationship to Person First Named	AGE	SEX	BLOOD	TRIBAL ENROLLMENT		
						Year	County	No.
✓	1 Kelton, Aven	Named	31	M				
✓	2 " Sarah	Wife	40	F				
✓	3 Anderson, Blummer	StepSon	21	M				
✓	4 " Julian	StepSon	16	M				
✓	5 " Bessie Lee H	Dau of No.3	2	F				
	6							
	7							
	8							
	9							
	10							
	11							
	12							
	13							
	14							
	15							
	16							
	17							

DISMISSED MAY 190

TRIBAL ENROLLMENT OF PARENTS

	Name of Father	Year	County	Name of Mother	Year	County
1	Frank Kelton		Non Citzn	Emma Kelton		Non Citzn
2	Jesse Montgomery		" "	Julia Montgomery		" "
3	James Anderson		" "	No2		
4	" "		" "	No2		" "
5	No.3			Mary Anderson		" "
6						
7	Admitted by United States Court at South McAlester September 9th 1897 Case 130					
8						
9	No1 admitted as "Julia Anderson"					
10						
11	Blummer Anderson and Mary Anderson divorced Dec 14, 1899					
12	No.3 is now the husband of Amanda A Zumwalt on Choctaw card #5202 who was denied					
13	No.5 Enrolled June 13th 1900					by C.C.C. [Illegible]
14	Nos 2,3 & 4 denied by Com in 1896 case No 26					
15	No1 " " " " 226					
16	Nos1,2,3 and 4 Denied March 24 '04 by C.C.C.C.					2/45
17						

DENIED CITIZENSHIP BY THE CHOCTAW AND CHICKASAW CITIZENSHIP COURT

252

Choctaw By Blood Enrollment Cards 1898-1914

RESIDENCE: Chickasaw Natn
POST OFFICE: Duncan, I.T.

Choctaw **Nation**   Choctaw **Roll**

CARD NO. **5053**
FIELD NO.

Dawes' Roll No.	NAME	Relationship to Person First Named	AGE	SEX	BLOOD	TRIBAL ENROLLMENT		
						Year	County	No.
1	Jones, Rutherford P	First Named	60	M				
2	" Reandes	Dau	19	F				
3	" Nellie	"	16	"				
4	Guest, May Candis	GrDau	4mo	F				
5								
6								
7								
8								
9								
10								
11								
12								
13								
14								
15								
16								
17								

TRIBAL ENROLLMENT OF PARENTS

	Name of Father	Year	County	Name of Mother	Year	County
1	J L Jones	Dead	Non Citzn	Elizabeth Jones	Dead	Non Citzn
2	No 1			Racel[sic] Jones	"	"
3	"			"	"	"
4	Joe S Guest		non-citizen	N° 3		
5						
6						
7						
8						
9						
10						
11						
12						
13						
14						
15						
16						
17						

Date of Application for Enrollment.

253

Choctaw By Blood Enrollment Cards 1898-1914

RESIDENCE: Chickasaw Natn
POST OFFICE: Tatum, I.T.

Choctaw **Nation** Choctaw **Roll**

CARD NO. **5054**
FIELD NO. 99

Dawes' Roll No.	NAME	Relationship to Person First Named	AGE	SEX	BLOOD	Year	County	No.
0	1 Scott, Lovie F			F		1896	Atoka	11693
0	2 " Hattie M	Dau	7	"		1896	"	11694
0	3 " Minnie R	"	4	"		1896	"	11696
0	4 " Archie M	Son	2	M		1896	"	11695
	5 " Glennis	Dau	1					
	6 " Joseph A	Son	5mo	M				
	7 " James I	"	6	M				

No1 Denied by

#6-7-12 DISMISSED JAN 23 1905

TRIBAL ENROLLMENT OF PARENTS

	Name of Father	Year	County	Name of Mother	Year	County
1	Jim Jones	Dead	Non Citz	Malinda Jones		Non Citz
2	G.W. [Illegible]		" "	No1		
3	" "		" "	No1		
4	" "		" "	No1		
5	" "		" "	No1		
6	" "		" "	No1		
7	" "		" "	No1		

8 Admitted by the U.S. Court, Ardmore, I.T.
9 Jan 17, 1898 Court Case No. 48

12 No5 was born Sept 30, 1897
13 No1 on 1896 roll as Lovey Scott
14 No2 " 1896 " " Myrtle
15 No3 " 1896 " " Burt
16 No4 " 1896 " " Arch
17 For child of No1 see NB #957 (Act Apr 26-06)

No.5 Re-enrolled April 13, 1900
No.6 Enrolled May 24, 1900
No.7 Born Sept 8, 1902; enrolled Oct 30, 1902

254

Choctaw By Blood Enrollment Cards 1898-1914

RESIDENCE: Chickasaw Natn
POST OFFICE: Tatum, I.T.

Choctaw **Nation** Choctaw **Roll**

CARD NO. **5055**
FIELD NO.

Dawes' Roll No.	NAME	Relationship to Person First Named	AGE	SEX	BLOOD	TRIBAL ENROLLMENT		
						Year	County	No.
1	Jones, William A		61	M				
2	" Garland R	Son	22	"				
3								
4								
5								
6								
7								
8	DECISION RENDERED.							
9	REFUSED							
10								
11								
12								
13								
14								
15								
16								
17								

TRIBAL ENROLLMENT OF PARENTS

	Name of Father	Year	County	Name of Mother	Year	County
1	J L Jones	Dead	Non Citz	Elizabeth Jones	Dead	Non Citz
2	No1			Mary J Jones		" "
3						
4						
5						
6						
7			Adopted by the U S. Court, Ardmore I.T.			
8			Jan 12, 1898 Court			
9						
10			Is not No2 Duplicate of No1 on Card #5288			
11						
12						
13						
14						
15						
16						
17						

255

Choctaw By Blood Enrollment Cards 1898-1914

RESIDENCE: Chickasaw Natn		Choctaw **Nation** Choctaw **Roll**				CARD NO. **5056**		
POST OFFICE: Duncan, I.T.						FIELD NO. C 101		

Dawes' Roll No.	NAME	Relationship to Person First Named	AGE	SEX	BLOOD	TRIBAL ENROLLMENT		
						Year	County	No.
1	Jones, John G	Named	49	M				
2	" Mary A	Dau	21	F				
3	" William O	Son	19	M				
4	" George D	"	16	"				
5	" Walter J	"	13	"				
6	" Lizzie B	Dau	11	F				
7	" Lilburn B	Son	6	M				
8	" Pearl V	Dau	4	F				
	DECISION RENDERED							
10	REFUSED							
11								
12								
13								
14								
15								
16								
17								

TRIBAL ENROLLMENT OF PARENTS

	Name of Father	Year	County	Name of Mother	Year	County
1	J L Jones	Dead	Non Citz	Elizabeth Jones	Dead	Non Citz
2	No 1			Lizzie Jones	"	"
3	No 1			" "	"	"
4	No 1			" "	"	"
5	No 1			" "	"	"
6	No 1			" "	"	"
7	No 1			" "	"	"
8	No 1			" "	"	"
9						
10						
11						
12						
13						
14	Admitted by the U.S. Court, Ardmore, I.T. Jan 17, 1898 Court Case No 111					
15						
16	Ardmore					153
17					Date of Application for Enrollment.	9-22-98

See Choctaw 5053

Choctaw By Blood Enrollment Cards 1898-1914

RESIDENCE: Chickasaw Natn
POST OFFICE: Duncan, I.T.

Choctaw **Nation**   Choctaw **Roll**

CARD NO. **5057**
FIELD NO. C 102

Dawes' Roll No.	NAME	Relationship to Person First Named	AGE	SEX	BLOOD	TRIBAL ENROLLMENT		
						Year	County	No.
1	Jones, Robert J		25	M				
2								
3								
4								
5								
6								
7								
8								
	DECISION RENDERED							
10								
11								
12								
13								
14								
15								
16								
17								

TRIBAL ENROLLMENT OF PARENTS

	Name of Father	Year	County	Name of Mother	Year	County
1	John G Jones		Non Citz	Elizabeth Jones		Non Citz
2						
3						
4						
5						
6						
7						
8						
9						
10						
11						
12						
13						
14						
15						
16						
17						

257

Choctaw By Blood Enrollment Cards 1898-1914

	RESIDENCE:	Chickasaw Natn				CARD NO. **5058**
	POST OFFICE:	Duncan I.T.	Choctaw **Nation** Choctaw **Roll**			FIELD NO. C 103

Dawes' Roll No.	NAME	Relationship to Person First Named	AGE	SEX	BLOOD	TRIBAL ENROLLMENT		
						Year	County	No.
0 0 ₁	Gamblin, John H	First Named	52	M	1/16	1896	Blue	4914
0 0 ₂	" James W	Son	29	M	1/32	1896	"	4919
0 0 ₃	" Hattie L	Dau	18	F	1/32	1896	"	4921
DP ₄	" Benny	Gr.Son	5mo	M	1/64			
₅								
₆								
#4 ₇	DISMISSED							
₈	JAN 2 1905							
₉								
₁₀	No 1 DISMISSED							
₁₁	FEB 14 1907							
₁₂								
Nos2,3&4 ₁₃	GRANTED							
₁₄	FEB 14 1907							
₁₅								
Nos2-3&4 ₁₆	Transferred to Choctaw card #D72							
₁₇								

TRIBAL ENROLLMENT OF PARENTS

	Name of Father	Year	County	Name of Mother	Year	County
₁	Joseph Gamblin	Dead	Non Citzn	Mahale Gamblin	Dead	Non Citz
₂	No 1			Liza A Gamblin	" "	" "
₃	No 1			" " "	" "	" "
₄	Nº 2			Lillie Gamblin	" "	" "
₅						
₆	Admitted by the U.S. Court at Ardmore, I.T.					
₇	Jan 17, 1898 Court Case 148					
₈						
₉	No1 on 1896 roll as "John A Gamblin"					
₁₀	No2 " 1896 " " "Walter " "				[Illegible]	
₁₁	No3 " 1896 " " "Hattie " "					
₁₂	Nº2 is the husband of Lillie Gamblin on Choctaw Card #D430					
₁₃	Nº4 Born Aug. 9, 1901; enrolled Jan. 4, 1902					
₁₄						
₁₅						
₁₆	For children of No3 see NB (Apr 26-06) Card #933					
₁₇	" " " " 2 " " " #996					

258

Choctaw By Blood Enrollment Cards 1898-1914

| RESIDENCE: | Chickasaw Natn | | | | Choctaw **Nation** | | Choctaw **Roll** | | CARD NO. **5059** | |
| POST OFFICE: | Dunca | | | | | | | | FIELD NO. | |

Dawes' Roll No.	NAME	Relationship to Person First Named	AGE	SEX	BLOOD	TRIBAL ENROLLMENT		
						Year	County	No.
0 0	₁ Reed, Amanda L	Named	21	F	1/32	1896	Blue	9920
0 0	₂ " Archie	Dau	5mo	"	1/64			
0	₃ " Glenn	Son	9mo	M	1/64			
	4							
	5							
	6							
#2-17 DISMISSED	7							
	8							
	9							
	10							
	11							
	12							
	13							
	14							
	15							
	16							
	17							

TRIBAL ENROLLMENT OF PARENTS

	Name of Father	Year	County	Name of Mother	Year	County
1	John H Gamblin		Non Citz	Liza Gamblin		Non Citz
2	Arch Reed		" "	Nol		
3	H. J. Reed		" "	Nº1		
4						
5						
6						
7						
8	Not admitted by the U. S. Court Atoka...					
9	Not wife of Arch Reed					
10						
11	No1 was born April 27, 1898					
12						
13	No3 Born Sept 10, 1903; enrolled July 28, 1902					
14	DENIED CITIZENSHIP BY THE CHOCTAW AND					
15	CHICKASAW CITIZENSHIP COURT					
16						
17						

| RESIDENCE: | Chickasaw Natn | | Choctaw **Nation** | Choctaw **Roll** | | CARD NO. | **5060** |
| POST OFFICE: | Comanche, I.T. | | | | | FIELD NO. | C 105 |

| Dawes' Roll No. | | D⁰ 7/16/0 NAME | Relationship to Person First Named | AGE | SEX | BLOOD | TRIBAL ENROLLMENT | | |
							Year	County	No.
	1	Brown, William N	First Named	39	M	1/16	1896	Blu	1691
	2	" Nancy J	Wife	36	D	1/16	1896	"	1692
	3	" Sarah	Dau	18	"	1/16	1896	"	1693
	4	" Becky	"	16	"	1/16	1896	"	1694
	5	" Mary	"	13	"	1/16	1896	"	1695
	6	" Mamie	"	11	"	1/16	1896	"	1696
	7	" Alice	"	8	"	1/16	1896	"	1697
	8	" George	Son	5		1/16	1896	"	1698
	9	" Susie	Dau	2	M	1/16	1896	"	1699
	10	Johnston William F	Grand son	3	F	1/32			
	11	Brown, Minnie G	Grand dau	2mo		1/32			
	12	" Fannie C	dau	3mo	F	1/32			
	13	" Henry Niten	Son of	4mo	F	1/32			
	14	Admitted by the U.S. Court Ardmore I.T. Jan 30, 1921 Court Case No 96								
	15	No9 was born July 1 1899					No1 to 8 denied (illegible)			
	16	No1 on 1896 roll as Wm Brown					No1 to 8 denied in 1896 case #14 18			
	17	No (illegible)					No12 Born May 21st 1902; Enrolled July 2nd 1902			

TRIBAL ENROLLMENT OF PARENTS

	Name of Father	County		Name of Mother	Year	County
1	William B Brown	Non Citz		Becky Brown	Dead	Non Citz
2	John Hern	Dead	" "	Arilla Hern	"	" "
3	No1			No2		
4	No1			No2		
5	No1			No2		
6	No1			No2		
7	No1			No2		
8	No1			No2		
9	No1			No2		
10	J A Johnston	Non-citizen		DEC 32 1904		
11	Eli W Brown	Choctaw D.432		No4		
12	No1			No2		
13	Eli W Brown	Choctaw #D 432		No4	MAR 18 1904	
14	No3 is now the wife of J A Johnson[sic]			No 9, Stricken from original judgment by order		
15	No4 is now the wife of Eli W Brown on			U S Court, Southern dist I.T. Jany 17th 1900		
16	Choctaw card D.432			Birth affidavits filed and attached		
17	No11 Enrolled Oct 19th 1900			hereto, April 2d, 1900		

No12 Enrolled May 16, 1901

No10 Enrolled Oct 13th 1905

Date of Application for Enrollment.

Choctaw By Blood Enrollment Cards 1898-1914

RESIDENCE:	Chickasaw Natn							CARD NO.	5061
POST OFFICE:	Comanche, I.T.		Choctaw **Nation**		Choctaw **Roll**			FIELD NO.	

Dawes' Roll No.	7/16/06	NAME	Relationship to Person First Named	AGE	SEX	BLOOD	TRIBAL ENROLLMENT		
							Year	County	No.
✓		Nichols Orin M	First Named	44	M	1/8	1896	Blue	9812
✓	2	" Amanda M	Wife	38	F	1/8	1896	"	9813
✓		" James W	Son	18	M	1/8	1896	"	9814
✓		" Maggie M	Dau	12	F	1/8	1896	"	9815
✓	5	" Mettie M	"	8	"	1/8	1896	"	9816
✓	6	" Lonie A	"	4	"	1/8	1896	"	9817
	7								
	8								
	9								
	10								
	11								
	12								
	13								
	14								
	15								
	16								
	17								

	TRIBAL ENROLLMENT OF PARENTS					
Name of Father		Year	County	Name of Mother	Year	County
1 Wilson Nichols		Dead	Non Citz	Delitha Nichols	Dead	Non Citz
2 J D Skelton		"	" "	Mary Skelton		" "
3 No1				No2		
4 No1				No2		
5 No1				No2		
6 No1				No2		

7 Nos1 to 6 denied by Com in 1896 case # 1418

8 Admitted by the U.S. Court, Ardmore, I.T. Dec 20, 1897 Court Case No 96

9 No5 "Mettie M" mitted as Myrtle

10

11 No1 on 1896 roll as Ora M Nichols

12 No2 " 1896 " " Amanda "

13 No3 " 1896 " " James A "   No3 is now the husband of Osa Nichols Card D #507 7/25-99

14 No4 " 1896 " " Maggie "

15 No5 " 1896 " " Myrtle "

16 No6 " 1896 " " Lona "

17   Date of Application

261

Choctaw By Blood Enrollment Cards 1898-1914

RESIDENCE: Chickasaw Natn
POST OFFICE: Comanche, I.T.

Choctaw **Nation** Choctaw **Roll**

CARD NO. **5062**
FIELD NO. C 107

Dawes' Roll No.	NAME	Relationship to Person First Named	AGE	SEX	BLOOD	TRIBAL ENROLLMENT Year	County	No.
1	Peck, Andrew		32	M	IW	1896	Blue	10517
2	" Polly A	Wife	30	F	1/8	1896	"	10518
3	" Florence	Dau	9	"	1/16	1896	"	10519
4	" Oscar	Son	7	M	1/16	1896	"	10520
5	" Benj G	"	5	"	1/16	1896	"	10521
6	" Andrew	"	3	"	1/16	1896	"	10522
7	" Otis David	"	2mo	"	1/16			
8	" Virgie	Son	2mo	M	1/16			
9								
10								
11								
12	No- 7&8							
13	No. 7&8							
14								
15								
16								
17								

DISMISSED
DEC 24 1904

TRIBAL ENROLLMENT OF PARENTS

Name of Father	Year	County	Name of Mother	Year	County
1 James Peck	Dead	Non Citz	Mary E Peck		Non Citz
2 Wm B Brown	"	" "	Becky Brown	Dead	" "
3 No 1			No 2		
4 No 1			No 2		
5 No 1			No 2		
6 No 1			No 2		
7 No 1			No 2		
8 No. 1			No. 2		

9 Nos 1 to 6 inclusive denied by Com in 1896 case # 1418
10 Admitted by the U.S. Court at Ardmore, I.T.
11 Dec 20, 1897, Court Case 96
12
13 No 7 was born July 2 1898
14 No 2 on 1896 roll as Pollie Ann Peck
15 No 3 " 1896 " " Minnie "
16 No 4 " 1896 " " Oscar "
17 No 8 born Oct 11th 1901: Enrolled Dec. 10, 1901
Dec 9 1901, PO Duncan

IT

Choctaw By Blood Enrollment Cards 1898-1914

RESIDENCE:	Chickasaw Natn		Choctaw **Nation** Choctaw **Roll**	CARD NO.	**5063**
POST OFFICE:	Comanche, I.T.			FIELD NO.	C 168

Dawes' Roll No.	NAME	Relationship to Person	AGE	SEX	BLOOD	TRIBAL ENROLLMENT		
						Year	County	No.
1	Campbell, Jane	First Named	56	F				
2	" James S	Son	22	M				
3	" Leanna I	Dau	18	F				
4	" Lucinda L	"	15	"				
5	" Walter S	Son	13	M				
6	" Ava Velia	Gr Dau	1yr	F				
7	Gaddie, Arminda B	GrandDau	1yr	F				
8								
9								
10	#6 - DISMISSED							
11	DEC 1 1904							
12								
13								
14								
15								
16								
17								

TRIBAL ENROLLMENT OF PARENTS

	Name of Father	Year	County	Name of Mother	Year	County
1	Wm Cooper	Dead	Non Citz	Barthena Cooper	Dead	Non Citz
2	G.W. Campbell	"	" "	No.1		
3	" "	"	" "	No 1		
4	" "	"	" "	No 1		
5	" "	"	" "	No 1		
6	No 2			Dora Campbell		noncitizen
7	Hugh E Gaddie		non-citizen	No.4		
8	Admitted by the U.S. Court at Ardmore, I.T. Dec 20, 1897, Court Case No 96					
9						
10	No 6 Enrolled Nov. 30, 1901					
11	No 3 admitted as "Lena Isabel"					
12	No 4 " " "Lucinda Lorilla"					
13	No.1 is now the husband of Dora Campbell a noncitizen. Residence of marriage filed Oct 8 1901					
14	No 2 born Nov. 24th 1900. Enrolled Nov. 30, 1901		NOV 29 1904			
15	No 4 is the wife of H.E. Gaddie a noncitizen. Evidence of marriage filed Dec 14 1901					
16	Nos 1 to 5 inclusive denied by Com in 1896 case # 1418					
17	1901 Duncan, I.T.			Date of Application for Enrollment		

No 2 Mood. Res 3/6/06

263

Choctaw By Blood Enrollment Cards 1898-1914

RESIDENCE: Chickasaw Natn
POST OFFICE: Comanche, I.T.

Choctaw **Nation**   Choctaw **Roll**

CARD No. **5064**
FIELD No. C 109

Dawes' Roll No.	NAME	Relationship to Person First Named	AGE	SEX	BLOOD	TRIBAL ENROLLMENT		
						Year	County	No.
1	Sanders, John N	First Named	44	M	1/16			
2	" Mary	Dau	19	F	1/32			
3	" William N	Son	18	M	1/32			
4	" Thomas W	"	16	"	1/32			
5	" Winnie R	Dau	10	F	1/32			
6	" Nancy E	"	8	"	1/32			
7	" John E	Son	12	M	1/32			
8	" Nellie May	Dau	5mo	F	1/32			
9								
10	Sanders, James Allen	Gr Son	4mo	M	1/32			
11	N⁰4 is now the husband of Mary M Sanders noncitizen. Evidence of marriage filed Oct. 9, 1902								
12	Nos 1 & 3 to 7 incl now in C.C.C.C. Case #731								
13					For child of No5 see NB (Apr 26'06) #1218			
14	DISMISSED		"	"	No 1	"	"	"	"	#1219
15	DEC 12 1904		"	"	No 2	"	"	"	#1220
16								
17	Affidavit as to marriage of Nos 1 and 2 filed this day May 21, 1901								

TRIBAL ENROLLMENT OF PARENTS

	Name of Father	Year	County	Name of Mother	Year	County
1	S.A. Sanders		Non Citizen	Artemncy Sanders		Choctaw
2	No 1			Martha C Sanders		Non Citz
3	No 1			" "		" "
4	No 1			" "		" "
5	No 1			" "		" "
6	No 1			" "		" "
7	No 1			" "		" "
8	No 1			" "		" "
9						
10	N⁰4			Mary M Sanders		non citz
11	No5 was admitted as "Minnie"	No 8 Enrolled May 21, 1901				
12	No7 was admitted under Supplementary[sic] Judgment rendered at Ardmore I.T.					
13	October 15, 1898, Court Case No 96 For child of #6 see NB #989 (Act Apr 26 '06)					
14						
15	Aug 15/99 No2 has this day been placed upon Card No 3412 with her					
16	husband Frank R Lantz by order of Commissioner McKennon					
17	P.O. address seems to be Alma I.T.					

DENIED CITIZENSHIP BY THE CHOCTAW AND CHICKASAW CITIZENSHIP COURT

Nos 1 to 6 denied in 96: case #1418

Date of Application for Enrollment.

264

Choctaw By Blood Enrollment Cards 1898-1914

RESIDENCE: Chickasaw Natn					Choctaw **Nation** Choctaw **Roll**		CARD NO. 5065	
POST OFFICE: I.T.							FIELD NO. C 110	

Dawes' Roll No.	NAME	Relationship to Person First Named	AGE	SEX	BLOOD	TRIBAL ENROLLMENT		
						Year	County	No.
1	Bowen, Jesse A Jr	Named	24	M				
2	" Rosa	Wife	24	F				
3	" Julia Ann	Dau	4	"				
4								
5	DISMISSED							
6								
7								
8								
9								
10								
11								
12								
13								
14								
15								
16								
17								

TRIBAL ENROLLMENT OF PARENTS

	Name of Father	Year	County	Name of Mother	Year	County
1	W. H. Bowen		Non Citz	Kizia Bowen		Non Citz
2	William Boen[sic]		" "	Jane Boen		" "
3	No1			No2		
4	Nos 1 & 3 denied in 1896 case # 1418					
5	Admitted by the U.S. Court Ardmore, I.T. Dec 20, 1897 Court Case No 96					
6						
7	No 2-3 were admitted under Suplementary[sic] Judgment rendered at Ardmore, I.T. Sept 24, 1898					
8	Court Case No 96					
9						
10	No2 wife of No1 as married to him in Arkansas seven years ago					
11	No3 is the daughter of Jesse A Jr and Rosa Bowen. They have					
12	lived in the Chickasaw Nation since September					
13						
14	DENIED CITIZENSHIP BY THE CHOCTAW AND					
15	1 & 3 CHICKASAW CITIZENSHIP COURT NOV 29 1901					
16						
17						

Date of Application for Enrollment.

265

| RESIDENCE: | Chickasaw Natn | | | | | Choctaw **Nation** | | Choctaw **Roll** | | CARD No. **5066** |
| POST OFFICE: | Tussey, I.T. | | | | | | | | | FIELD No. C 111 |

Dawes' Roll No. 6\06	NAME	Relationship to Person First Named	AGE	SEX	BLOOD	TRIBAL ENROLLMENT		
						Year	County	No.
DP ✓	1 Brown Caswell M		34	M	1/16	1896	Blue	1701
✓	" Maudie	Dau	10	F	1/32	1896	"	1703
✓	3 " Willie	Son	6	M	1/32	1896	"	1704
✓	" Amanda	Wife	31	F	1/32	1896	"	1702
DP	5 " Elbert K	Son	3mo	M	1/32			
	6							
	7							
	8 #5 DISMISSED							
	9							
	10							
	11							
	12							
	13							
	14							
	15							
	#1,2,3,4 16							
	17							

DENIED CITIZENSHIP BY THE CHOCTAW AND CHICKASAW CITIZENSHIP COURT

CANCELLED

AUG 13 1906

TRIBAL ENROLLMENT OF PARENTS

	Name of Father	Year	County	Name of Mother	Year	County
1	W. B. Brown		Non Citz	Becky Brown	Dead	Non Citz
2	No1			Amanda Brown		" "
3	No1			" "		" "
4	John Kelley		Non Citz	Cynthia Kelley		" "
5	[illegible]			[illegible]		
6	Nos 1 to 4 denied in 1896 case # 1418					
7	Admitted by the U.S. Court Ardmore, I.T. Dec 20, 1897 Court Case No 96					
8						
9	No4 was admitted by Suplementary [sic] Judgement [sic] rendered at Ardmore,					
10	I.T.					
11	September 28, 1898, Court Case No 96.					
12						
13	No4 has lived in Territory					
14						
15	No1 on 1896 roll as C. M. Brown"					
16	No4 " 1896 " " Mandy " "					2/71
17	Oct 17-1899 PO Homer IT					

Choctaw By Blood Enrollment Cards 1898-1914

RESIDENCE: Chickasaw Natn
POST OFFICE: Comanche, I.T.

Choctaw **Nation**   Choctaw **Roll**

CARD NO. **5067**
FIELD NO. C 112

Dawes' Roll No.	NAME	Relationship to Person First Named	AGE	SEX	BLOOD	TRIBAL ENROLLMENT Year	TRIBAL ENROLLMENT County	TRIBAL ENROLLMENT No.
1	Higgins, Rosa I		21	M[sic]				
2	" Susie M	Dau	8mo	F				
3	" Oscar Edward	Son	5W	M				
4								
5								
6								
7								
8								
9								
10								
11								
12								
13								
14								
15								
16								
17								

DISMISSED
DEC 12 1904

TRIBAL ENROLLMENT OF PARENTS

	Name of Father	Year	County	Name of Mother	Year	County
1	W. H. Bowen		Non Citz	Kizia Bowen		Non Citz
2	L. J. Higgins		" "	No1		
3	" " "		" "	No1		
4						
5						
6	No.1 denied in 1896, case #1418					
7	Admitted by the U.S. Court Ardmore, I.T. Dec 20, 1897 Court Case No 96					
8						
9						
10	No2 was born Jan 16, 1898					
11	No3 Enrolled February 5, 1901					
12	Post office address now seems to be Addington Ind Ter. 3/5-1901					
13						
14						
15						
16	Feb 2' 1901 PO Addington IT					
17	For child of No1 see NB 1189- (Act Apr 26- '06)					

DENIED CITIZENSHIP BY THE CHOCTAW AND
CHICKASAW CITIZENSHIP COURT

267

Choctaw By Blood Enrollment Cards 1898-1914

Dawes' Roll No.	NAME	Relationship to Person First Named	AGE	SEX	BLOOD	TRIBAL ENROLLMENT Year	County	No.
✓	1 Pearcy, Triphena E		78	F				
	2							
	3							
	4							
	5							
	6							
	7							
	8							
	9							
	10							
	11							
	12							
	13							
	14							
	15							
	16							
	17							

TRIBAL ENROLLMENT OF PARENTS

	Name of Father	Year	County	Name of Mother	Year	County
1	Wm McGurnis	Dead	Non Citz	Triphena McGurnis	Dead	Non Citz
2						
3						
4						
5						
6	No. Denied in 1896 case #299					
7	Admitted by the U.S. Court Ardmore, I.T. Feby 1, 1898 case #134					
8						
9	Correct surname is Piearcy (sic)					
10						
11						
12						
13						
14						
15						
16						2/73
17					Date of Application for Enrollment.	9-22-98

Choctaw By Blood Enrollment Cards 1898-1914

RESIDENCE: Chickasaw Natn   **Choctaw Nation**   Choctaw **Roll**   CARD NO. **5069**
POST OFFICE: Wilson, I.T.   FIELD NO. C 114

Dawes' Roll No.	NAME	Relationship to Person First Named	AGE	SEX	BLOOD	TRIBAL ENROLLMENT		
						Year	County	No.
✓ 1	Pearcy, Joseph A	First Named	49	M				
✓ 2	" Bettie	Wife	43	F				
✓ 3	" Joseph A Jr	Son	19	M				
✓ 4	" John F	"	17	"				
✓ 5	" Luvisa	Dau	14	F				
✓ 6	" Elijah	Son	12	M				
✓ 7	" Ida M	Dau	9	F				
✓ 8	" Mary E	"	7	"				
DEAD ✓ 9	" Addie	"	6	"				
✓ 10	" Blanche	"	4	"				
11								
12								
13								
14								
15								
16								
17								

TRIBAL ENROLLMENT OF PARENTS

	Name of Father	Year	County	Name of Mother	Year	County
1	Williamson Pearcy	Dead	Non Citz	Triphena E Pearcy		Non Citz
2	Wm Dixon	"	" "	Louvisa Dixon		" "
3	No 1			No 2		
4	No 1			No 2		
5	No 1			No 2		
6	No 1			No 2		
7	No 1			No 2		
8	No 1			No 2		
9	No 1			No 2		
10	No 1			No 2		
11	Denied by Com in 1896 case # 299					
12	Admitted by the U.S. Court Ardmore, I.T. Feb 1, 18-- Case #134					
13						
14	No5 was admitted as "Louisa" Correct surname is Piearcy					
15						
16	Oct 4/99. As to death of No9, see affidavit attached					
17	to Card No C115					

Choctaw By Blood Enrollment Cards 1898-1914

Dawes' Roll No.	NAME	Relationship to Person First Named	AGE	SEX	BLOOD	TRIBAL ENROLLMENT Year	County	No.
DEAD 1	Piearcy, William A	First Named	24	M				
2	" William F	Son	4	M				
DP 3	" Nora E	Dau	2	F				
0 4	" Mary C	"	9mo	"				
5								
6								
No 4 7	DISMISSED							
8	SEP 15 1904							
9								
10 #3	DISMISSED							
11								
12								
13								
14								
15								
16								
17								

TRIBAL ENROLLMENT OF PARENTS

	Name of Father	Year	County	Name of Mother	Year	County
1	J. A. Pearcy		Non Citz	Bettie Pearcy		Non Citz
2	No 1			Christine Pearcy	" "	" "
3	No 1			" "	" "	" "
4	No 1			" "	" "	" "
5	Nos 1&2 denied by Com in 1896 case # 299					
6	Admitted by the U.S. Court Ardmore, I.T. Feb 1898 Court Case #134					
7	[Illegible]					
8	No3 was born Feby 22, 189[?] [Illegible]					
9						
10	Oct 4/99 As to death see affidavit attached					
11						
12	No4 enrolled Oct 30/99 subject to receipt of evidence of marriage of					
13	parents. Letter requesting same, this day. Correct surname is Piearcy					
14	CITIZENSHIP BY THE CHOCTAW AND					
15	No 1.2 CHICKASAW CITIZENSHIP COURT					
16						
17	PO Wilson IT				Date of Application for Enrollment. 9-22-98	

Choctaw By Blood Enrollment Cards 1898-1914

RESIDENCE: Chickasaw Natn

POST OFFICE: Purcell, I.T.

Choctaw **Nation**   Choctaw **Roll**

CARD NO. 5071

FIELD NO.

Dawes' Roll No.	NAME	Relationship to Person First Named	AGE	SEX	BLOOD	TRIBAL ENROLLMENT		
						Year	County	No.
1	Kelly, Mary Ann	Named	48	F				
2	Boone, Hampton	Son	17	M				
3								
4								
5								
6								
7								
8								
9								
10								
11								
12								
13								
14								
15								
16								
17								

TRIBAL ENROLLMENT OF PARENTS

	Name of Father	Year	County	Name of Mother	Year	County
1	Hamp Lindsey	Dead	Non Citz	Elizabeth Lindsey	Dead	Non Citz
2	W. H. Boone	"	" "	No 1		
3						
4						
5						
6	Nos 1&2 denied in 1896 case #18					
7	Admitted by the U.S. Court Ardmore, I.T. Dec 21, 1898 Court Case No 88					
8						
9						
10	No1 was married to Wm Kelly July 21. 1897 and was admitted as					
11	"Mary Ann Kelly"					
12	Nos 1 and 2 C.C.C.C. Case #64T 3/10/03					
13						
14						
15						
16						
17						

Choctaw By Blood Enrollment Cards 1898-1914

| RESIDENCE: | Chickasaw Natn |
| POST OFFICE: | Orr, I.T. |

Choctaw **Nation** Choctaw **Roll**

CARD NO. **5072**
FIELD NO. C 117

Dawes' Roll No.	NAME	Relationship to Person First Named	AGE	SEX	BLOOD	TRIBAL ENROLLMENT		
						Year	County	No.
1	Hill, John H	*	40	M				
2	" Louisa T	*	38	F				
3	" John W	*	Son	14	M			
4	" Lycurgus S	*	"	12	"			
5	" Louada B	*	Dau	10	F			
6	" Charley G	*	Son	8	M			
7	" Edith M	*	Dau	6	F			
8	" Robert D	*	Son	4	M			
9	" Nola C	*	Dau	2	F			
10	" Archie L		Son	5mo	M			
11	" Jesse Marvin		Son	2wks	M			
12								
13								
14								
15								
16								
17								

Nos 10 & 11 DISMISSED

SEP 15 1904

DENIED CITIZENSHIP BY THE CHOCTAW AND CHICKASAW CITIZENSHIP COURT

Nos 1 to 9 inc

TRIBAL ENROLLMENT OF PARENTS

	Name of Father	Year	County	Name of Mother	Year	County
1	Wᵐ Hill	Dead	Non Citz	Jane Hill	Dead	Non Citz
2	J T Davenport		" "	Queen S Davenport	"	" "
3	No 1			No 2		
4	No 1			No 2		
5	No 1			No 2		
6	No 1			No 2		
7	No 1			No 2		
8	No 1			No 2		
9	No 1			No 2		
10	No 1			No 2		
11	No 1			No 2		
12						
13	Nos1 to 9 inclusive, denied by Com in '96 case # 465					
14	Admitted by the U.S. Court Ardmore, I.T. Dec 22, 1898 Court Case No 104					
15						
16	No10 was born April 8, 1898					
17	No.11 was born Dec. 18, 1901 : Enrolled Dec 31, 1901					

Date of Application for Enrollment 9-22-98

Choctaw By Blood Enrollment Cards 1898-1914

RESIDENCE: Tobuskey[sic] County

POST OFFICE: I.T.

Choctaw **Nation**   Choctaw **Roll**

CARD NO. **5073**

FIELD NO.

Dawes' Roll No.		NAME	Relationship to Person First Named	AGE	SEX	BLOOD	TRIBAL ENROLLMENT		
							Year	County	No.
✓ ✓	1	Askew, William Q		66	M	1/8			
✓ ✓	2	" Martha	Wife	49	F	IW			
✓ ✓	3	" Mattie	Dau	9	"	1/16			
✓ ✓	4	" Ellen	"	7	"	1/16			
✓ ✓	5	" Tom	Son	6	M	1/16			
	6								
	7								
	8								
	9								
	10								
	11								
	12								
	13								
	14								
	15								
	16								
	17								

TRIBAL ENROLLMENT OF PARENTS

	Name of Father	Year	County	Name of Mother	Year	County
1	Tom Askew	Dead	Non Citz	Betsey Askew	Dead	Non Citz
2	Joe Burnwell	" "	Becky Burnwell	"	" "
3	No1			No2		
4	No1			No2		
5	No1			No2		
6						
7	Nos 1 to 5 inclusive, denied in 1896 case #1					
8	Nos 1,3,4 and 5 Admitted by the U.S. Court Ardmore, I.T. Dec 21, 1897 Court Case No 71					
9						
10	No2 was admitted as an intermarried citizen by supplemental judgment					
11	U.S. Court March 1st 1898			DECISION RENDERED		
12						
13						
14	No1 denied by C.C.C.C. as William Quint Askew					
15						MENT.
16						2/114
17						9-22-98

Choctaw By Blood Enrollment Cards 1898-1914

Dawes' Roll No.	NAME	Relationship to Person First Named	AGE	SEX	BLOOD	TRIBAL ENROLLMENT		
						Year	County	No.
✓ ✓	1 Askew, George W	Named	28	M	1/16			
✗ ✓	2 " Dora	Wife	30	F	IW			
✓ ✓	3 " Sophia	Dau	7	"	1/32			
✓	4 " Alice	S"	1	"	1/32			
	5							
	6							
	7							
	8							
	9							
	10							
	11							
	12							
	13							
	14							
	15							
	16							
	17							

#4 DISMISSED

NOV 12 1904
DECISION RENDERED.

DISMISSED

RECORD FORWARDED DEPARTMENT.

Notice and decision [Illegible]

See Petition #[Illegible]

TRIBAL ENROLLMENT OF PARENTS

	Name of Father	Year	County	Name of Mother	Year	County
1	W. S. Askew		Non Citz	Martha Askew	Dead	Non Citz
2	Perry Toibert	Dead	" "	Lizzie Toibert		" "
3	No1			No2		
4	No1			No2		
5						
6	Nos1,2 and 3 Denied by Dawes Com in 1896 Case #1					
7						
8						
9						
10						
11						
12						
13	DENIED CITI [Illegible] AW AND					
14						
15	CHICKA [Illegible] URT					
16	No.1 denied by C.C.C.C. as George Washington Askew					2/117
17	For child of No 1&2 see NB 962 (Act Apr 26-'06)				Date of Application for Enrollment	9-22-98

274

Choctaw By Blood Enrollment Cards 1898-1914

RESIDENCE:	Chickasaw Natn						CARD NO.	**5075**
POST OFFICE:	Foster, I.T.		Choctaw **Nation**		Choctaw **Roll**		FIELD NO.	

Dawes' Roll No.	NAME	Relationship to Person First Named	AGE	SEX	BLOOD	TRIBAL ENROLLMENT		
						Year	County	No.
1	Forsyth, William J	Named	56	M	1/8			
2	" William F	Son	15	"	1/16			
3	" Lorena	Dau	11	F	1/16			
4	" Laura	"	9	"	1/16			
5	" Ernest	Son	7	M	1/16			
6	" Walter	"	5	"	1/16			
7	" Lizzie	Dau	3	F	1/16			
8	" Roland C	Son	8mo	M	1/16			
9	" Lula May	Dau	6mo	F	1/16			
10	" Clarence Arthur	Son	3mo	M	1/16			
11								
12								
13								
14								
15								
16								
17								

Nos 8-9-10 **DISMISSED**
SEP 15 1904

TRIBAL ENROLLMENT OF PARENTS

	Name of Father	Year	County	Name of Mother	Year	County
1	T [?] Forsyth	Dead	Non Citz	Nancy Forsyth	Dead	Non Citz
2	No 1			Caroline Forsyth	"	" "
3	No 1			Roxie A Forsyth	"	" "
4	No 1			" "	" "	
5	No 1			" "	" "	
6	No 1			" "	" "
7	Nº 1			" "	" "

8 Admitted by the U.S. Court Ardmore, I.T. Dec 22, 1898 Court Case No 104

9

10 No8 was born Feby 20, 1898   Nº10 Born Feby 3,1902: enrolled April 29, 1902

11   Nos 1 to 7 denied in 1896 case #465

12 The above named people moved into the Territory in August, 1898

13

14 No9 enrolled Nov 7/99, subject to receipt of evidence of marriage of

15 parents. Letter, requesting same, this day

16

17

Date of Application for Enrollment   9-22-98

275

Choctaw By Blood Enrollment Cards 1898-1914

RESIDENCE: Chickasaw Natn
POST OFFICE: Foster, I.T.

Choctaw **Nation**   Choctaw **Roll**

CARD NO. **5076**
FIELD NO. C 121

Dawes' Roll No.	NAME	Relationship to Person First Named	AGE	SEX	BLOOD	TRIBAL ENROLLMENT Year	County	No.
1	Shannon, Mary Ann	Named	31	F				
2	Thompson, Ella	Dau	9	"				
DP 3	Shannon, Embers E	Son	2wk	M				
4								
5								
No 6	DISMISSED							
7	SEP 15 1904							
8								
9								
10								
11								
12								
13								
14								
15								
16								
17								

TRIBAL ENROLLMENT OF PARENTS

	Name of Father	Year	County	Name of Mother	Year	County
1	W. J. Forsyth		Non Citz	Caroline Forsyth	Dead	Non Citz
2	DeCosa Thompson		Choctaw Citz	No1		
3	J. W. Shannon		Non Citz	No1		
4						
5	Nos 1&2 denied in 1896 case #465					
6	Admitted by the U.S. Court Ardmore, I.T. Dec 22, 1897 Court Case No 105					
7						
8						
9	No1 was married to Jim Shannon in December, 1897, and was					
10	admitted as "Mary Ann Thompson"					
11						
12	No3 was born October 3, 1898. Not in [illegible]					
13	DENIED CITIZENSHIP BY THE CHOCTAW AND					
14	No1 is same person as Ellen Thompson on Choctaw card #501					
15	CHICKASAW CITIZENSHIP COURT					
16						
17					Date of Application for Enrollment	9-22-98

276

Choctaw By Blood Enrollment Cards 1898-1914

RESIDENCE: Pickens County Chick Natn
POST OFFICE: Ardmore, I.T.

Choctaw **Nation**   Choctaw **Roll**

CARD NO. **5077**
FIELD NO.

Dawes' Roll No.	NAME	Relationship to Person First Named	AGE	SEX	BLOOD	TRIBAL ENROLLMENT		
						Year	County	No.
1	Tucker, Susie		24	F				
2								
3								
4								
5								
6								
7								
8								
9								
10								
11								
12								
13								
14								
15								
16								
17								

TRIBAL ENROLLMENT OF PARENTS

	Name of Father	Year	County	Name of Mother	Year	County
1	J. W. Hoffman		Non Citz	Mary Hoffman		Non Citz
2						
3						
4						
5						
6	No.1 denied in 1896 case # 1345					
7	Admitted by the U.S. Court Ardmore, I.T. Dec 22, 1898 Court Case # 137					
8						
9	Husband of No 1 on Choctaw doubtful card #D392					
10						
11						
12						
13						
14						
15						
16						
17					Date of A for Enroll	9-22-98	

Choctaw By Blood Enrollment Cards 1898-1914

RESIDENCE: Pickens County Chick Natn
POST OFFICE: Ardmore, I.T.

Choctaw **Nation** Choctaw **Roll**

CARD NO. **5078**
FIELD NO. 123

Dawes' Roll No.	NAME	Relationship to Person First Named	AGE	SEX	BLOOD	TRIBAL ENROLLMENT Year	County	No.
1	Hoffman, J. W.	Named	66	M	IW			
2	" Mary	Wife	46	F	3/4			
3	" Mollie	Dau	20	"	3/8			
4	" Daniel	Son	16	M	3/8			
5	Florice, Charles	S Son	28	"	3/8			
6	" Yourland	Son of No5	10mo	M	3/16			
7	Cude, Timothy J	Son of No3	1mo	"	3/16			
8								
9	#6-7- DISMISSED							
10	JAN 22 1905							
11								
12	No5 denied by C.C.C.							
13	as "Charles Florice or Chas Florice"							
14	No3 denied by C.C.C. as "Mollie Cude (nee Hoffman) or							
15	Mollie Hoffman"							
16								
17								

TRIBAL ENROLLMENT OF PARENTS

	Name of Father	Year	County	Name of Mother	Year	County
1	Dan'l Hoffman	Dead	Non Citz	Elizabeth Hoffman	Dead	Non Citz
2	Frank Puskachumey	"	Choc Ind	Kittie Puskachumey	"	Choc Ind
3	No 1			No2		
4	No 1			No2		
5	Sous Florice	Dead	Non Citz	No2		
6	No5			Eva J Florice	dead	non-citizen
7	W.A. Cude		non-citizen	No 3		
8	Nos 1 to 5 denied in 1896 case #1345					
9	Admitted by the U.S. Court Ardmore, I.T. Dec 22, 1898 Case #137					
10	No.5 is the husband of Eva Florice on Choctaw card #D.393					
11	Evidence of marriage of No.5 and Eva Florice filed with Choctaw #D.393					
12	No.6 born Dec. 31, 1900: Enrolled Oct 11, 1901					
13	No7 Born Sept 11, 1902, enrolled Oct. 20, 1902					
14	No3 is now the wife of W.A. Cude, non-citizen. Evidence of marriage					
15	requester Oct. 20, 1902. Received and filed Oct. 29, 1902					
16	Judgment of U.S. Court admitting Nos 1 to 5 incl vacated and set aside by Decree [illegible]/1531					
17	Nos1 to 5 incl now in C.C. C.C. Case #377		Date of A for En		9-22-98	

278

Choctaw By Blood Enrollment Cards 1898-1914

RESIDENCE: Chickasaw Natn   Choctaw **Nation**   Choctaw **Roll**   CARD NO. **5079**
POST OFFICE: Ardmore, I.T.   FIELD NO.

Dawes' Roll No.	NAME	Relationship to Person First Named	AGE	SEX	BLOOD	TRIBAL ENROLLMENT		
						Year	County	No.
1	Puscachummy, Frank	Named	53	M	3/4			
2								
3								
4								
5								
6								
7								
8								
9								
10								
11								
12								
13								
14								
15								
16								
17								

TRIBAL ENROLLMENT OF PARENTS

	Name of Father	Year	County	Name of Mother	Year	County
1	Puscachummy	Dead	Choc Ind	Kittie Puscachummy	Dead	Choc Ind
2						
3						
4						
5						
6						
7						
8	No1 denied by Com in 1896 case # 1345					
9	Admitted by the U.S. Court Ardmore, I.T. Dec 22,			Case # 137		
10						
11						
12						
13						
14						
15						
16						
17				Date of application for Enrollment.	9-22	

Choctaw By Blood Enrollment Cards 1898-1914

RESIDENCE: Chickasaw Natn
POST OFFICE: Ardmore, I.T.

Choctaw **Nation**   Choctaw **Roll**

CARD NO. **5080**
FIELD NO. C 125

Dawes' Roll No.	NAME	Relationship to Person First Named	AGE	SEX	BLOOD	TRIBAL ENROLLMENT Year	County	No.
1	MᶜClerg, Victoria,	Named	30	F				
2	" Susie	Dau	5	"				
3	" Lillie	"	4	"				
4	" Haney	"	3	"				
5	" Jack D	Son	1	M				
6	Wallis, Henry	"	8	"				
7	MᶜClerg, Halley B	"	4mo	"				
8								
#5-7-	DISMISSED							
10								
No1 Denied by C.C.C.C. as								
12	"Victoria MᶜClerg							
13	(nee Florice)"							
14								
15								
16	See C-726							
17	Record in Choctaw #5078							

TRIBAL ENROLLMENT OF PARENTS

	Name of Father	Year	County	Name of Mother	Year	County
1	Sous Florice	Dead	Non Citz	Mary Hoffman		Non Citz
2	O. W. MᶜClerg		" "	No 1		
3	" "		" "	No 1		
4	" "		" "	No 1		
5	" "		" "	No 1		
6	Henry Wallis		" "	No 1		
7	O. W. MᶜClerg		" "	No 1		
8		Nos 1 to 4 inclusive and No.6 denied in 1896, case #1345					
9		Admitted by the U.S. Court Ardmore, I.T. Dec 22, 1897 Case # 137					
10		Judgment of U.S. Ct admitting No vacated and [remaining illegible]					
11		No5 was born September 3, 1897					
12							
13		No4 was admitted as "Henry"					
14		No6 " " " "Handy"					
15	DENIED CITIZENSHIP BY THE CHOCTAW AND					
16	No1,2,3,4,5,6					²/155
17	CHICKASAW CITIZENSHIP COURT			for Enrollment.		9-22-98

Choctaw By Blood Enrollment Cards 1898-1914

RESIDENCE: Chickasaw Natn
POST OFFICE: Hewitt, I.T.

Choctaw **Nation**   Choctaw **Roll**

CARD NO. **5081**
FIELD NO.

Dawes' Roll No.	NAME	Relationship to Person	AGE	SEX	BLOOD	TRIBAL ENROLLMENT		
						Year	County	No.
✓ *	1 Sessums, W. R. Jr	First Named	37	M				
✓ *	2 " Mary J	Dau	10	F				
✓ *	3 " William F	Son	6	M				
✓	4 " Lillie R	Dau	9mo	F				
✓	5 " Dolly Palaw	Dau	2mo	F				
✓ *	6 " Lelia	Dau	11	F				
	7							
	8							
4 & 5	9 DISMISSED							
	10 MAY 27 1904							
	11							
	12							
	13							
	14							
	15							
	16							
	17							

TRIBAL ENROLLMENT OF PARENTS

	Name of Father	Year	County	Name of Mother	Year	County
1	W. R. Sessums		Non Citz	Liza A Sessums		Non Citz
2	No 1			Sarah E Sessums		" "
3	No 1			" " "		" "
4	No 1			" " "		" "
5	No 1			" "		" "
6	No. 1			" "		" "
7	Nos 1,2&3 denied in 1896, case # 452					
8	Admitted by U.S. Court, South McAlester, I.T.					
9	Court Case No 10					
10						
11	No4 was born December 19, 1898					
12	No.5 Enrolled Sept 17, 1901					
13	Evidence of marriage of No1 to Sarah E Sessums					
14	No.6 admitted as Sallie Sessums					
15	No.6 Enrolled Jany 21st, 1902					
16						
17						

DENIED CITIZENSHIP BY THE CHOCTAW AND CHICKASAW CITIZENSHIP COURT

Date ... tion ... nrollment. 9-15-98

281

Choctaw By Blood Enrollment Cards 1898-1914

RESIDENCE:	Chickasaw Natn		Choctaw **Nation**	Choctaw **Roll**		CARD No.	**5082**
POST OFFICE:	Earl, I.T.					FIELD No.	C-127

Dawes' Roll No.		NAME	✓	Relationship to Person	AGE	SEX	BLOOD	TRIBAL ENROLLMENT		
								Year	County	No.
✓ ✓ *	1	Stepp, Mattie		First Named	19	F				
✓	2	" James R	✓	Son	1	M				
✓	3	" Cora Oma	✓	Dau	1mo	F				
	4									
	5									
	6									
#2-3	7	DISMISSED								
	8	MAY 27 1904								
	9									
	10									
	11									
	12									
	13									
	14	See C - 117								
	15									
	16									
	17									

TRIBAL ENROLLMENT OF PARENTS

	Name of Father	Year	County	Name of Mother	Year	County
1	W. R. Sessums		Non Citz	Liza A Sessums		Non Citz
2	J. F. Stepp		" "	No1		
3	" "	DENIED CITIZENSHIP BY THE CHOCTAW AND		No1		
4		CHICKASAW CITIZENSHIP COURT				
5				ACTION APPROVED BY		
6	No1 denied in 1896 case #452			SECRETARY OF INTERIOR. FEB 2 1 1907		
7	Admitted by the U.S. Court South McAlester, I.T. January 10, 1898					
8	Court Case #10			NOTICE OF DEPARTMENTAL ACTION		
9				NOTICE OF DEPARTMENTAL ACTION FORWARDED ATTORNEYS FOR CHOCTAW		
10				AND CHICKASAW NATIONS. MAY 1 8 1907		
11	Married to J.F Stepp in November 1897 and was admitted as			NOTICE OF DEPARTMENTAL ACTION		
12	"Mattie Sessums"			FORWARDED ATTORNEY FOR APPLICANT. MAY		
13			No.3 Enrolled Feby 25th, 1901			
14	* No1 denied by C.C.C.C. Case #36 March 9 '04			NOTICE OF DEPARTMENTAL ACTION MAILED APPLICANT.		
15				No2 enrolled MAY 30/99		
16	For children of No1 see NB (Apr 26 '06) #1267					2/166
17				Date of Application for Enrollment.	9-15-98	

Choctaw By Blood Enrollment Cards 1898-1914

RESIDENCE:	Chickasaw Natn		Choctaw **Nation**		Choctaw **Roll**		CARD NO.	**5083**
POST OFFICE:	Earl, I.T.						FIELD NO.	128

Dawes' Roll No.	NAME	Relationship to Person First Named	AGE	SEX	BLOOD	TRIBAL ENROLLMENT		
						Year	County	No.
✓ * 1	Bratcher, Effie A	First Named	17	F				
✓ 2	" Mary D	Dau	10mo	"				
✓ 3	" Bessie E	"	3mo	"				
✓ 4	" Elbirtia	Dau	5mo	F				
5								
6								
#2-3-4 7	DISMISSED							
8								
9								
10								
11								
12								
13								
14								
15								
16								
17								

TRIBAL ENROLLMENT OF PARENTS

	Name of Father	Year	County	Name of Mother	Year	County
1	W. L. Bailey	Dead	Non Citz	Mary Bailey		Non Citz
2	J. E. Bratcher	" "		No 1		
3	" " "	" "		No 1		
4	" " "	" "		No 1		
5						
6						
7	No.1 denied in 1896 case #452					
8	Admitted by the U.S. Court South McAlester, I.T. January 20, 1898					
9	Court Case No10					
10						
11	Married to J.E. Bratcher Jan 24, 1897 and was admitted as "E. A. Bailey"					
12	No4 Enrolled Aug 24, 1901					
13						
14						
15						
16			No3 enrolled Oct 30/99			²/169
17						9-22-98

DENIED CITIZENSHIP BY THE CHOCTAW AND CHICKASAW CITIZENSHIP COURT

283

Choctaw By Blood Enrollment Cards 1898-1914

RESIDENCE: Chickasaw Natn
POST OFFICE: Earl, I.T.

Choctaw **Nation**   Choctaw **Roll**

CARD NO. **5084**
FIELD NO. C 129

Dawes' Roll No.	NAME	Relationship to Person First Named	AGE	SEX	BLOOD	TRIBAL ENROLLMENT Year	County	No.
✓ *	1 Ramsey, Rosa A		17	F				
✓	2 " James Henry 2	Son	8½mo	M				
	3							
	4							
	5							
	6							
	7							
	8							
	9							
	10							
	11							
	12							
	13							
	14							
	15							
	16							
	17							

DISMISSED
MAY 27 1904

TRIBAL ENROLLMENT OF PARENTS

	Name of Father	Year	County	Name of Mother	Year	County
1	J. T. Sessums		Non Citz	Lizzie Sessums		Non Citz
2	J.W. Ramsay[sic]		" "	No 1		
3						
4	No 1					
5						
6						
7	No.1 denied in 1896, case No 452					
8	Admitted by the U.S. Court South McAlester, I.T. Jan 20, 1898					
9	Court Case No 10					
10						
11						
12	Married to J.W. Ramsey, Jan 15, 1898 and was admitted as					
13	"Rosa Ann Sessums"					
14						
15	No.2 Born June 21, 1901; enrolled March 11, 1902					
16						
17						

DENIED CITIZENSHIP BY THE CHOCTAW AND CHICKASAW CITIZENSHIP COURT

Date of Application for Enrollment 9-22-98

284

RESIDENCE: Chickasaw Natn   Choctaw **Nation**   Choctaw **Roll**   CARD NO. **5085**
POST OFFICE: Earl, I.T.   FIELD NO. C 130

Dawes' Roll No.	NAME	Relationship to Person First Named	AGE	SEX	BLOOD	TRIBAL ENROLLMENT Year	County	No.
✓ *	1 Sessums, J. F.	First Named	41	M				
✓ *	2 " Myrtle	Dau	15	F				
✓ *	3 " May	"	11	"				
✓ *	4 " Ethel	"	6	"				
✓ *	5 " William D	Son	4	M				
✓	6 " Charley L	"	8mo	"				
✓	7 " Jacob Carroll	Son	2mo	M				
	8							
	9							
6 & 7	10 DISMISSED							
	11							
	12							
	13							
	14 Petition No W 69							
	15 Ser C 27 incl 69							
	16							
	17							

TRIBAL ENROLLMENT OF PARENTS

	Name of Father	Year	County	Name of Mother	Year	County
1	W. R. Sessums		Non Citz	Liza A Sessums		Non Citz
2	No 1			Elizabeth Sessums		" "
3	No 1			" "		" "
4	No 1			" "		" "
5	No 1			" "		" "
6	No 1			" "		" "
7	N° 1			" "		" "
8	Nos 1 to 5 denied in 1896, case # 452					
9	Admitted by the U.S. Court South McAlester I.T. Jan 20, 1898					
10	Court Case No 10					
11						
12	No 3 was admitted as "Mary"					
13	No 4 " " " "Ethie"					
14	No 5 " " " "Daniel"		For child of No 3 see NB #1063 (Act Apr 26 '06)			
15	N° 7 Born Feby 14, 1902; enrolled April 22, 1902					
16						2/160
17						

DENIED CITIZENSHIP BY THE CHOCTAW AND CHICKASAW CITIZENSHIP COURT

PO Maxwell IT

Date of Application for Enrollment.

Choctaw By Blood Enrollment Cards 1898-1914

| RESIDENCE: | Chickasaw Natn | | | | | | CARD NO. | **5086** |
| POST OFFICE: | Purcell, I.T. | | Choctaw **Nation** | Choctaw **Roll** | | | FIELD NO. | C 131 |

Dawes' Roll No.	NAME	Relationship to Person First Named	AGE	SEX	BLOOD	TRIBAL ENROLLMENT		
						Year	County	No.
1	Boone, Hughton	Named	26	M			D	
2	" Florence	Wife	22	F			D	
3	" Marie	Dau	3	"			D	
4	" Lillie	"	9mo	"				
5								
6	#4 DISMISSED							
7								
No1 Denied by CCCC as "Hollard Boone or Hulen Boone"								
" 3 9 " " " " "Maria Boone or								
10	Marie Boone"							
11								
12								
13								
14								
15								
16								
17								

TRIBAL ENROLLMENT OF PARENTS

	Name of Father	Year	County	Name of Mother	Year	County
1	W. H. Boone	Dead	Non Citz	Mary Boone		Non Citz
2	J. V. Crow	" "	Elsie Crow	Dead	" "
3	No1			No2		
4	No1			No2		
5	Nos1,2&3 denied in 1896, case #18					
6	Admitted by the U.S. Court Ardmore, I.T. Dec 21, 1897 Court Case No 88					
7						
8						
9	No4 was born Dec 6, 1897					
10						
11	No1 was admitted as "Hollord Boone"					
12	No3 " " " "Maria Boone"					
13						
14						
15	DENIED CITIZENSHIP BY THE CHOCTAW AND					
16	CHICKASAW CITIZENSHIP COURT					
17						

Choctaw By Blood Enrollment Cards 1898-1914

RESIDENCE: Chickasaw Natn			Choctaw **Nation**			Choctaw **Roll**	CARD NO. **5087**	
POST OFFICE: Wilson, I.T.							FIELD NO. C 132	

Dawes' Roll No.	NAME	Relationship to Person First Named	AGE	SEX	BLOOD	TRIBAL ENROLLMENT		
						Year	County	No.
1	Wainscot, B B	First Named	54	M				
2	" Julia C	Dau	2	F				
3	" Melvin	Son	9mo	M				
4								
5								
6	#2-3 DISMISSED							
7								
8								
9								
10								
11								
12								
13								
14								
15								
16								
17								

TRIBAL ENROLLMENT OF PARENTS

	Name of Father	Year	County	Name of Mother	Year	County
1	C C Wainscot	Dead	Non Citz	Hannah Wainscot	Dead	Non Citz
2	No1			Lourana Wainscot	" "	
3	No1	DENIED CITIZENSHIP BY THE CHOCTAW AND				
4		CHICKASAW CITIZENSHIP COURT				
5						
6						
7	No.1 denied in 1896, case #18					
8	Admitted by the U.S. Court Ardmore, I.T. Dec 22, 1897					
9	Court Case No 88					
10						
11						
12	No3 enrolled Dec 18/99. Affidavit irregular and					
13	returned for correction. Recd & filed Jany 7, 1900					
14	No3 Evidence of marriage of			Filed Jany 15, 1900		
15						
16						
17						

Choctaw By Blood Enrollment Cards 1898-1914

						TRIBAL ENROLLMENT		
Dawes' Roll No.	NAME	Relationship to Person First Named	AGE	SEX	BLOOD	Year	County	No.
✓	₁ Gamel, Kate		63	F				
✓	₂ Witt, Carrie	Dau	29	"				
	₃							
	₄							
	₅							
	₆							
	₇							
	₈							
	₉							
	₁₀							
	₁₁							
	₁₂							
	₁₃							
	₁₄							
	₁₅							
	₁₆							
	₁₇							

RESIDENCE: Chickasaw Natn
POST OFFICE: Ardmore, I.T.

Choctaw **Nation** Choctaw **Roll**

CARD NO. **5088**
FIELD NO. C 133

TRIBAL ENROLLMENT OF PARENTS

Name of Father	Year	County	Name of Mother	Year	County
₁ John Rutledge	Dead	Non Citz	Betsy Rutledge	Dead	Non Citz
₂ Geo Gamel	" "		No1		
₃					
₄					
₅					
₆					
₇	Nos 1 &2 denied in 1896, case # 24				
₈	Admitted by U.S. Court Ardmore, I.T. Dec 21, 1898	Court Case			
₉					
₁₀					
₁₁	No 1 admitted as "Kate Gammel"				
₁₂					
₁₃					
₁₄					
₁₅					
₁₆					
₁₇	For child of No2 see NB #1055 (Act Apr 26 '06)				

Date of Application for Enrollment 9-22-98

Choctaw By Blood Enrollment Cards 1898-1914

RESIDENCE: Chickasaw Natn
POST OFFICE: Ardmore, I.T.

Choctaw **Nation**   Choctaw **Roll**

CARD NO. **5089**
FIELD NO. 134

Dawes' Roll No.	NAME	Relationship to Person First Named	AGE	SEX	BLOOD	TRIBAL ENROLLMENT		
						Year	County	No.
1	Williams, Minnie	Named	21	F				
2	" Floyd	Son	2mo	MM				
3	" Ebb jr[sic]	Son	4mo					
4								
5								
6	DISMISSED							
7	SEP 15 1904							
8								
9								
10								
11								
12								
13								
14								
15								
16								
17								

TRIBAL ENROLLMENT OF PARENTS

	Name of Father	Year	County	Name of Mother	Year	County
1	Geo Gamel	Dead	Non Citz	Kate Gamel		Non Citz
2	Ebb Williams		" "	No1		
3	" "		" "	No.1		
4	No1 denied in 1896, case # 24					
5	Admitted by the U.S. Court Ardmore, I.T. Dec 23, 1898 Court Case					
6						
7	No2 was born July 8, 1898					
8						
9	No.3 Born Dec 4, 1901; Enrolled April 11, 1902					
10						
11						
12	DENIED CITIZENSHIP BY THE CHOCTAW AND					
13	CHICKASAW CITIZENSHIP COURT					
14						
15						
16						
17						

Choctaw By Blood Enrollment Cards 1898-1914

RESIDENCE: Chickasaw Natn
POST OFFICE: Pauls Valley, I.T.

Choctaw **Nation** Choctaw **Roll**

CARD NO. **5090**
FIELD NO. 43

Dawes' Roll No.	NAME	Relationship to Person First Named	AGE	SEX	BLOOD	TRIBAL ENROLLMENT Year	County	No.
1	Bousman, Sallie		48	F				
2	" Ed	Son	17	M				
3	" Frank	"	15	"				
4	" Kennie	Dau	13	F				
5	" Mabel	"	9	"				
6	" Kate	"	7	"				
7								
8								
9								
10								
11								
12								
13								
14								
15								
16								
17								

Nos 2 & 9 DISMISSED OCT 20 1904

TRIBAL ENROLLMENT OF PARENTS

	Name of Father	Year	County	Name of Mother	Year	County
1	Tom Cruce	Dead	Non Citz	Kate Cruce		Non Citz
2	Louis Bousman		" "	No 1		
3	" "		" "	No 1		
4	" "		" "	No 1		
5	" "		" "	No 1		
6	" "		" "	No 1		
7						
8						
9						
10						
11	Nos1 to 6 denied in 1896, case # 24					
12	Admitted by the U.S. Court Ardmore, I.T. Dec 21, 1898 Court Case No 109					
13						
14	The above names appear in the Decree of the Court as Boseman					

DENIED CITIZENSHIP BY THE CHOCTAW AND CHICKASAW CITIZENSHIP COURT

Date of Application 9-23-98

290

Choctaw By Blood Enrollment Cards 1898-1914

RESIDENCE: Chickasaw Natn   Choctaw **Nation**   Choctaw **Roll**   CARD NO. **5091**
POST OFFICE: Ardmore, I.T.   FIELD NO.

Dawes' Roll No.	NAME	Relationship to Person First Named	AGE	SEX	BLOOD	Year	County	No.
Void	1 Blake, L. L.		54	M	IW	1896	Chick Dist	14365
	2 " Thedia D	Wife	45	F				
	3 " John Y	Son	18	M				
	4 " Julia C	Dau	15	F				
	5 " Nellie	"	13	"				
	6 " Lafayette	Son	8	M				
	7 " Virginia	Dau	6	F				
	8 " Ruth	"	3	"				
	9							
	10							
	11							
	12							
	13							
	14							
See Chickasaw card #1806								
for #3 John Y.F. Blake	16							
	17 See Petition #C-55							

ACTION APPROVED BY   FEB 27 1907
SECRETARY OF INTERIOR.
NOTICE OF DEPARTMENTAL ACTION
FORWARDED ATTORNEYS FOR CHOCTAW   APR 3 1907
AND CHICKASAW NATIONS.
NOTICE OF DEPARTMENTAL ACTION   R 3 1907
FORWARDED ATTORNEY FOR APPLICANT.
NOTICE OF DEPARTMENTAL
ACTION MAILED APPLICANT   R 3

TRIBAL ENROLLMENT OF PARENTS

	Name of Father	Year	County	Name of Mother	Year	County
1	T. K. Blake	Dead	Non Citz	Clara T Blake	Dead	Non Citz
2	N. C. Crowder	" "	Rosella Crowder		" "
3	No1			No2		
4	No1			No2		
5	No1			No2		
6	No1			No2		
7	No1			No2		
8	No1			No2		
9						
10	Nos 1 to 8 inclusive denied in 1896, case #902					
11	Admitted by the U.S Court Ardmore, I.T. Dec 21, 1897 Court Case No 122					
12						
13	No2 was admitted as "Thedia"					
14	No4 " " " "Julia C"					
15	Nº3 is now the husband of Callie Chase on Chickasaw card #590 April 25, 1902					
16	Evidence of marriage of No.3 filed with Chickasaw #590				3/27
17						

291

RESIDENCE:	Chickasaw Natn						CARD NO. **5092**
POST OFFICE:	Duncan Ind. Terr.	Choctaw **Nation**		Choctaw **Roll**			FIELD NO. 137

Dawes' Roll No.	NAME	Relationship to Person First Named	AGE	SEX	BLOOD	TRIBAL ENROLLMENT		
						Year	County	No.
1	Jones, William J	Named	28	M				
2	" Sallie M	Wife	23	F				
3	" Alta F	Dau	6mo	F				
4	" Noma Lila	"	2	"				
5								
6	DECISION RENDERED.							
	REFUSED							
8								
9								
10								
11								
12								
13								
14								
15								
16								
17	See Choctaw 5053							

TRIBAL ENROLLMENT OF PARENTS

	Name of Father	Year	County	Name of Mother	Year	County
1	Wm Albert Jones		Non Citz	Jennie Jones	Dead	Non Citz
2	John G Jones		" "	Eliza Jones		" "
3	No1			No2		
4	No1			No2		
5						
6						
7				ACTION APPROVED BY SECRETARY OF INTERIOR		
8			No3 was born Mch 5 - 1898			
9						
10			Admitted by the U.S Court Ardmore. I.T.			
11			Jan 17 - 1898 Case 148			
12						
13						
14						
15						
16				Application	9-22-98	1/54
17						

Choctaw By Blood Enrollment Cards 1898-1914

RESIDENCE: Chickasaw Natn
POST OFFICE: Comanche I.T.

Choctaw **Nation**   Choctaw **Roll**

CARD NO. **5093**
FIELD NO.

Dawes' Roll No.	NAME	Relationship to Person First Named	AGE	SEX	BLOOD	TRIBAL ENROLLMENT Year	County	No.
1	Sanders Jesse W		42	M				
2	" Lizzie	Wife	24	F				
3	" James R	Son	18	M				
4	" John N	Son	16	M				
5	" Joseph M	Dau	14	M				
6	" Izey M	Dau	3	F				
7	" Ida J	son	6mo	F				
8	" Luther Bynum	Son	1mo	M				
9	" Freemont	G.Son	2mo	M				
10	" Delmer Waldo							
11	Admitted by the U.S. Court Ardmore, I.T.							
12	Dec 20, 1897 Court Case 96			Nos 1 to 6 denied in 1896, case # 1418				
13	Joseph M Admitted as "James M"							
14								
15	#7-8-9-10- DISMISSED							
16								
17								

(left margin, vertical:) Jno of Jno Newton Sanders or Jesse Wilson Sanders John Newton Sanders or "Jesse Walsh Sanders Denied by C C C C No 4 Denied No 1

TRIBAL ENROLLMENT OF PARENTS

	Name of Father	Year	County	Name of Mother	Year	County
1	S. F. Sanders		Non Citz	Artie M Sanders		Non Citz
2	Sam Harris	Dead	" "	Julia Harris		" "
3	No1			Malinda Sanders		" "
4	No1			" "		" "
5	No1			" "		" "
6	No1			No2		
7	No1			No2		
8	No1			No2		
9	No1			No2		
10	Nº3			Willie Sanders		non citizen
11	No7 was born Feb 14-1898					
12	Nº3 was married to Willie Henson white woman Sept.1,1901. Evidence of marriage					
13	No8 Enrolled May 24, 1900					
14	No9 Born April 17th 1902 Enrolled June 18th 1902					
15	No10 Born Aug 29,1902. Enrolled Oct 29, 1902					
16				Date of Application for Enrollment:	9-22-98	159
17	For child of No3 see NB #1927 (Act Apr 26 '06) (For child of Nos1&2 see NB (Apr 26'06) #1221					

6/16/02 PO Terral IT

293

Choctaw By Blood Enrollment Cards 1898-1914

RESIDENCE: Chickasaw Natn						Choctaw **Nation** Choctaw **Roll**		CARD NO. **5094**	
POST OFFICE: Comanche, I.T.								FIELD NO. C 139	

Dawes' Roll No.	NAME	Relationship to Person First Named	AGE	SEX	BLOOD	TRIBAL ENROLLMENT		
						Year	County	No.
1	Bowen William H	Named	49	M				
2	" Kesiah	Wife	49	F				
3	" Nancy B	Dau	15	F				
4	" Elizabeth J	Dau	12	F				
5	" James S	Son	10	M				
6	Bennett, Royal E	Granson[sic]	2wk	M				
7								
8								
9	DISMISSED							
10	DEC 1904							
11								
12								
13								
14								
15								
16								
17								

TRIBAL ENROLLMENT OF PARENTS

	Name of Father	Year	County	Name of Mother	Year	County
1	Jesse Bowen	Dead	Non Citz	Polly Bowen	Dead	Non Citz
2	Spencer Horner	Dead	" "	Melia Horner	Dead	" "
3	No1			No2		
4	No1			No2		
5	No1			No2		
6	W.S.A. Bennett		Non-citizen	No.3		
7	Nos 1 to 5 denied in 1896, case # 1418					
8	Admitted by the U.S. Court Ardmore, I.T.					
9	Dec 20 - 1897 Court Case 96					
10						
11	No3 is now the wife of W.S.A. Bennett, a non-citizen					
12	No6 Enrolled Aug 30th, 1900					
13						
14	DENIED CITIZENSHIP BY THE CHOCTAW AND					
15	CHICKASAW CITIZENSHIP COURT NOV 29 1904					
16					9-22-98	2/63
17					Date of Application for Enrollment.	

294

Choctaw By Blood Enrollment Cards 1898-1914

RESIDENCE: Chickasaw Natn
POST OFFICE: Comanche I.T.

Choctaw **Nation**   Choctaw **Roll**

CARD NO. **5095**
FIELD NO. C 140

Dawes' Roll No.	NAME	Relationship to Person First Named	AGE	SEX	BLOOD	TRIBAL ENROLLMENT Year	County	No.
1	Brown George G	Named	26	M	1/16	1896	Blue	1705
2	" Sarah	Wife	21	F		1896	"	1706
	" Willie Emma	Dau	3	F				
4								
5								
6								
7								
8								
9								
10								
11								
12								
13								
14								
15								
16								
17								

TRIBAL ENROLLMENT OF PARENTS

	Name of Father	Year	County	Name of Mother	Year	County
1	Wm Brown		Non Citz	Rebecca Brown	Dead	Non Citz
2	Perry Johnson		"	Bett Johnson	"	"
3	No1			No2		
4						
5						
6	Nos 1&2 denied in 1896, case # 1418					
7	Admitted by the U.S. Court Ardmore, I.T.					
8	Dec 20 - 1897 Court Case 96					
9						
10						
11	No1 on 1896 Roll as Geo G Brown					
12						
13						
14						
15						
16					Date of Application for Enrollment	9-22-98 2/64
17						

CANCELLED

DENIED CITIZENSHIP BY THE CHOCTAW AND CHICKASAW CITIZENSHIP COURT

295

Choctaw By Blood Enrollment Cards 1898-1914

| RESIDENCE: | Chickasaw Natn | | | | | CARD NO. | **5096** |
| POST OFFICE: | Tussy I.T. | Choctaw **Nation** | | Choctaw **Roll** | | FIELD NO. | C 141 |

Dawes' Roll No	NAME	Relationship to Person First Named	AGE	SEX	BLOOD	TRIBAL ENROLLMENT		
						Year	County	No.
1	Brown William B	Named	61	M	1/8	1896	B	1688
2	Nancy A	Dau	23	F	1/16	1896	"	1689
3	McCarly Bettie	Dau	19	F	1/16	1896	"	1670
4	McCarly Mary E	Grand dau	1mo	F	1/32			
5								
6								
7								
8								
9								
10	#4- DISMISSED							
11								
12	Dec 12 - 04							
13								
14	No3	NAME STRICKEN FROM ORIGINAL JUDGMENT BY ORDER OF U. S. COURT						
15								
16								
17								

TRIBAL ENROLLMENT OF PARENTS

	Name of Father	Year	County	Name of Mother	Year	County
1	Jesse Brown	Dead	Non Citz	Mary Brown		Non Citz
2	No1			Rebecca Brown	Dead	" "
3	No1			" "	"	" "
4	Oliver McCarly		non-citizen	No3		
5						
6	Nos 1&2 denied in 96 case # 1418					
7	Admitted by the U.S. Court Ardmore, I.T.					
8	Dec 20, 1897 Court Case 96					
9						
10	No1 on 1896 roll as Wm B Brown					
11	No2 " 1896 " " Nancy A "					
12	No3 " 1896 " " Bettie "					
13	No3 is now the wife of Oliver McCarly, a non-citizen No3: Name stricken from original judgment					
14	Jan 20 1902 by order of U.S. Court Southern District I.T.					
15	No.4 born Dec 8, 1901; placed on this card Jan 20 1902 Ardmore Jany 17,1900 Court Case 96					
16					Date of Application for Enrollment	2/64
17	1 2 3				9-22-98	

Choctaw By Blood Enrollment Cards 1898-1914

RESIDENCE: Chickasaw Natn
POST OFFICE: Center I.T.

Choctaw **Nation**   Choctaw **Roll**

CARD NO. **5097**
FIELD NO. C 142

Dawes' Roll No.	OP 7/16/06 NAME	Relationship to Person First Named	AGE	SEX	BLOOD	TRIBAL ENROLLMENT		
						Year	County	No.
√ 1	Nichols, John W B		24	M	1/8	1896	L...	9809
2	" √ Bessie	Wife	18	F	I.W.			
3	" Louie Herman	Son	2wk	M	1/16			
4	" Golda Ula	Dau	2wk	F	1/16			
5								
6								
7	#2-3-4- DISMISSED							
8								
9								
10								
11								
12								
13								
14								
15								
16								
17								

TRIBAL ENROLLMENT OF PARENTS

	Name of Father	Year	County	Name of Mother	Year	County
1	J. B. Nichols		Non Citz	Nancy Nichols		Non Citz
2	Levi Deaton		"	R. O. Deaton		" "
3	No.1			No.2		
4	No.1			No.2		
5	John W B ...hols married to Bessie Sept 11-1898					
6	No.1 denied in 1896, case # 1418					
7	Admitted by the U.S. Court Ardmore, I.T.					
8	Dec 20 - 1897 Court Case 96					
9						
10						
11						
12	No1 on 1896 roll as Johnnie Nichols					
13	No.3 Enrolled Sept 1st, 1900					
14	No.4 born Dec. 15, 1901: Enrolled Dec. 27, 1901					
15	DENIED CITIZENSHIP BY THE CHOCTAW AND					
16	No1 CHICK AS AW CITIZENSHIP CO... 9-22-98 NOV 29 ?/69					
17	Aug 30-1900 Comanche IT				Date of Application for Enrollment NOV 29 1904	

Dec 24-1901   "   "

RESIDENCE: Chickasaw Natn		Choctaw **Nation**	Choctaw **Roll**	CARD No. **5098**
POST OFFICE: Wilson I.T.				FIELD No. C 143

Dawes' Roll No.	NAME	Relationship to Person First Named	AGE	SEX	BLOOD	TRIBAL ENROLLMENT		
						Year	County	No.
✓	1 Pearcy John W		60	M				
DEAD.	2 " Sarah E	Wife	20	F				
	3 " Sarah Eveline	Dau	6mo	"				
	4 " Andrew Jackson	Son	7mo	M				
	5							
Nos	6							
3 & 4	7 DISMISSED							
	8 SEP 15 1904							
	9							
	10 No. 2 HEREON DISMISSED UNDER							
	11 ORDER OF THE COMMISSION TO THE FIVE CIVILIZED TRIBES OF MARCH 31, 1905							
	12							
	13							
	14							
	15							
	16							
	17							

TRIBAL ENROLLMENT OF PARENTS

	Name of Father	Year	County	Name of Mother	Year	County
1	Williamson Pearcy	Dead	Non Citz	Triphena Pearcy		Non Citz
2	Aisley	Dead	" "	Aisley	Dead	" "
3	No1			No2		
4	No [sic]			Ada Prercy[sic]		noncitizen
5						
6	Admitted by the U.S. Court Ardmore I.T. Feb. 1st 1898 Case #134					
7						
8						
9	No.1 denied in 1896, case # 299					
10	Correct surname is Pearcy					
11	No.2 died Sept 28, 1898 Proof of death filed Aug 13 1901					
12	No1 is now the husband of Ada Piercy a noncitizen. Evidence of marriage filed Aug 10,1901					
13	No.4 Enrolled Aug 13, 1901					
14						
15						
16					Date of Application for Enrollment	9-22-98 2/77
17						

Choctaw By Blood Enrollment Cards 1898-1914

RESIDENCE: Chickasaw Natn   Choctaw **Nation**   Choctaw **Roll**   CARD NO. **5099**
POST OFFICE: Province I.T.   FIELD NO. C 144

Dawes' Roll No.	NAME	Relationship to Person First Named	AGE	SEX	BLOOD	TRIBAL ENROLLMENT Year	County	No.
✓	1 Belcher Martha E	First Named	45	F				
	2							
	3							
	4							
	5							
	6							
	7							
	8							
	9							
	10							
	11							
	12							
	13							
	14							
	15							
	16							
	17							

TRIBAL ENROLLMENT OF PARENTS

	Name of Father	Year	County	Name of Mother	Year	County
1	Williamson Pearcy	Dead	Non Citz	Triphena Pearcy		Non Citz
2						
3						
4						
5						
6						
7	No 1 denied in 1896, case # 299					
8	Admitted by the U.S. Court Ardmore, I.T. Feb 1ˢᵗ 1898 Case #134					
9						
10						
11						
12						
13						
14						
15						
16			Date at Application	9-22-9?	374	
17						

299

Choctaw By Blood Enrollment Cards 1898-1914

RESIDENCE:	Chickasaw Natn						CARD NO. 5100		
POST OFFICE:	Comanche I.T.		Choctaw **Nation** Choctaw **Roll**				FIELD NO. C 145		

Dawes' Roll No.	NAME	Relationship to Person First Named	AGE	SEX	BLOOD	TRIBAL ENROLLMENT		
						Year	County	No.
1	Nichols James B	First Named	48	M	1/8	1896	Blue	9807
2	" Nancy C	Wife	42	F	1/8	1896	"	9808
3	Scott Della M	Dau	14	F	1/8	1896	"	9810
4	Nichols Nancy V	Dau	7	F	1/8	1896		9811
5	Scott[sic]							
6								
7								
8								
9								
10								
11								
12								
13								
14								
15								
16								
17								

TRIBAL ENROLLMENT OF PARENTS

	Name of Father	Year	County	Name of Mother	Year	County
1	Wilson Nichols	Dead	Non Citz	Delithe Nichols	Dead	Non Citz
2	Bethel Guest	"	" "	Tinzy Guest	"	" "
3	No 1			No 2		
4	No 1			No 2		
5						
6	Nos 1 to 4 denied in 1896 case #1418					
7	Admitted by the U.S. Court, Ardmore, I.T.					
8	Dec 20, 1898 Court Case 96					
9						
10						
11	No 1 on 1896 roll as J B Nichols					
12	No 2 " 1896 " " Nancy "					
13	No 3 " 1896 " " Della "					
14	No 4 " 1896 " " Velma "					
15						
16	Date of Application for Enrollment			9-22-98	2/69	
17						

300

319